You Are Becoming A
Galactic Human

VIRGINIA ESSENE
and
SHELDON NIDLE

 S.E.E. Publishing Company, Santa Clara, California, USA

This book is manufactured in the United States of America.

Cover Art: Lightbourne Images
Book Design and Illustrations: Miriam de Vera Nidle

ISBN# 0-937147-08-7
Library of Congress Catalog Card Number: 94-066226

Spiritual Education Endeavors
Publishing Company
1556 Halford Avenue, #288
Santa Clara, CA 95051
USA
(408) 245-5457

First Printing June 1994
Second Printing October 1994

You Are Becoming A
Galactic Human

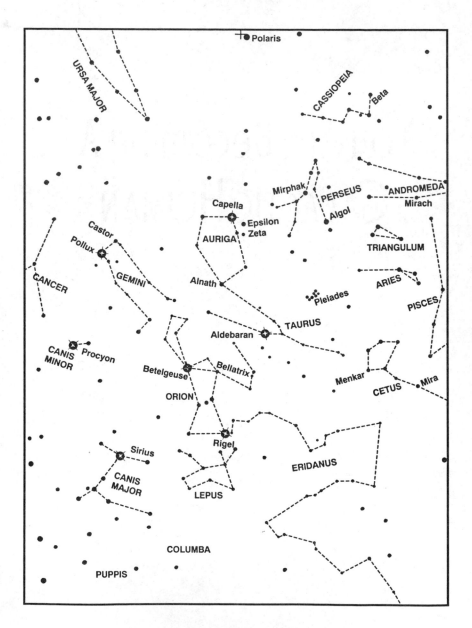

*What is your galactic origin? Is there a particular star
that attracts your interest?*

Dedication

Dedication from Sheldon

This book is dedicated to God, the Time Lords, Spiritual Hierarchies, the Galactic Federation, my Sirian galactic family, Washta and his Sirian Council, my son little Narturi (the munchkin pie), Gort'An Shar'a, and especially to Miriam de Vera Nidle whose undying devotion and love made this work possible.

". . . It is best to understand the Universe and its song, for its harmony plays your inner truth."
- from Sirian **Codice of Understanding**

Dedication from Virginia

My work in this book is dedicated to the One Creator, whatever its many names may be . . . to the Spiritual Hierarchies of all times, dimensions and places . . . to the Time Lords. . . and to all lifeforms everywhere who contribute to the expansion of life, love and wisdom.

This book is also dedicated to the positive galactic humans who are assisting our solar system and planet Earth to reach greater consciousness and light . . . most especially to those Sirians who have truly persevered on behalf of Earth's humanity!

Finally, I honor my fellow brothers and sisters of Earth who share a common heritage and an ever expanding cosmic journey with me.

Sheldon's Acknowledgments

The physical preparation of this book's manuscript was made possible through the efforts of a great many dedicated people who came to assist in the arduous birthing process of this book. First of all, I would like to acknowledge and sincerely thank Virginia Essene for following Spirit's wishes and for allowing this book to become a reality. I wish to thank Daniel Riqueros for donating his transcription services in the midst of his personal difficulties. We couldn't have completed this book in such a short time without his efforts. I deeply wish to thank Miriam de Vera Nidle for illustrations, production, and coordination of everyone's efforts.

I acknowledge Tom and Gwen Aragon for introducing us to Daniel. I am extremely grateful to Ron of S.E.E. Publishing and Lenora Grant Mayer for their copyediting assistance . . . Roland G. Mayer for numerous errands in support of the book . . . Yves Martin for desktop publishing assistance in the last few weeks of final production . . . Lucille Martin for the use of her car and Yves' time and for those healing magnets that helped relieve my back pain!

I am very grateful to Tony McGettigan for several long-hour days of typing and copyediting as well as to Colleen Ann Marshall, Anand SaRA, and Kate-Melissa Ague for taking a day off to do typing. I also thank Sheri DiSalvo for assigning one of her office staff—Sharinn Christie—to do a one-day rush transcription. I wish to acknowledge ChowChow Imamoto for her healing treatments and for letting us use her computer for a day. My deepest heartfelt thanks go to Peggy McConnell for her spiritual insights, constructive feedback, and for facilitating my healing process so I could get back on my feet. I could not have completed this book without her assistance.

Virginia's Acknowledgments

I particularly want to acknowledge the longtime association of my spiritual brother, Urs Winzenreid, whose continuing support of the SHARE Foundation's work has made many endeavors possible.

Special appreciation also goes to Don, Shirley and Willie, Dorothy, Phil and Anne, and Emily for their ongoing Love Corps assistance. And to many others too numerous to list!

I also wish to acknowledge the superb contributions of Ron, our S.E.E. Publishing editor, for his efforts in this book's preparation and production phase, and to both Daniel Riqueros and Yves Martin for their special dedication in bringing the material into publishable form. Thanks also to Carol for some copyediting hours.

As always, I honor the SHARE Foundation's present and past board members for their encouragement . . . all present and past employees for their efforts . . . and the many helpful volunteers who have assisted us since 1985 when our publishing work first began. To one and all, you have my heartfelt gratitude.

Finally, I want to thank all of the awakening friends and compatriots who have brought their unique talents and love to assist in this extraordinary Earth adventure—and whose caring for all life has enriched my own journey so much. I especially salute our magnificent children whose Christ light ignites an even more profound remembrance of who we truly are and why we have come!

Preface

The task of translating a series of spoken audio tapes recorded with a verbal stream of consciousness is always a formidable task because the *spoken* message lacks the structured sentences, paragraphs, and official rules of grammar, punctuation, etc., required by our *written* language communication. This is especially true if the written communication has length and needs both organization for continuity and flow of expression, as a book does. So we'd like to explain the methods we used to create this material.

Sheldon's messages were first channeled and then directly typed onto hard paper copy as an initial starting point. The question and answer portion of each chapter was taped with Virginia asking questions of Washta through Sheldon.

These materials then had to be edited many times for clarity of thought and written comprehension. Of course this had to be accomplished without losing the intended meaning.

In the middle of all this, Miriam had to create certain illustrative materials in order to assist in clarifying novel, basic concepts vital to the reader's understanding. This was a true labor of love and adds immeasurably to the book's value.

The final text was composed on a computer using a page layout program which was then laser printed and sent to a vendor for printing and binding.

We are now pleased to place the book's contents into the public forum and release the Sirian message to those who feel called to listen.

Any question about Washta's ideas or comments should be addressed directly to Sheldon Nidle at the address in the back of the book rather than to the publisher or Virginia.

Recorded April 23, 1994.   Virginia Essene

Contents

List of Illustrations

Virginia's Introduction

The questions that haunt humanity's existence—the ones that have remained for the last 10,000 years and don't vanish even though we may believe we know their answers—are merely these: Who are we? Who or what created us? And why are we alive today on planet Earth?

Some religions of recorded history tell us that God is our Creator and that it was he, she, or it who supplied the spiritual energy with which to power a unique physical body at the matter level of existence. Many teachings say that this physical body can wear out and experience what is called death, or non-awareness, even though the soul, or spiritual consciousness, does not die. But others imply that we need not experience physical death at all. So what is the truth about this critical human issue?

As we know, at least one being has appeared on Earth who claimed he was here to model love and overcome physical death. He taught that it was this love that would bring peace and wisdom, forever changing humanity into a fully conscious state of spiritual awareness . . . often referred to as heaven.

This great one called Jesus said we need not die but could have eternal life through a resurrection process, or what is called ascension. Love and forgiveness were the way, he said—not war and confrontation. Indeed, resurrection and ascension required love. (Love not merely law.) They required forgiveness rather than blame and retribution. Yet Jesus' message was delivered to a society of human beings whose genes may have been damaged by the Atlantean genetic experiments thousands of years before his arrival.

These people who lived in the Middle East were certainly courageous, and we probably cannot imagine the terrors they went through. But we see from present-day history that they were ignorant of their own local history—hardly cognizant of the Egyptian, Sumerian and Babylonian civilizations and their relationships with what we call star people or extraterrestrial visitors.

That Middle East remnant was not only separated from their own full consciousness as human beings, but most of their regional history had been destroyed in the biblical flood so they had no records of what had gone before. Imagine what it would be like if, today, we had all of our personal and societal belongings and records destroyed. How long could we remember our past? Would it soon be forgotten except through oral stories and myths? How could human continuity be retained with distorted genetic codes?

Because of that great watery inundation, then, those located in the Middle East lost whatever data they had known about themselves and also about the nations in Asia, especially the greatest of all Earth civilizations—Lemuria. Since they had lost virtually all knowledge of Lemuria, they also had lost the records of Lemuria's later adversary—Atlantis. And it was the Atlanteans whose autocratic structure and cooperation with renegade extraterrestrials reduced the human species to a debilitated DNA genetic mutation of minimal capabilities.

Thus most of our struggling ancestors coped as best they could without their own former 12-helix DNA strands which were now reduced to only two strands, a mere 1/6th of their previous capability. And all of this occurred right in the middle of a devastating planetary upheaval we can scarcely comprehend!

Indeed, this "fall" meant that the human knowledge about who we are was no longer remembered or even historically recorded. Nearly every morsel of information was lost to everyday mental recollection. Without their former psychic abilities such as mental telepathy, seeing and hearing spiritual energies, communing with nature, and so forth, how could they now retrieve this former human history? Since we, today, are only a little better off in the soulful ways and psychic sensitivities of higher consciousness, the truth of who

2

we are and why we are here is also still deeply hidden. That is why I believe we keep sensing there is a core mystery that needs to be solved—the greatest human mystery of all times! A mystery daring us to remember and reclaim our original God-given nature.

Yes, many people genuinely feel there is an unknown chapter awaiting our discovery. For them, the question of who we are and why we were born receives continuing attention. Many of us attempt to find those answers that could ease our inner quest just so we can live our lives with comfort and trust. Yet we may feel we exist in an uncomfortably foreign world that somehow leaves us hungering for a once-known purity and power.

Although some individuals find a peace and joy to base their lives upon, others are racked with painful circumstances such as war, violence, and starvation. Many experience few moments of the bliss that our religions promise. Thus there are many who deny a God that allows such injustice to the innocent, to the babies and children, and to those who are the pawns of murderers and charlatans. Such miseries have caused deep fear, anger and depression, especially without a belief in karma and reincarnation. Such agony to body, mind, and spirit does little to encourage humanity's belief in an invisible being who is very powerful as a Creator—yet who abandons the people to the excesses and cruelties of other humans who somehow gain power and control over the weak and helpless. Many have asked, *"Who could love or respect such a God?"*

Now we cannot promise that reading this book will confirm your belief in God, or that you will love and respect God more earnestly. However, we will not skirt the issue of what created us, how we arrived in this world of negativity and what potential changes the future holds. It is our intention to focus on what is happening right this instant for the entire human population and offer hope to everyone who will listen. Good things are coming! The time of resurrection is here! Individually, and en masse, humans are moving from the past limitations into a sublimely exciting future.

To quote from *New Cells, New Bodies, New Life!*, "Is it possible that in some encoded but suspended animation, we have held the memory of our original genetic origin and its awesome capabilities until we could evolve back in consciousness? Is this the present momentous experience in which our inner waters—beyond blood to the flowing electromagnetic energy of molecular life—can be reclaimed?"

3

My own answer to that question is an emphatic "YES". . . this is the time of that momentous experience when full molecular capability will be reclaimed! This is the historical juncture when we offspring of an awesome Creator reclaim the cellular credentials of galactic birthright. But to welcome the occasion with the vitality and assurance that it deserves, we must truly be willing to surrender our rigid earth-based history and look into the galactic history with which we are associated. "How is this possible?" you may wonder. We are fortunate, indeed, that we have at least five ways to remember or learn what our true origins and Earth's history have been.

Five helpful ways we can discern the truth on a daily basis:

1. We can extricate information from our own inner resources through meditation, dreams, visions, breath and body work, metaphysical study, polarity balancing and all safe energy balancing practices that help us heal spiritual, mental, emotional and physical limitations. Then we can join together frequently—especially on a weekly basis—with others who are also doing their inner cleansing and healing. By this activity we are greatly empowered! Indeed this chalice of light allows enormous comprehension of the truth we seek. And it also enhances our manifesting capabilities for healing ourselves, resolving planetary problems and achieving peace.

2. We can examine various religious writings and teachings for common agreements rather than for separate attitudes, and we can then update their meaning for our 20th-Century times. We can also utilize the inspired information currently coming to us from our many invisible helpers in spirit and the physical galaxy.

3. We can evaluate true scientific discoveries for their possible value and application in our everyday, conscious lives. We can insist that only noble people should be seeking to discover and use natural laws for positive applications.

4. We can read and listen to the great world myths, epics, legends, folk tales and stories from all cultures—especially noting the incredible information stored in the oral traditions of indigenous peoples whose wise elders are now releasing many helpful secrets.

5. We can dare to believe that our planet is a living being in need of stewardship and that the whales and dolphins are not only her caretakers, but intelligent beings capable of communicating with us humans.

This very moment while much of humanity sleeps, we may even choose to recall that we humans must be involved in that "dominion role" so clearly defined in the Christian Bible and many other belief systems.

Because many humans deny the indigenous people's valuable information and refuse to believe who the whales and dolphins really are, much of what we need to know is lost. Just as refusing to acknowledge our planet as a living being is a major error! But these three sources of assistance will be increasingly valuable in the days ahead if we will but open our minds to include them. Knowledge, safety and joy can be added to our lives as we awaken and consciously attune to all of them.

It goes without saying that a major resource for help can be found in the many religious teachings already given to guide our path—and many kind and sincere people do practice a religion based upon the teachings of past masters and saints. Yet we may not be willing to examine what those great beings have said in their holy writings with today's scientific and technological mind; i.e., with 20th-Century knowledge about the way physical things operate— whether it is aircraft, TV, radio and communication devices, computers and so forth. We must look at those past scriptures with present-day comprehension to really understand them—considering especially the way energy devices of all kinds work. If we are willing to look at spiritual teachings for their moral and ethical values, and also at the physical circumstances they describe, we may find many new answers or receive clearer perceptions about the messages we've been given. Perhaps our increased perception about the so-called "end time" and what that really portends will be clarified by such a search.

Having investigated such matters and found new answers or clearer perceptions, humans might dismiss the monstrous mayhem scenario many expect—and accept a relationship with our wise galactic human family presently living on nearby planets and stars.

But can we hold onto love after we learn our true and long-hidden Earth history?. . . after we discover that we are mutant starseed creations?. . . and that there really has been a war in the lower realms where we exist? Can love then remain in our hearts? For love is the key to conscious reclamation of our higher origins and capabilities, and those who do not express love's powerful nature will

5

not easily flow into the accelerated advancement humanity is now being offered by spirit and the galactic human family.

Right now, this moment, dare we accept that the inspired directives and guidelines of nearly all religions contain guidance from the stars? If we're genuinely willing to look at the precious pages we call holy with the knowledge of present-day scientific equipment, then new meanings may be found in them that clarify today's divine plan.

Then let us join together in this perceptive exploration of sacred scriptures to see what they promise, and to consider who has brought these explanations to humanity. I must caution us, however, to open our minds and hearts to the possibility that no one religion has had all the truth. And in fact, that many cultures, over thousands and thousands of years, have had moral and ethical values which they competently lived and expressed. Because self-righteousness will negate our passport to higher consciousness, then, let us agree to pause a moment and let our love and open-mindedness permeate our search for truth.

(Please feel comfortable in ignoring this challenge if you are not at ease with this exploration of new ideas and/or new perceptions of the old. Perhaps these new ideas or interpretations may not serve you just now. But if you feel the longing to explore human history more fully, come join our explorer's alliance and get ready to soar together because we have much to consider and ponder.)

❊ ❊ ❊ ❊ ❊ ❊

It should be no embarrassment that we don't know our own human history and the circumstances of the planet's creation.

❊ ❊ ❊ ❊ ❊ ❊

It is imperative that we do not feel guilty that our text books are inadequate, often mistaken, and generally incomplete at best. As researchers we are looking to find the gaps and fill them so others who don't have time to become thoughtful explorers can benefit from our contributions. Our love and willingness to learn will not only help ourselves, but others, as well. Therefore, this material is not just for us, personally, but for the planet and all of her other life forms!

Many of us who live in what are called the western technological countries tend to have a rather superior attitude about ourselves.

Sometimes we think our way of living is the best or our religion is the best. The Orient is generally considered inferior, although the current Japanese business competition may have changed some attitudes. India, in particular, is not considered very important to our way of life, yet it is from India that we have the oldest records (after Egypt and Sumeria)—and it is from Asia that our greatest spiritual impetus has been brought. The teachings of meditation, in particular, along with the concept of mind over matter and many alternative healing practices, have triggered a very profound influence in our everyday lives. It is fortunate for us, indeed, that Kipling's quotation, "East is East and West is West, and never the twain shall meet," was erroneous, because much of our recent spiritual inspiration was sparked by these various Eastern beliefs and practices, especially meditation and non-attachment.

Surely these Eastern practices have reminded Westerners that one can experience—in the silence—a profound religious meaning. A way, it would seem, that most Christians were not experiencing in the 20th Century even though all previous great saints and teachers practiced contacting an inner source. Jesus, himself, showed the power of seclusion and meditation in everyday affairs and also by his 40-day trek in the wilderness. Isn't it interesting that the contemporary Catholic church, and other Christian denominations, have not usually elevated meditation and the importance of daily silence for the masses to the level recommended by our early saints and teachers?. . . and that the vital message of turning within every day had to be stimulated by visitors from lands across the sea?

So cross-fertilization of ideas and experiences is valuable, and travel to other countries can be very stimulating. For example, those travelers who have viewed the sculptured forms of earlier human bodies found in Egypt will notice that most of their heads were noticeably different than our head shapes today. More elongated, with greater brain capacity, these heads pictorialize the way humans looked before the tragic circumstances of Atlantean genetic engineering reduced our brain structure to its smaller, limited size. Yet who tells us these things in our current history books? How many generations have been denied an understanding of their true heritage because the experts have no evidence, no proof? The few open-minded scientists who dare suggest there are other pieces of evidence or who go against the unimaginative beliefs presently accepted, are often cruelly maligned, attacked, and ridiculed.

All this resistance has occurred in spite of the Zoroastrian cosmology, the translations of Egyptian hieroglyphics and various Sumerian-Babylonian tablets that have clearly recorded extraterrestrial spacecraft appearances. They have recorded appearances that brought wars upon the earth to control humans, both genetically and behaviorally. How could anyone with a desire for truth fail to acknowledge the cuneiform and pictographic evidence that exists about spacecraft presence and influence? There are, today, illustrative Sumerian tablets that describe the various groups who used space flight with great skill and who came to earth and interacted with certain human leaders and groups in the Middle East. And the Sumerian *Epic of Gilgamesh* describes beings with little concern for human well-being.

In Semitic descriptions about these earlier historical events, we are led to the inescapable belief that humanity has been visited and possibly controlled by certain extraterrestrial beings. Moreover, it could be that an actual planet our scientists have yet to physically identify could once more appear in present time. Even in what we call the Bible (especially in the book of Revelation) John suggests this planetary object to be Wormwood.

And speaking of the Bible, I would strongly recommend that you take time to read a number of passages that are descriptions by or about Moses, Enoch, Noah, Elijah, Ezekiel, and even Daniel and Zechariah, describing the incoming angels and messengers who interacted with them or others around them. Using our knowledge as 20th-Century people, we can see that some of these biblical passages describe contact by, and with, extraterrestrial beings who gave prophecy and guidance to a few prayerful humans of pure-hearted intention. I believe you will find that the Bible has descriptions of spacecraft sincerely explained as something else by those whose lives had no contact with the weapons and various air machines that we, today, see all the time on TV, in movies, videos, magazines and newspapers. I believe you will read their earlier descriptions and words with greater knowledge simply because in those thousand years past, the general public had no knowledge of things that are commonplace for us in our historical time.

Surely we can grasp how our technical awareness allows us to comprehend the cosmic meaning of some scriptural events. This perspective was not available to those pure-hearted ones who had no such technical experience. Remember that we, ourselves, had never seen our planet from space until the late 1960's, and would have been hard-pressed to grasp an explanation given to us by someone who knew and described what Earth looked like from space! Images based upon modern experience are essential as we read our Bibles and the stories told about angels and messengers by those technically inexperienced minds. Our challenge is not to deny that humans have been guided by God, by a loving intention, and by a wiser influence including great spiritual beings such as Jesus, Buddha and others. Rather, it is to understand that the Creator has made many different life forms throughout what we call the reaches of space, and to accept that there are a vast number of consciousness levels and physical beings contained therein. To think otherwise is a limitation humanity cannot afford, since our own sightings of UFO's have increased dramatically since World War II when we dropped the atomic bomb.

In looking at the contents of the Bible, then, let us delve into the Old Testament with a willingness to see what the language of a non-technical person might be describing to his non-technical listener. As the descriptions of "angels" and "messengers" and "God" and "Lord" are given, using terms such as wind or whirlwinds, lightning and very bright lights, smoke and thunder and fire, not to mention the ever-present clouds—what are Jews of a pre-Christian historical period saying? Not as mental inferiors but as honest reporters of an experience so powerful they must describe it as best they can.

From these interactions referred to in the Bible, we soon determine there is more to the scriptures than earlier generations could grasp since they had no experience to assist them. Let's examine one particularly precise description from Exodus 19:16-21. "And on the morning of the 3rd day there were thunders and lightnings, and a thick cloud upon the mountain . . . and a very loud trumpet blast so that all who were in the camp trembled. Then Moses brought the people out of the camp to meet God, and they stood at the foot of the mountain. Mount Sinai was wrapped in smoke because the Lord descended upon it in fire and the smoke of it went up like the smoke of a kiln and the whole mountain greatly quaked. As the sound of the trumpet grew louder and louder, Moses spoke and God answered him in thunder. Yea, the Lord came down upon Mount Sinai, to the top of the mountain, and Moses went up to meet him. And the Lord said to Moses, 'Go down and warn the people lest they break through to the Lord to gaze and many of them perish'."

If we ask ourselves who has descended in this description, it does not sound very gentle or what might be termed angelic, does it? Quite the opposite. It has a feeling of things mechanical and dangerous. Could it be this is a space craft putting out radiation that would endanger the populace?. . . a space craft with the noise of rockets, or some kind of landing procedure that creates immense dust, fiery exhaust and incredible noise?. . . an event that causes Moses to believe he is speaking directly to God? I mean no disrespect to the great Moses. But who wouldn't be confused under the circumstances described? Who might not confuse such an event with actual contact by God? This visitor, God or not, seems to care about the safety of the people, and later on, passes to Moses specific rules and recommendations required for moral behavior.

At the least this is a messenger who brings teachings of precise attitudes and applications for everyday living. The visitation, in fact, sets into motion a long-term relationship which Moses is expected to present and place into action. One might wonder if there is a need to suspect subterfuge on the part of these galactic visitors. Who are they really? And who benefits from their visit? Are they physical extraterrestrials or true representatives of a spiritual power? They had a message to deliver—and deliver it they did. This fiery, smoking, noisy event implanted a new direction for peoples of the Middle East that has lasted into our own time.

There are numerous other descriptions in the Bible which bear close examination, and like all things, can be viewed from a variety of perceptions. Each one of us can well re-visit the Book of Isaiah, Ezekiel, Daniel, and even the words of the prophet, Zechariah, not to mention the ever-curious Revelation as told us by John.

Christians might read Isaiah's remarks about "These that fly as a cloud" with 20th Century experience and see whether his cloud description sounds only like a vision or could be a description about an aircraft with very physical characteristics? If there is the chance that this is a physical object being pictured for us, what do we think it might be? Where did it come from?

Is it possible that along with various dreams and visions, which were very real personal experiences, the Bible also contains actual descriptions of physical events and circumstances?. . . events explained in the only language available by our earlier human family who had no experience with mechanical things like aircraft and communication devices? Or do the scriptures possibly contain some of both? Perhaps when Enoch walked with the energy reported to us as God, we might consider that it was not *the* God (the Creator of All Life), but a lesser, still very important being of value to humans.

Can it be that the prophets we respect and appreciate so very much had both dreams and visions plus actual physical experiences with individual beings who were not invisible or highly etheric? Could it be that they were merely galactic human beings with far more sophistication and knowledge about technological crafts, instruments, and communication devices?

Would these possibilities really demean the value of our wonderful prophets and ancestors?. . . or merely indicate that they were doing their very best, as humans who had been genetically abused, to understand events, circumstances and information brought to them from the solar system or the galaxy?. . . from a place where they had no astronomical instruments to view—as our astronomers of today can at least partially do. No, it does not demean them at all. If anything, we must marvel at their soulful willingness to report what they experienced to groups of unsophisticated folks who were most likely far less literate than we are today. Prophecy requires an enormous commitment, in my opinion, and I can only honor those who did their very best to inform, warn, and nurture an unconscious human family who were even more genetically disempowered than we are today.

Imagine walking with God, and knowing about the fallen angels, as Enoch did, and then trying to describe your experience for other people. Now that would be a challenge! And how else could Ezekiel describe his experience other than with a phrase like, "Wheels within wheels"? How expressive could we be, today, trying to explain to human beings living hundreds of years from now, what we experienced if we saw "Gods" with an extraterrestrial aspect? What attitude would those more advanced humans—those more galactic humans—think of our simple inept descriptions? Hopefully they will have understanding minds and hearts as elder brothers and sisters. Perchance they will be grateful for our own willingness to grow and learn and express the commitment of our hearts even with the most simplistic explanations.

Then let's honor Daniel's conversations with beings who may have been galactic humans of high technical ability, when he walked along the River Tigris. And honor Zechariah and his fascinating experience with what he termed "flying scrolls." Indeed, all of the prophets and their various messages could be either very personal inner dream and vision experiences, telepathic communications intended for the whole planet, or physical contact by living extraterrestrial beings. In some cases might it even have been a combination of these?

Surely, in this presumed time of John's *Revelation,* we can read the material with the eye of a 20th-Century human who has come to accept the idea of space flight, UFO's, and objects that lift off the earth for higher destinations. I hasten to add that not everyone believes in what we term UFO's, although an examination of topics covered in the Gallup polls over the past several decades definitely shows an advancing belief in them. By the 1984 poll, here in America, Gallup reports that some 80 percent of the population believes in something called "flying saucers."

Then we acknowledge the gifts of our biblical ancestors—those great men and women who were trying their best to love and trust in God. We honor them even when their knowledge of things mechanical was extremely limited and they would be hard pressed to recognize God with a big "G" back then. But I challenge our own generations, even now, to know how to recognize God with the big "G." How much do we know today about this Creator of life that would assure we would recognize God if we ever met? Aren't we more likely to be contacting some kind of intermediaries who can mentally or physically be with us?

Yes, even Jesus said he could call 10,000 angels, and haven't you ever wondered what they would have looked like if they'd come? Or more appropriately for us today, if he comes back to us—even as he's promised to do—what will he look like? And who will we see in the company of this loving and ever-supportive Lord of Light? Aren't you curious who might show up? Can't you imagine how our historians might struggle to describe such an extraordinary event? . . . especially in a meaningful language that future generations could easily understand.

Some people believe that the Star of Bethlehem was not a star as we would scientifically define it, but a great UFO starship. They argue that the normal procedure for stars does not allow them to move and then hover. And so the perception of all past written descriptions left to guide our paths can separate us, often by violence, as we seek to be right and control or destroy those who disagree.

As we continue exploring the purpose of this book, then, we need to look at information from many cultures that help answer the basic questions that haunt our hearts and minds. Who are we? Where did we come from? Why are we here? Where are we going? For instance, it is fascinating to read the vast history contained in the early Vedic scriptures from India, and not merely focus on Western religions and scriptures. The Vedic scriptures offer a much clearer and quite obvious explanation about their belief in spacecrafts, wars in the heavens and on earth, and the influence of these galactic beings who are more advanced than their earth observers.

The Sanskrit language from India also has a much more precise vocabulary for the various stages of consciousness—some 50 levels or more compared to our few English language words—many of which can be attained in meditation. The Hindus shine in this field. And the reading of their Vedic scriptures gives us yet another perception of God and the heavens and our past major earth events. Thus we find tales of the great being from India called Krishna who had a laser-like disc called Sudarana. As reported in the Hindu scriptures, specifically the *Vishnu Purana*, he was able to use this weapon to destroy his enemies with what are described as nuclear devices and sonic reflectors.

But there is further evidence that India had a superior civilization with frequent extraterrestrial contacts and flying devices called Vimana. In fact, in the *Vymanika Shastra*, there is an explanation of ancient vehicles with terrible weapons and of crafts operated by motive power generated by solar rays.

Another ancient text called the *Samarangana Sutradhara* explicitly describes the principles needed to build a Vimana and gives explanations about its uses in war and peace. There are also reports of Indian gods and heroes fighting with piloted flying devices made from special heat absorbing metals called Somaka . . . and utilizing a kind of visual shield called a Pinjula Mirror to prevent pilots from being blinded by "evil rays." Either Earth humans, galactic humans or both had very advanced technical equipment at their disposal back in those days. Of this I am certain.

There are also commentaries about a weapon named Marika

which indicate a culture of high technological achievement at least 4,000 to 5,000 years ago in India. All major teachings in India such as the *Mahabharata, Ramayana* and *Rigveda* discuss a multitude of flying ships with many different shapes and sizes. Frequent descriptions appear with phrases like . . . "It was large, many-storied and self-propelled. It flew through the air with a singing sound." Or they may remark that "Gods from the sky came to the earth in these machines and because of them, human beings can fly in the air." But the Hindus aren't our only source of information.

We must not assume that the epics, legends and oral stories from many other earth cultures are foolish reports by primitive peoples, even if their religions are not powerfully present upon the planet today. Think of the enormous body of Greek literature with their innumerable gods and goddess stories—or the Nordic tales. What was happening here? Who is being described as powerful, influential, and from higher realms?

Many ancient South and Central American indigenous civilizations such as the Mayans have innumerable descriptions of sky people, or visitors from beyond the planet, who influenced them quite profoundly. And just as the Great Pyramid stands in Egypt, so also are there pyramids throughout Guatemala and Mexico . . . many more in number and mostly ignored by Western nations as unimportant. Because of their astronomical data, pyramids, and teachings (especially about time), these former cultures outrank most early European and North American civilizations except perhaps those like the Hopi in the U.S. Southwest.

These Hopi remnants still remember and report that they had ancestors from the sky—in many times and experiences—who are scheduled to return once again, perhaps very soon. In one of their stories they relate that when the iron bird flies, their human family from across the sea will join them once more in peace and familyhood—an event that will announce the return of the high world's intervention into the affairs of earth again. This event requires a serious purification before the moment of this intervention—an intervention by Pahana, who will bring a long-awaited planetary millennium of harmony and peacefulness.

Stories among the Mayan, Aztec and Incas also speak of the time of preparation before the return of their saviors and gods Names like Viracocha, Quetzalcoatl, and Kukulkan may not flow from Western tongues as easily as Jesus and Mary, Abraham and Moses, but the reading of the remarks made by these great beings is stirring indeed. (I was not at all acquainted with these teachings until I stumbled upon a museum exhibit that had a display of major poetic commentaries and teachings left behind for their peoples by some of these great beings. I still recall the inner soul response I had while reading some of the profound truths they espoused in such a rhythmic way. But then I must confess to reading certain of the Hindu Vedic scriptures and finding passages similar to the Beatitudes spoken by our beloved Jesus.)

None of this takes away from our Christian heritage, in my opinion. Rather it is reassuring that many civilizations, peoples, and their beliefs have consistently offered aid, nurturing and the kiss of hope, regardless of how terribly humans have behaved at certain times and places. No matter how far we have fallen from the state of cosmic heritage and consciousness, we will soon reclaim it! That is, we will if those of us in the Western countries, in our new cultures of very short duration (compared to others that have existed), don't remain complacent but open our minds and hearts to what has gone before. Many times the value of even so-called primitive tribes shows itself to be quite profound.

In evidence of this I offer the Dogon people of North Africa who have retained astounding information about astronomical matters they presumably have no way of knowing. In fact, their information about the star cluster we call Sirius was not known by astronomers until years after the Dogon reported precise facts about the Sirius star group such as their rotations, relative positions and relationships with each other. Identical information about Sirius A and Sirius B has only very recently been confirmed by present-day astronomical findings! Kept in safe-keeping by certain responsible spiritual leaders of ancient oral traditions, the Dogons inspire us to honor what they know about space. They further entice our curiosity about how a so-called primitive tribe's shaman could draw pictures of previously unknown Sirian planetary cycles, as well as other heavenly movements, that our astronomers hadn't yet found.

We can also learn much from those we call primitive people, for their healing practices using natural plants, herbs, and "mind over matter" techniques. A profound example of the power and simplicity of native people comes from the Australian Aborigines—those who have remained pure in consciousness and natural living for nearly 60,000 years. While the so-called civilized nations wreaked havoc and inflicted unspeakable horrors upon each other, these beings remained loyal to Mother Earth and all of life. No wonder their last remnants will soon advance into the higher spiritual dimensions!

Then by examining reports from a vast number of other non-Western cultures—many of them from indigenous people like the Mayans and the Hopi—a tapestry of information emerges regarding UFO appearances and influences in human affairs. Yes, there are spiritual beings from etheric or invisible realms who teach and love humans, sometimes appearing in dreams and visions or in physical meetings. But there are also the physical contacts with those we term extraterrestrials and possibly other life forms less well-known to us. Perhaps, as pictured in some of the movie and TV footage from "Star Trek" and other space age programs, we are being introduced to the various life forms beyond our own planet?

As Westerners, then, it is vital that we surrender our self-righteous attitudes about having all the answers and examine an ever-growing body of evidence about past Earth history that our current books do not include. Just because there is little or no physical proof or evidence in the major sciences like biology, geology, anthropology, astronomy, and so on, it does not mean there has been no history. That destructive flood surely demolished an enormous amount of life and physical evidence, too.

It is the true role of science, as mentioned in *New Teachings for an Awakening Humanity*, to find the truth we need by humbly seeking it. Indeed, this is an intuitive seeking—an attitude of wonderment and open-minded exploration of energy in all its manifestations and characteristics—that is necessary. Only in this way can we safely postulate "Who or what kind of energy gives us life?". . . and explore the limits, if any, of the energy qualities and uses our human species possess.

While I am not a scientist, I have great respect for those who are nobly dedicated to the scientific exploration of these basic questions, and I often find certain quotations and comments that touch my mind and heart. One of them by the illustrious Albert Einstein—"I only want to know the thoughts of God. Everything else is a footnote," has always intrigued me. Another of his comments, referring to energy in the human being, was "human emanations exist that are still unknown to us for the knowledge about man is still in infancy."

Have you already answered the question of who you are to your own satisfaction? Possibly you know who created you and the process by which this was accomplished. Maybe you are well-acquainted with both electric and magnetic field energies and also those invisible but influential energies we call subtle. (Those invisible powers that may be the currents of creation and manifestation.) As we are beginning to discover, however, it may require a cooperative bonding of the subtle and those four known physical forces that science has already identified, to achieve the enormous manifesting powers that our spiritual teachers have insisted are humanly possible.

Whatever the secret bridge may be, it seems we have not identified it for everyday use by the common man. It is still a mystery, but its latent nature cannot be hidden forever. New paradigms await human discovery and application, of this I am sure. Nearly every major religion has promised we could use 'God' energy at a mental level to control our thoughts and the subsequent effects they produced. And many religious prophecies, as well as worldwide legends, epics, and folklore, have promised us a thrilling new Golden Age—a brighter tomorrow—in spite of what has befallen us.

Let's accept that this is that promised time indicated to us from many sources, and that we really are the prodigal Earth humans regaining and reclaiming our galactic origins and powers. Nonetheless, there is research to do in finding the major missing chapters in our history books, in learning about ourselves and other life forms, and in discovering why things are the way they are on planet Earth. Happily, we are now busily determining what those truths are! Indeed, the vital information that we need in order to grasp the true enormity of Earth life and our purpose here is within reach of every opening mind and heart. Isn't it wonderful that we have embarked upon the most extraordinary search a human could undertake?. . . and that we are doing it together in many places and in many ways?

Our intention in presenting the material in this book, then, is to explore these extraordinary but historically splintered ideas and evidences for the good of all humankind. Who we humans are and why we're here on planet Earth will be a repetitive theme throughout our sharing. You have your own perceptions and guidance, which we applaud. Now we seek to challenge your intellect and have what is shared by your intuition or inner knowing brought into balance.

17

That place of heart resonance and feeling that's brought you this far will continue to guide your path, of course. That is why it feels essential to offer food for thought and expansive considerations, even if they are considered controversial, as channeled or inspired material usually is.

The idea of inspired or channeled information being received by people currently alive right now, during our own lifetime, seems difficult for people to accept. There seems to be this lingering belief that prophets, visionaries, spiritual disciples and psychic wonders only happened long ago and to a very few special humans.

Today, however, with an ever-increasing population and world-wide communication capabilities present everywhere, aren't there likely to be more and more people with these unusual gifts and talents? . . . and more and more of them becoming widely known to the public?

Whether psychic, visionary, or telepathic talents are really possible is no longer the main issue for me personally. The focus for me now is on the *quality* of the information being shared and where that information emanates from—angels, great spiritual beings, space beings, or our own deceased human comrades. In the final analysis, however, it is you who must decide whether channeling is real and if it has value for you. Then you must contemplate whether this material is of the quality level you seek.

We cannot prove much of what you will read in this book—not if you compare it with present Earth history books, certainly. But that is part of this document's value. It is a challenge to your mind, heart and soul . . . and we offer it with our respect and love.

Now let me introduce Sheldon Nidle, who will present his own story and then begin sharing the galactic information his sources have provided.

In love and service,

Virginia Essene

Chapter 1
In the Beginning

A glorious day is dawning for planet Earth and for this global civilization. It may well be the "end time" mentioned in Biblical and other religious and indigenous people's prophecies. This "end time" will bring our ascension/transformation into a fully conscious galactic human and the creation (on Earth and in this solar system) of a true human galactic civilization with full membership in the Galactic Federation. Before we discuss these wondrous occurrences that are now emanating from our space brothers and sisters, let me share my own story of how I learned of the wonders that are shortly to be given to this world.

My name is Sheldon Nidle and I have been appointed as a representative of the Galactic Federation. This position was given to me by a Sirian counselor and galactic presence named Washta. Washta explained to me that the information that follows is a message from the Sirians and their Council of Ascended Masters on what is about to happen to my fellow Earth humans in the next few years.

The inauguration of my encounter with our space family, especially the Sirians, began when I was about nine years old. My family had just moved from our rented home in Buffalo, New York to our own home in a nearby suburb. Life was fairly normal once we got settled and then, after about two months, something very strange and, in the beginning, very frightening, began to happen. At that time, I experienced the sudden appearance of two bluish–white balls directly over the head of my bed. These two strange lights were about the size of an adult fist and would appear like clockwork just before I went to bed.

At first I was scared and bothered by them. Eventually, I became determined to discover their origins and to put an end to their nightly appearances over my bed's headboard. The blackout shades, duct tape and other similar devices I used to cut off all visible light left my room looking more like a dark tomb than a bedroom. Yet the more I darkened my bedroom the more the globular bluish-white lights would glow in an even and beautiful way.

As this strange activity continued, I really worried as to what was happening to me. Was it an illusion? Was some kind of unreal apparition surrounding me? It became one of the most frightening times of my life. My questions deepened and my amazement steadily grew until one evening, a very beautiful and loving male voice suddenly spoke outloud in my bedroom. The voice said that it was from a star in our galaxy known as Sirius B and that it was here to begin my instructions. These teachings would later prove to be the foundation for my present mission to this planet and explain some very incredible things that are about to happen on Earth during the course of the next few years.

Back in the mid-'50s, however, this voice was a perplexing experience for me because I perceived it as being some sort of hallucination. The voice understood this disbelief and said that its purpose was to educate me by using love and light. It also promised me proof of its reality through a simple experiment. I was asked to take off the taped blackout shades that had created near darkness in my room and to look out the window into the night sky. When I pulled up the shade, to my amazement, there suddenly appeared a V-shaped formation of nine UFO ships high in the atmosphere that seemed to glow like some strange and unusual stars. Washta (the source of the voice) told me that this unique starry-like configuration would move into any formation that I imagined.

After making these ships change formation many times, I asked if this was a once in a lifetime appearance or if it was something that would happen regularly. Washta told me with a voice that evoked both love and compassion that this particular activity was being done so that I could accept his presence as a reality and be ready to believe his messages. I later asked if I could share this amazing light show with my younger sister and Washta approved. She was willing to play, and the two of us began our mutual involvement with the Sirians by nightly engaging in the joint activity of moving ships into any type of formation that we chose.

These nightly incidents eventually led us to visiting the Sirian mother ship either in the form of an out-of-body experience or as an actual physical (in-body) experience. Over the course of the next few years, these visits and their accompanied verbal instructions led my sister and myself to a belief that we were not raised by our parents but by the Sirians under the direction of Washta. These events caused a kind of surrealistic existence and made it very difficult for either one of us to understand fully what was occurring. It confused us and yet it was also an incredibly beautiful experience filled with a great caring love. It demonstrated yet another way to view human civilization and the application of human consciousness.

Nonetheless, these messages and experiences began to create some degree of conflict within me. Sirians continued to demonstrate an advanced science that appeared to be almost magical, and they explained concepts about the formation of the galaxy that made Earth human cosmology completely erroneous in its theories about the universe. As they told me more about the elements of their science, it accentuated my conflict between their knowledge and that of Earth science and its related cosmology. This conflict was created by my many years of involvement in summer science achievement programs that were established during the immediate post-sputnik era (1958-1961), and by my own voracious reading in all branches of science. (I was reading university physics texts and advanced college texts on anthropology at age seven.)

It seemed to me that an unresolvable schism was slowly developing in me between the science of Earth and the science of the stars. In fact, as opportunities began to develop for a career in science, I felt I had to make a choice, so by the beginning of my junior high school years I made the dreaded decision that the time had come for the Sirians to leave me. For while their science was incredible and amazing, it was one that tore me apart from the Earth-type science with which I had become deeply involved. I therefore asked them to leave. This they did but with an admonition that they would return at an appropriate time and place in my life.

I then began to further develop my interests in science by taking advanced courses in calculus, physics, and chemistry. However, this opportunity was ended by my freshman year in college when a deep personal conflict developed between the vice-chairman of the physics department and myself. We disagreed over the formulation of Isaac Newton's mechanics theorems and their usage in modern cosmology as well as in subatomic physics. This conflict forced me to change my major from physics to political science with minors in anthropology, sociology and various area study programs. During my senior year I felt drawn to specialize in South East Asia history studies which include the nations of Malaysia, the Philippines and Indonesia.

After completing my MA in 1970, I left academia in search of work. But tough economic times and my ability to obtain only dead-end jobs led to a decision to study for a Ph.D. in Southeast Asian Studies. In 1973, I returned first to Illinois and then to the University of Southern California where I obtained another Master's degree in political science with a specialization in international public administration and American government. By late 1975 I only needed to complete my dissertation to obtain a Ph. D.; however, I never finished it because I became interested in the development of a television documentary—as well as a possible motion picture—on the life and discoveries of Nikola Tesla. Tesla was the genius who invented the electrical technology that presently dominates our world.

Nikola Tesla had been my hero during all the various summer science study programs that I had undertaken in elementary and junior high school. At that time, I decided that he was indeed one of the great unsung heroes of modern science because he was the father of modern electricity and all the incredible inventions that mark the twentieth century's technology. I, therefore, jumped at the chance to study Tesla again and possibly to bring forth a television documentary that would help people understand Tesla's many gifts to humanity.

These events also allowed me to study some unusual Tesla devices such as the wireless power technology, called the magnifying transmitter, in greater detail. This research gave me access to information as to how Tesla's theories were being used by both the Soviet Union and the United States to create a weather war that has continued from the mid-1970s to the present time. My investigation of Tesla also led to the development of various zero-point energy devices created by myself and some newly acquired friends.

As I began to do various projects on alternate technologies, it slowly began to dawn on me that these projects, although capable of producing useful technology, would not be allowed to see the light of day. This opinion was developed by my encounters with various power company executives and the Department of Energy's *Alternative Energy Program*, as well as my observation of the destruction of various companies that attempted to produce or develop various devices in Europe.

However, even though these devices would not be allowed to become a commercial success, they did give me another opportunity to evaluate the way society was structured. I began to wonder what I was going to do in my life—what my true purposes were. Simultaneously, I began to consider some interesting data about the influence that extraterrestrials had on shaping the world that now surrounds us.

When Comet Wilson, the companion to Comet Halley, was mentioned in the newspapers, I wondered if some strange predictions that I had begun to dream of in 1985 had any relationship to Comet Wilson. During the course of doing several free energy projects, I had made a number of friends who were also interested in fringe theories of science and who had developed a strong interest in evaluating the true nature of Comet Wilson. We started to network and discovered that indeed a starship was approaching Earth disguised as Comet Wilson. We wondered what this reality truly meant—not only for us but for the planet as well.

As I further researched the meanings of Comet Wilson, I started to meet many researchers who told me about the Sirians and their relationship to the cetaceans (the whales and the dolphins). They also told me of a possible relationship between the indigenous peoples of this planet and the cetaceans based on ancient myths as well as tribal traditions and customs. I began to wonder if such a connection really did exist. I was then told by a researcher (who studied planet Earth's connection with Sirius) that a new shift in our planet's polarity was occurring in 1987. Indeed, it was being accomplished by the Sirians so Earth could be put safely into a belt of photon light that was approaching this solar system. I wondered what all this data meant to me and especially to our civilization on planet Earth.

Around the year 1988, I again heard the voice of Washta. He told me that the time had come to reactivate me and that what they had said during my childhood would now indeed begin to happen. The first part of my lessons was to understand the relationship of Sirius to Earth throughout Earth's history. Washta said that at a certain time in the near future, a moment would come when I could utilize what they were telling me. The present period was for instruction, preparation and seclusion during which Washta began to tell me fascinating information about the Galactic Federation and its history.

He told me about the wars in space and the major catastrophes predicted for this planet. He assured me that the Sirians would not allow these catastrophes to happen. Washta said they were in the process of pushing various protocols through important Federation Councils. These protocols would allow for a positive change in the approach to this planet and its human civilization. As these thoughts whizzed around me, I began to understand that their procedures were preparing me to become a channel as well as a representative for the Galactic Federation on this planet. They intended to connect me with others who were also on the verge of activation. Although this operation brought me in contact with a few people initially, for the most part I was in an almost hermit-like seclusion.

During the next three years, Washta began the activation process needed to have me become a channel for the Sirian information. Yet I felt very strange about these wondrous things that were being told to me. Were they real or weren't they? I developed a great need to know. I needed proof that what I was about to do was indeed a truthful mission and not a fantasy. When I asked for proof, Washta stated that the way to obtain this proof was to go to Seattle in the early part of 1992 and to have a hypnotic regression. He said important events would happen from this hypnotic regression and through it, I would begin my mission.

I arrived in Seattle in a driving rain storm filled with trepidation about what was to happen to me. My sister's worries over what my beliefs could lead to did not aid my uneasiness. During the next two weeks, I arranged for a series of hypnotic regressions as prescribed by Washta. These sessions led me to my own personal comfort and verification. I was then invited by the person who did the hypnotic regressions to give a talk before her group. This meeting was an incredible success, so I gave several additional lectures. These first lectures were just the beginning and a preparatory phase. At that point, Washta told me that some personal situations would have to be resolved before my mission could truly begin. Consequently, I left Seattle in May to return to the San Francisco Bay Area and spent the next year resolving these personal issues and preparing for the mission that I was to begin in the late summer of 1993.

In July of 1993, a friend of mine named Aya (we had met in mid-April, 1993) arranged for me to resume lecturing on the future changes in store for this planet and the role of the Galactic Federation in our civilization. I first lectured for her friends in Santa Cruz, California; next, at her home in Atascadero, and then back again in Santa Cruz. The initial three lectures led me to realize the importance of my mission—to deliver the Galactic Federation's message for this planet. I also concluded that the changes occuring to our planet and solar system were an important activity for the Galactic Federation. My task was to eventually inform large numbers of people about the Sirian contact, and then to activate a certain number of them who would be drawn either to my own lectures and/or to those of my associates. The key was to set an information campaign in motion that would give people an opportunity to define their role in creating a new galactic civilization on planet Earth.

It was in August of 1993 that I unexpectedly began to give readings. After I had delivered a lecture for a packed house in Aya's home, she informed me that she had scheduled appointments for me to do three readings the next day. She asked me how much I would charge. I said, "I don't do readings." She said, "You do now." And that was the start of another aspect of my mission—giving channeled information through private readings—which included a description of one's recent star of origin along with one's relationship to the present mission of the Galactic Federation.

It was during one of my lectures, in September of 1993, that I met Virginia Essene and, shortly after, we began discussing the possiblity of presenting all the information I've been given in a book. At the same time, I also started to scrutinize the deepest meanings of galactic time with the hope of learning to understand the processes that surround it. My lengthy association with the Galactic Federation, along with the current circumstances to be described in this

YOU ARE BECOMING A GALACTIC HUMAN

book, have provided me a broader understanding of what is now happening on this planet.

In the rest of this book, I will convey the knowledge that Washta and his specially-assembled board of six Sirian counselors have asked me to share so that you may understand and evaluate it. Please know that what I have to say is based upon the truths that these Sirian counselors have given me and that they have been verified through others. I hope you will take this information and utilize it if you find it valuable. Kindly take those necessary actions needed to prepare for these changes. I hope you will share this information with others and allow them to determine those actions that they should take.

Chapter 2
The Photon Belt

Washta and two other Sirian Council members would now like to discuss an incredible physical as well as spiritual event that is presently approaching Earth. *(Washta is a galactic presence who is in training as a new Sirian ascended master. When he completes this book project, Washta will be promoted to a full-fledged ascended master.)* He is joined in this presentation by Aumtron and Teletron—Sirian experts on science and history—but throughout the book Washta will be the only Council speaker.

We are here to share the fact that your solar system is presently poised to enter a vast region of light called the photon belt sometime during a period between March of 1995 and December of 1996. This photon belt—a huge mass of light—will be the vehicle for your restoration to full consciousness and for the complete transformation of your DNA and chakra systems. These unbelievable changes will forever alter not only yourselves, but also your planet and your solar system. This is because the photon belt will move your solar system into a higher dimension (from 3rd to the 5th), allowing your planet, within the solar system, to move to a new position in space closer to the Sirius star system. At this point, you may be asking. . . what is this photon belt? Why haven't I heard about it before? If it's this important, why aren't our scientists discussing it?

The photon belt, a huge torroid shaped object composed of photon light particles, was first discovered by your scientists in 1961

27

near the vicinity of the Pleiades by satellite instrumentation. *(See Figure 1: Configuration of Photon Belt.)* Throughout this book we usually speak of your Earth entering the photon belt—and sometimes, of the photon belt moving toward Earth. The reality is that your solar system and the photon belt are moving toward each other.

For those who do not know what a photon light particle is, you should realize that it is the result of a collision between an anti-electron (positron) and an electron. This split-second collision causes the two particles to destroy each other. The resulting mass of this collision is completely converted into energy that registers as photons or light particles. In the first quarter of this century, an English physicist, Paul Derac, postulated that for every single particle a similar anti-particle should exist. In 1932, Dr. Carl David Anderson, who won a Nobel prize in 1936, discovered the first of these anti-particles—the positron or positive electron. By the 1950s, anti-protons as well as anti-neutrons had been discovered by your scientists.

The importance of these discoveries is not just that it proves Derac's theories. More importantly, it allows a new and unprecedented form of energy to be discovered by Earth's scientists. This energy that results from the collision between an anti-particle and a particle (for example, the collision of an anti-proton and a proton) is known as photon energy and will be the major source for all of your energy requirements in the future. In fact, the new energy age being established for this planet can be called the "Photon Energy Age."

The photon belt was initially discovered when a series of studies on the Pleiades were begun in the early 18th Century by the famous British astronomer, Sir Edmund Halley. Halley is famous for the discovery of Comet Halley that seemed to prove Newton's laws of planetary motion. Halley discovered that at least three of the stars in the Pleiadean star group are not in the same positions as recorded in classical times by various Greek astronomers. The difference in position had become so great by Halley's time that it was impossible to state whether the Greeks or Halley were wrong. Halley therefore concluded that the Pleiades moved within a prescribed system of motion.

This concept was later proved correct one century later with some astute observations by Frederick Wilhelm Bessel. It was his discovery that all stars in the Pleiades had a proper motion of

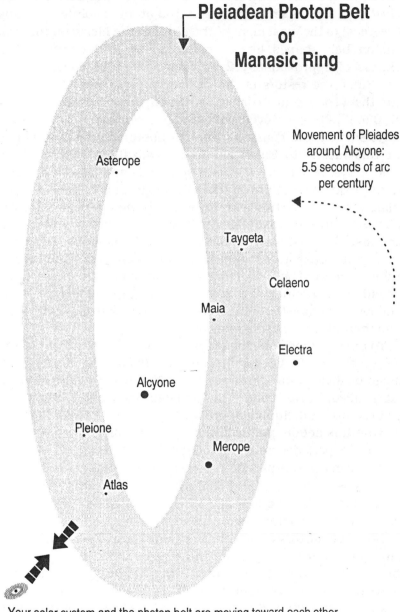

Figure 1: Configuration of Photon Belt

approximately 5.5 seconds of arc per century. Paul Otto Hesse also studied the Pleiades and discovered that at an absolute right angle (90 degrees) to the movement of the stars in the Pleiades, there was a photon belt shaped like a torroid or huge doughnut with a thickness of approximately 2,000 solar years or 759,864 billion miles. Since the results of the observations of Bessel and Hesse about the Pleiades are correct, your Earth is now completing a 24,000 to 26,000-year cycle with this photon belt.

As Earth is now going to enter this photon belt, you must know what this means to Earth's human civilization. Many of your astrologers as well as many of your scientists and historians believe that the next millennium marks the beginning of a new age for humankind. To Earth's astrologers, this new age is the Age of Aquarius, a time for vast changes in your science, technology and your consciousness. To your scientists and historians, it is an age of vast difficulties that your civilization's societal and political structures may not be able to handle. In any case, it may now appear to be either the prelude to a new wondrous age or the time of your extinction. The question remains—what part will the approaching photon belt play in these scenarios?

To answer these questions let us now look at the photon belt itself. *(See Figure 2: A Cross Section of the Photon Belt.)* The photon belt can be divided into three sections. You will first enter through what is called the null zone. This procedure will take roughly 5 to 6 days to complete including approximately 3 days of total darkness. Following this action, you will move into the main part of the belt itself and experience unending daylight (24 hours a day). This journey normally lasts around 2,000 years and ends when your solar system exits at the other end of the belt by going through the null zone exit for the same 5 to 6 day period. *(See Table 1: Your Human Experience in the Photon Belt.)*

However, in this cycle, the Supreme Creator Force (God) has arranged for your solar system to enter an interdimensional rescue bubble that will thrust it out of the photon belt through the 5th dimension and into a position about three light years from the Sirius star system (at present Sirius is approximately 8.3 light years from Earth). This bubble will be reached around the years 2012-2013 AD. That period of approximately 17 years (1996-2013 AD) will mark the end of your 24-hour daylight experience and bring the return of an

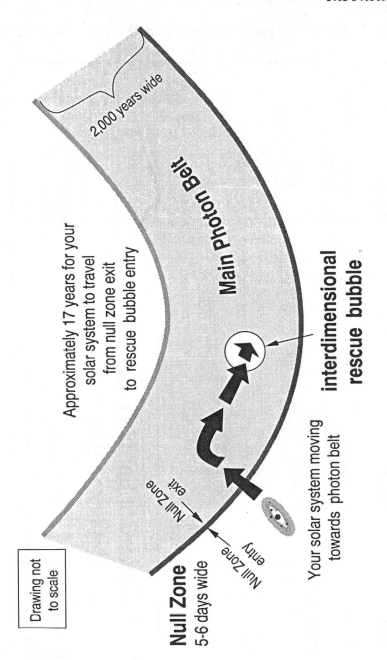

Figure 2: A Cross Section of the Photon Belt

Table 1: Your Human Experience in the Photon Belt

Day1:	Day 2:	Day 3-4:	Day 5-6:
Enter null zone	Atmosphere compressed everyone will feel bloated	Atmosphere dimly lit like dawn	Transition into a 24-hour daylight period.
Alter body type of all living things	Sun cools down	Start photon effect	Exit null zone, enter main photon belt zone
Non-operation of any electrical device	Earth climate cools "ice age"	Photon energy devices are operable	Every living thing is invigorated
Total darkness		Stars will reappear in sky	Earth climate warms
			Photon beam-powered ships can travel in space
			Incredible psychic abilities telepathy, telekinesis, etc.

Summary of Earth's Entry into the Photon Belt

Total of 144 hours or 5-6 days

approximate 12-hour daylight/12-hour nighttime schedule.

As we have just stated, surrounding the photon belt there is a huge barrier called the null zone. If you could look at the null zone, you'd see it really contains a region of incredible energy compression. It is a place where magnetic fields are so tightly strung together that it's impossible for any type of 3rd-dimensional magnetic field to pass through it without being altered. This fact means that the magnetic field of the Earth and your Sun must be transformed into a new type of interdimensional magnetism. You should therefore expect a change in Earth's electrical, magnetic, and gravitational fields. Such a change is occurring right now.

Over the past few decades, the magnetic field of the Earth has been decreasing gradually to almost zero. Many Earth humans have used this phenomenon to prove that a major polar shift is going to occur by the end of this century. However, this council and the Sirian scientists of this council can assure you that *a polar shift will not occur!* This change in the Earth's magnetic field is a by-product of the pressure being put on your solar system by the photon belt.

When the photon belt is fully manifested, it will not allow any electrical device to function. Such a development will mean that neither batteries nor electrical circuits will operate when Earth is in the photon belt. You will require a new form of energy—photon energy—to operate your former and soon-to-be altered electrical devices.

Another major development that is expected to occur as you approach the null zone is an increase in pressure on the planet's atmosphere and upon its surface. This aspect is also beginning to happen as noted by the increase in seismic activities that stretch from the 1960s to the present time. Earth is presently in a period in which seismic activities across the planet have increased. The same thing can be said for volcanism. There has also been a dramatic change in your planetary weather patterns that put pressure on the traditional water cycle. Thus, the droughts in California, Sub-Saharan Africa (the Sahal), South Central India, and the northern part of Chile are examples of how the jet stream and the ocean's internal currents have been altered by this event. In addition, the opening of the ozone hole in the late 1970s and the early 1980s signals another critical change created in part by the approaching photon belt. More importantly, this coming event has also affected your solar system by deeply altering the sunspot cycle and even the overall surface temperatures on the Sun. Now let us look at the Sun and see what has been happening to it.

In 1987 and 1988 the Sirians switched the polarity of the subtle bodies of the Sun so that the photon belt could not in any way adversely affect your solar system. First, we switched the polarity of the solar subtle bodies by realigning them to the new grids being created by the Time Lords (the creator supervisory force of God that deals with the continual creation of this physical universe). This will allow Earth a safe entry into the photon belt. Secondly, our Galactic Federation scientists altered the timing of the sunspot cycle to more easily allow the Sun to adjust to its new subtle body realignment. In an effort to create solar harmony, they therefore produced a different kind of Sun. This new Sun responded with an increase in solar flare activity and with a general stellar cooling. By accomplishing this action, the vast pressures on your solar system have been alleviated. If this shift in interdimensional polarity had not been done, the Sun would have been destroyed by the null zone of the photon belt and Earth vaporized. Thus, as you near Earth's entry into the photon belt, you can be comforted by the fact that the Sun has been significantly changed and is now capable of successfully entering the photon belt.

There were two reasons why the Sun was adjusted and safely positioned so that it can go directly into the photon belt. First, the photon belt is an interdimensional event that requires that the Sun enter it in a properly phased position. (The Sun must be in a relatively low level of activity and able to easily adjust itself to the rapid changes that entering the photon belt will entail.) Secondly, the Earth must be monitored and procedures put into place that will align the interdimensional energy bodies of your planet to the rapid degree of changes that will take place before and just after entering the null zone. The alterations that will allow this event to occur have been put into place though the use of an interdimensional *hologram*.

This interdimensional envelope of light was placed around your Sun so as to properly align the solar system with this new event (the photon belt), and to also use this hologram to successfully regulate your Earth's entry into the photon belt. The hologram will later be used to move your solar system into its new position near our star system (Sirius). Thus, we needed to adjust the Sun's entry fields by enlarging your planet's hologram to include your Sun and solar system. This adjustment will allow a safe entry into both the photon belt and into your new position in this galaxy. *(See Figure 3: Sirius and Your Solar System.)*

These procedures were accomplished through a number of very important processes which we would like to emphasize. First, the Sun's polarity was changed. Second, the Galactic Federation has put into position various atmospheric research ships and specially prepared survey teams who integrated their activities with the actions from the Earth's interdimensional hologram. Their sole purpose is to monitor the ozone hole and to make sure that it does not get too untenable for life on your planet. In addition, these ships and their teams are able to monitor and correct major Earth seismic and plate activities now going on as your planet and solar system approach and enter the photon belt's null zone.

Nevertheless, it is you on Earth who will be entering the photon belt and losing the electromagnetic fields when they are nullified. And as we have explained, this means that when you enter the photon belt you won't be able to utilize electrical equipment anymore. Therefore, you must begin to prepare for this major change in your lives as new forms of gravitational and electrical fields are established. What appears to you as a loss will actually be a benefit that allows photon energy fields to be altered at the subatomic level and become the basic energy drivers of your solar system. As all atoms and molecules are changed, you Earth humans will be vastly modified in your very nature. You will become something quite different—excitingly improved—from what you presently are.

Therefore, let's go over the entire scenario of the photon belt experience and get an idea of what is about to happen. As mentioned, it will likely occur sometime between March of 1995 and December of 1996. Your planet will experience a great field of darkness as it approaches the null zone and your solar system becomes immersed in the zone. Suddenly, the twilight level of darkness will be replaced by complete *darkness*. It will be as though the entire planet has been thrown into an incredibly huge closet and the door closed behind you. The Sun will have disappeared from view and you will be unable to see stars in the pitch black sky. Day will have suddenly turned to night as the null zone's compression of solar and stellar light will blot out the Sun and even the stars. *(Return to Table 1: Your Human*

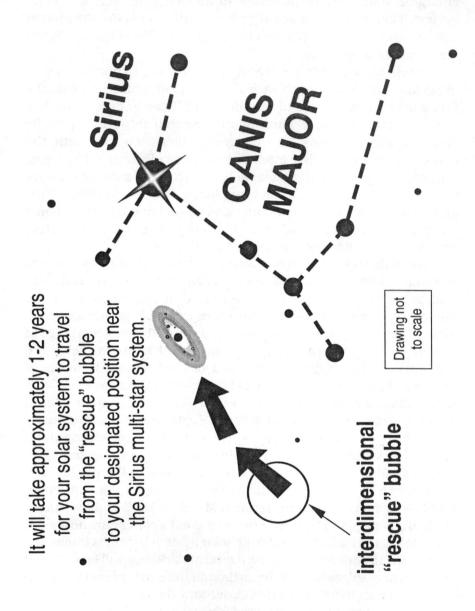

It will take approximately 1-2 years for your solar system to travel from the "rescue" bubble to your designated position near the Sirius multi-star system.

Sirius

CANIS MAJOR

Drawing not to scale

interdimensional "rescue" bubble

Figure 3: Sirius and Your Solar System

Experience in the Photon Belt.)

You will know by the total darkness that you have now entered the null zone and begun the transformation process. As you begin to accept the shock of this utter darkness, you will find that something else has happened. Not only are you in the dark but none of your electrical devices will work anymore. Once the pumps quit and the water tanks are empty, water will not run and toilets will not flush. Lights cannot be turned on. Cars will not start. Hence, you are now in a whole new world. Despite these incredible difficulties, something has happened to your bodies, something wonderful.

When the collapse of the planet's electrical and magnetic fields occurs, it will also allow all atoms on Earth to be changed. The atoms in your body will be modified to form a new body—a body that is semi-etheric—and the veil of consciousness around you will be removed. You will no longer be living in the limited 3rd-dimensional reality. You will now be human beings living in the reality of the galactic light. You will now have physical and psychic gifts that you were meant to have ever since the time you humans first left the Lyran constellation to spread your knowledge and guardianship throughout this galaxy. You will have begun the process of "coming home" to the 5th dimension.

When the atmosphere begins to compress by the second day, you will experience the sensation of being compacted by the pressures from the null zone on Earth's gravitational field and you will feel bloated. This bloating will only last for about two days, however.

As your atmosphere is compressed and all materials become denser, the big danger will be from nuclear materials since there is the possibility for either nuclear chain-reactions or huge and deadly radioactive explosions of fissionable materials. This compression of nuclear energy could possibly cause massive fire storms in addition to explosions around the planet, or nuclear chain reactions. Therefore, to avoid these dangers, the Galactic Federation will allow a special landing of technical ships and personnel so that these potential nuclear dangers can be alleviated.

The next change that you will feel is coldness caused by the complete absence of the Sun. (This temperature drop will be profound—like an Ice Age type of cold.) This will occur because the Sun will be undergoing a change in its interdimensional polarity which will prevent the Sun's heat from reaching planet Earth's surface.

By the third day of change, however, you will begin to see a dawn-like glimmer surrounding your planet. You will then have the beginnings of the "photon effect." This photon effect is very important because it will allow you to have a new energy source. This new energy source will permit the end of your planet's fossil fuel dependency. It will also allow the capability for space travel since photon drive technology is the power system for all starships operated by the Galactic Federation. By the third and fourth day, then, you will have reached the time for your first introduction to photon energy, weak though it may be.

As the fourth day quickly draws to an end and the fifth day now begins, the climate will begin to warm and bright light will return. The photon effect which began toward the end of the third day will now be in full effect. You will now be able to use photon-beam power equipment. Every living thing will now be invigorated by the photons streaming in from the main part of the photon belt. You will have entered a new age with a new body. You will now be ready for the next phase in which your psychic abilities will be heightened by the photon effect. These photon energies will not only provide your bodies with maximum efficiency of energy use, but they will also be used for energizing your homes and your industries. You will have entered the photon age! Space travel will now become quite simple and a preferred mode of transportation.

Once you begin living in the photon belt you will be in a fully-realized space age. With the power provided by photon beam energy, the stars and other planets will soon seem to be as near as a trip across town. With this new energy, it will be as easy to travel to Sirius, or any other nearby star, as it is now to travel from California to New York. In addition, you will now have in your midst those you have long called the extraterrestrials who *are* your elder brothers and sisters and your counselors and guides during this transitional period.

The return of your space family, then, marks an important change in Earth's spatial relationship to your universe. The Time Lords who control this particular entry into the belt will cause your planet to have both a shift in consciousness and physical relationship and also a shift into a higher dimension.

This shifting from a largely 3rd-dimensional world to a 5th-dimensional world is an enormous gift, because as a result of this change, you will be removed from Pleiadean control and situated under Sirian influences. This 5th-dimensional reality means that you will be nearer to Sirius—that you can adopt the Lyran/Sirian culture and be under the protection of Sirius as you were in the time of Lemuria, some 25,000 years ago. (See *Figure 4: Star System of Sirius.*)

As you reflect upon your true Earth history, you will also learn from the Galactic Federation how to use this new spatial relationship that the 5th dimension will give you access to. Hence, your society approaches an almost indescribable Golden Age that various Earth religious prophecies have forecast over the past 2,000 years.

This coming Golden Age is one in which every Earth human will have the opportunity to become all that he or she was meant to be. It is a time when you, the people, will at last have the opportunity to understand your planet's true history and recover your lost full consciousness abilities. The approaching photon belt will mark the end of your present civilization as you know it. Moreover, with the photon belt's coming, the 10,000+ year period of limited consciousness and negative hierarchical government control (that has existed since the end of Atlantis) will conclude. At last, you are presently in the final period of a global Piscean age civilization that will lead you to truly wondrous times. *(See Table 2: Galactic Influence on Earth.)*

Table 2: Galactic Influence on Earth

Sirian Influence 2 million BC	Pleiadean Influence 25,000 BC	Joint Influence of Sirian and Pleiadean November 1992
Began in colonies of Hybornea and Lemuria. Ended when Atlantis destroyed Lemuria.	Began when Atlantis destroyed Lemuria and used the Pleiadean model for Earth human civilization.	Began as a result of the Pleiadean Star League decision to switch to the Lyran/Sirian culture.

The new wondrous times that you are about to enter will allow the reclamation of your fully consciousness potential. This fact is forecast in the biblical revelations, and it is an age when you will talk and walk with all who have lived on your planet. It is a time when you will be one with the Earth's Spiritual Hierarchy. It is also a time when you will return to work cooperatively with your planet's cetaceans to be co-guardians of Earth, and eventually with your rehabilitated solar system, as well.

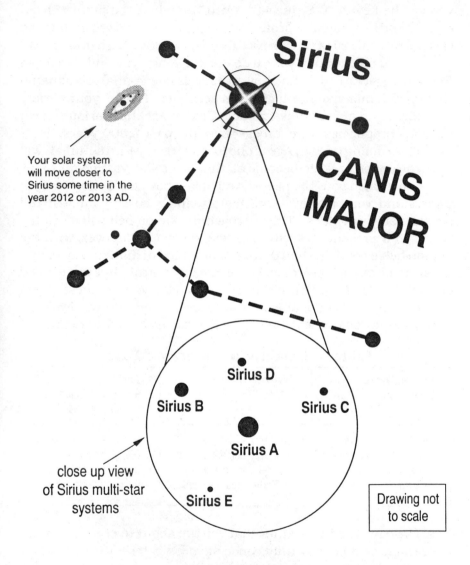

Your solar system will move closer to Sirius some time in the year 2012 or 2013 AD.

close up view of Sirius multi-star systems

Sirius D

Sirius B

Sirius C

Sirius A

Sirius E

Drawing not to scale

Figure 4: Star System of Sirius

You are also in the midst of discovering your true selves, and your true selves are capable of understanding and utilizing many psychic abilities. Yes, psychic abilities such as telepathy and telekinesis, clairaudience, clairvoyance, etc., are a former heritage of every human. You are also heir to new concepts about how you should empathetically relate to one another, and how these correct personal human relationships will determine constructive practices in governing your society in a peaceful and caring way. With these personal and societal changes will also come new technologies and a new science that can be safely known and applied. In effect, a whole new planet, a whole new galactic civilization and a whole new galactic human, are about to be born.

The Earth human that you have been is now ready for an incredible new era, even better than what you created in Lemuria. By aiding the Spiritual Hierarchy in this solar system, you will return to your soul focus as true guardians of all life on planet Earth as well as other planets in your solar system.

But there is another point that is also important for you to understand. You are on the verge of these great changes and new beginnings because of our future "first contact" landings on Earth. This Spiritual Hierarchy and Sirian-led first contact will enable your entire solar system to take its place in the Galactic Federation so you will become all that we have just described—a galactic civilization. Through wisdom and love applied here on Earth, you may be sure that at sometime in the future you will be able to share your knowledge with other star systems—and so the sharing continues in the ever expanding power and presence of God. You are indeed on the verge of an amazing and wondrous time.

Now we are sure that you have many questions about what we just covered. In the next chapter, Virginia asks Washta and his Sirian Council many questions about this Photon Belt material.

Chapter 3
Photon Belt
Questions & Answers

(Due to the vital information about the photon belt—we will now present an entire chapter of questions and answers intended to clarify the information.)

Virginia: I greet the Sirian Council today and would like identification of who is here.

Washta: First is Washta who is before you. There are three of us here. I am joined by my science associate Aumtron and the historian Teletron who come to aid in understanding those things which must be known this day. *(Aumtron is the senior priest/ counselor of the science-engineering clan and one of the Sirian representatives on the Central Sun Council, headed by Metatron. Sirian names which end in "tron" indicate a galactic title such as Lord or Teacher.)*

Virginia: Before listening to the information you bring us, I would like to have a little introduction for our readers. Kindly state how many members there are on this Sirian Council and what Washta's role or position is, please. Also, it would be helpful to understand why these particular beings you mention today, or others, have come to assist us and what they do. We need to ask the question of who you are and why you are doing this work, so our readers will be able to ascertain a sense of your council's commitment, expertise, and concern for humanity.

Washta: Let us begin by giving an overall view of what this Sirian Council is. We are a total of six persons but only four of us will be making physical contributions to this book. The two other members are here to hold energies, to interact with the Spiritual Hierarchy, and to act as intermediaries between the Sirius star system and your solar system. Of the four who are contributing members of the council, three (Washta, Aumtron, Teletron) are here to give you whatever technical information may be needed for this chapter. In Chapter 4 you will meet Sirai, our female council member.

We are here for two basic reasons. The first is to demonstrate that this particular project is being done by the Sirians out of great love for the children that they seeded on your world many, many thousands of years ago in ancient Lemurian times. Our present interest is but a continuation of the overseeing of your spiritual development—along with the cooperation of the spiritual hierarchies of your planet and your solar system—so present day Earth humans can acquire full consciousness once again. Secondly, we come to introduce the Galactic Federation that was created to bring the profound light of the Supreme Creative Force into this glorious galaxy.

We are therefore here in love and in light, to oversee, to aid, and one might say to midwife a new civilization. Those of us on this council are able and eager to do this task for we have been appointed by a higher council that might be called in your language, ascended masters, and in our language (as translated into English), galactic presences.

We, and beings from many higher levels of existence, have interacted with other various ascended masters, angels and archangels of many dimensional realms of this physical universe on your behalf. They are all helping to create a new energy of love and wisdom across this entire galaxy because the time has now come again for your planet to belong to this diverse galactic family. Yes, you are to experience this great leap forward into a new Age of Light and to let the interdimensional Christ Consciousness touch you more fully. This Christ Consciousness originates from the very core of creation to this world. It comes so that more love and light can now be brought into full consciousness, and so that all the men and women on your planet can act as guardians for planet Earth and its accompanying solar system.

Virginia: Yes, thank you for that introduction and we give our gratitude to all of you who are serving in this helping capacity. Now I want to ask the council, through Washta—Do we have any other words in the English language that define *photon belt* or is this a totally new concept that we need to acquire?

Washta: Well, the photon belt itself could be called "the great light that is coming." Photon is a particular kind of energy you haven't identified as yet. Right now, the photon belt energies are located at an angle where they are very difficult to be seen except by very powerful astronomical instruments. The governments of your planet have largely prevented those who have access to such instruments from sharing their findings in the public light. This suppression has led to a great deal of confusion among those who have been given information about its true cause and nature. Since your instruments are still very limited in properly identifying photon energy, just think of it as the great light that has been talked about in many prophecies, by many peoples, throughout the past few thousand years of recorded human history on your planet.

Virginia: Is this what we normally refer to as the God light or the energy of God? What level or dimension does it come from?

Washta: It is a lower vibratory level of the energies of pure God light; however, it is still a great celestial energy. It was put into place for the purpose of bringing various star systems into alterations of consciousness, of bringing them through changes and shifts in dimensions. This is what is going to occur here once again on Earth. You are about to re-experience this drama that the Earth and its solar system have entered many times, because there is roughly a 26,000 year cycle involved in this whole process.

The last photon belt experience happened around the time of the destruction of Lemuria, approximately 25,000 years ago; however, it was not the cause of that destruction as we will later explain.

Virginia: Could you say more about the quality of this energy and give it a dimensional designation we can understand?

Washta: It is an energy that operates in a 3rd- and a 4th-dimensional reality. It is a great energy of light that changes and alters itself and creates great openings into dimensional time portals—which is what the 4th dimension is about. Therefore, whenever the Earth and your solar system go through the photon belt's alterations, great shifts occur in the radioactive activities of your planet and in its electrical and magnetic fields. Some shifts have occurred that have caused great catastrophes so it is basically what one might call an awesome omen of change in the sky which your planet has passed through from time to time.

Virginia: In the photon belt illustration *(See Figure 1, Chapter 2, Configuration of Photon Belt)* it looks like a doughnut containing energies and particles. Has it always maintained that same shape?

Washta: It has changed from time to time, for it is an interdimensional energy. What is shown here, however, is one of its recent aspects of reality. This is about as close a general drawing as we can give. Earth scientists who have actually discovered the photon belt, and who have secretly been allowed to discuss it, have noticed that it gives off enormous amounts of gamma rays and other massive radiation particles. Because these radiations exist along the entire edge of this particular belt, the scientists are very worried about it. However, we will inform you of the whole process so that you may understand.

Your planet is inside a great light bubble, a hologram, which was created in 1972 by the Sirians. The hologram was created in response to the actions of the dark forces who altered your Sun's polarity in a negative way. To protect your solar system and your planet from the harmful effects of your Sun, the hologram was created and your Sun's polarity was reversed. This occurred between 1987 and 1989, in preparation for the coming of the photon belt.

Various alterations and changes are constantly occurring because of the vast energy shifts now being created in this solar system by both the Time Lords and the Spiritual Hierarchies. Therefore, the actual entry date into the belt will not be known until just two to six months before it actually occurs. We will come in our mass landings to protect your entire planet from negative physical events and to teach you how to utilize photon energy. We do bring help and hope! But the dates of our arrival are based upon the energy patterns and changes in human consciousness upon your planet. We advise you that the crucial energy pattern, which will determine the final entry point for your planet and its solar system into this incredible photon light, is now approaching.

Virginia: Could you indicate why this shape of the torroid (the manasic ring) is important?

Washta: It is important because it is what might be called a halo in the galaxy. It acts much as a halo would act over the head of an ascended one having energies around his or her crown. This halo represents, in both a symbolic and physical way, what this energy will do to those whom it will encounter. It will create a great God test, a great change in their realities. It will cause those who encounter the belt to ascend into new realities and dimensions, and it will prepare them for a great challenge they are capable of passing through.

Virginia: That halo image is a wonderful one! Please further clarify why Earth's human family and the planet are being helped at this particular time.

Washta: The first reason is the great increase humans made in consciousness, beginning in the 1950s, accelerating in the 1960s and the 1970s—and most especially in the late 1980s. Secondly, because the Spiritual Hierarchy of Lady Gaia (the name we give to the Earth and all of its angels, archangels and ascended masters) decided to save your planet's civilization, contrary to the Galactic Federation's Sirian Regional Council's opinion. The cetaceans and the Earth's Spiritual Hierarchy first requested, back in the early 1970s, that some of the solar difficulties of this particular cycle of the photon belt experience be alleviated for your civilization.

We, Sirians, are deeply committed to aid the Spiritual Hierarchy of your planet and solar system and always do what we feel is desired by the great will of the God Force. Therefore, we began petitioning on your behalf among other council members within the Galactic Federation's Sirian Regional Council to protect your physical world from the unspeakable catastrophe that would surely occur because of the upcoming photon belt. The photon belt would have created the great catastrophic scenario that many of your psychics have been warning about during the last decade and a half. However, because of the intervention of the Earth's Spiritual Hierarchy and because of the rise in human consciousness since the 1950s, this new scenario was given priority and is now being implemented.

Virginia: Thank you for that energy and effort. So in other words, if the cetaceans, the Spiritual Hierarchy, and you Sirians had not called upon the Sirian Regional Council of the Galactic Federation for leniency then the destruction would have continued?

Washta: Yes. You see, many members in the Galactic Federation's

47

Sirian Regional Council (that have jurisdiction over your particular planet and solar system) had previously agreed that it was necessary for humans to experience the photon belt. This was because the mutant human civilization on your planet was not raising its consciousness to the desired level—a level required for it to be saved on a mass basis. However, because of the intervention of the Spiritual Hierarchies (including your great spiritual leaders such as Lord Jesus, etc.), the intervention of the cetaceans, as well as we Sirians pleading on your behalf with the Galactic Federation—Sirian Regional Council members allowed this dreadful photon belt to be shifted after voting for the adoption of the present positive plan we bring.

Virginia: I'm sure I speak for many other humans when I say thank you for that intervention! Many Earth people who hear about the potential electrical device's inoperability during the 5-6 day null zone experience say they'll use campfires, Coleman stoves and heaters, and so on, as substitutes. Could you speak about the use of fire and possible electrical device substitutes?

Washta: Regular carbon-based heating equipment will still operate, however we would ask all humans on this planet to accept our suggestions. Before this photon belt experience occurs, and this great halo of change becomes the reality for everyday life on this world, know that we will come to help you. Yes! There will be a mass landing by those who represent this Galactic Federation in what is called the First Contact Team.

We will be coming in large numbers to your planet for one purpose only. That purpose is to help your entire planetary civilization ascend into the next dimensional civilization which is galactic—to help you be transformed into galactic humans. We will therefore be providing units for electrical energy needs, for basic housing needs, also for clothing, food and so forth. This will allow all of you on your planet to take care of your basic needs and necessities. Consequently, since we have to thoroughly clean your toxic atmosphere, we would prefer that all utilization of carbon-based technology be minimized. This means that campfires and other forms of burning carbon-based fuels such as kerosene lamps and Coleman-type stoves should be eliminated or curtailed as much as possible.

Virginia: You mentioned the pressure on this planet during the upcoming changes, although you say there will not be a pole shift. Some people feel that this pressure will create a tectonic plate interaction and seismic activity of major proportion, etc. Is this likely or what comment might you make to clarify this?

Washta: Let us clarify that the incoming photon belt is causing a great deal of stress on your entire solar system, not merely planet Earth. However, you have three levels of assistance helping you with this problem. One comes from the great spiritual caregivers and angels on many different dimensions. A second comes from those in human form who assist the God forces. And then, of course, we have been aiding you by instituting protective energy patterns around your planet. This enormous, combined effort keeps the amount of seismic activity to a minimum. This is why various earthquakes around your planet have not been as dangerous in magnitude as they could have been.

However, while seismic activity on your planet will be kept as low as possible, there must be some activity for there is a natural energy release pattern that the Earth normally goes through. And humans have done destructive bombings above and below ground that have taken their toll, have they not? Some humans on this planet may experience death or dislocation in spite of our best efforts because there are some poorer countries where the housing structures and public buildings cannot withstand even the smallest tremors. This is because they are inexpensively constructed or improperly erected to resist earth movement. We regret that any loss of life as a natural act of nature must happen and assure you we are doing amazing things to minimize what would otherwise be a near total planetary disaster!

Virginia: Yes and we thank you for that help and concern! Nonetheless, can you imagine what the average human person thinks who hears you say that the Galactic Federation scientists are able to do something so powerful as to realign the Sun? To most of us, the Sun is such a major aspect of life that it seems permanent, or at least available for billions of years. Could you just briefly describe how such a seemingly unbelievable thing was accomplished?

Washta: The explanation is as follows: All celestial objects, or heavenly bodies, as they are called in your basic science, have interdimensional portals around them. These exist in various angles

49

around the entire orb. For example, the Sun—which is the one you wish to discuss—is a very special star for Earth's existence, but it is a star nonetheless. As a star, it has a longevity much as every human on your planet has one. Because the Sun is now in what might be called a late middle-age period, it has already matured, so to speak, and has established these energy portals. These energy portals control its very existence—in fact, physical planets and stars like your Sun are a different life form than what you presently think. They are a new type of living organism that you will learn about as your science increases its willingness to know the truth.

You will begin to understand that what I am about to say is not only logical but simple science. How one goes about the entire process is as follows. First, the energy portal points on a particular star are energized and examined. Then once the degree of imbalance is completely analyzed, one can then set apart various counter energy points in these portals. When the Sun's energy portals are activated, these energy patterns then flash over it in a vast high frequency light across the entire solar magnetosphere—which extends out and includes its entire solar system, all its planets, its asteroids, its comets, etc. Basically, this is what was done. We could explain this in greater detail, but would like to keep our explanation simple and avoid advanced mathematics for the average reader, which is not necessary right now.

Virginia: Are you saying that you had these abilities to alter the portal points? Or did those you call the Time Lords have to be involved in such maneuvers?

Washta: These maneuvers—concerning the positive alteration of your Sun—required not only our science but also the great intervention of the Spiritual Hierarchies. These Spiritual Hierarchies control the 3rd, 4th, and 5th interdimensional portals (gates) that surround your Sun. Once these maneuvers were completed, the final stages of these positive alterations could proceed.

Virginia: Thank you. Is there any way that our Earth scientists would be able to determine that this is now a different kind of Sun than what they could view astronomically in prior times?

Washta: They would notice that the star they called the Sun has gone through vast changes in its magnetosphere, that its cronosphere has greatly changed and that Sun spot activity patterns have been altered. These phenomena occurred because they are the physical manifestations of the interdimensional shifts that were required to bring the Sun and its great promenades under control, thus avoiding a near disaster for your planet. We interceded so that your planet and solar system could gradually move toward the photon belt and the safer destiny recommended by your Spiritual Hierarchy. Know that angels, spiritual masters, the Time Lords, and ultimately the great God Force itself, have saved your planet through this process.

Virginia: I was told that in 1972 the light and the dark forces were vying for control over our Sun and its planets (primarily Earth) and that in order to save this solar system, the light forces changed our reality. Is this just what you've explained? What kind of reality have we been living in since the Sun was changed and we were placed in a protected hologram?

Washta: Those of the dark forces, as you call them, did not want the transformation of humanity to occur nor did they want us to bring this entire solar system into the light. They attempted to interfere with the Sun in such a way as to cause its entire system to be vastly altered—so that their reality could determine the future destiny of the entire solar system. Therefore, our intervention was required since it had been agreed by the Earth's Spiritual Hierarchies that whatever happened to your planet must be done within its own destiny patterns, not those patterns brought from some other place.

So we Sirians, along with the Galactic Federation, brought in those of science and a pure spirit to alter this entire system. The result is that your planet now sits in the midst of a hologram causing your reality to appear to be unchanged. However, a vast shift has already occurred because of Galactic Federation intervention, though you don't know it yet. What is now happening to you is unprecedented but protects you from psychological overload and distress. Within the planetary hologram you are being allowed to gradually move through changes and shifts in reality. These changes will allow you to reclaim what was meant to be your destiny as a fully conscious person in a civilization existing within a fully conscious, multidimensional world.

Virginia: Could you indicate if these dark forces you mentioned were the "grays" from Zeta Reticuli who had considerable negative activity here?

Washta: These people that you have just mentioned were unfortunately the tools being used by the dark forces to create a horrendous disaster for your solar system—especially for your particular planet. They were attempting to create a new type of solar system that would allow their kind and their reality to maintain its permanence, and end any intervention by galactic humans in your solar system. This would also have vastly altered the origins and realities of your solar system because it would have affected the destiny for which that origin and reality are based.

Virginia: Would these dark forces be the reptoids and/or dinoids? Or are you referring to a totally different energy source?

Washta: These grays are but the instruments of this dark energy which has flowed through present creation from its beginnings. This energy is now being dissipated as was promised as part of the great prophecy. That prophecy said that all life in creation would pass through ages of darkness and then eventually reach light when the reunion with the higher realms became possible. Creation thus goes through many cycles of light and darkness until the final light is ready to appear. This is what is occurring at this time. You are now securing a period of light in your particular solar system. The darkness that has held you in unconsciousness for so long has been put to a great retreat. The dark energy is presently acting in a very minimal way in your solar system, although on your planet its last vestiges are still great, even as we now speak.

Virginia: The average person who thinks about the Sun probably thinks about the words heat and light. Has there been any shift or change in what we would call the Sun's output of heat or light?

Washta: Heat and light from the Sun have been changed because portions of its energy have been drawn off to support this new hologram placed around your entire solar system. This hologram will protect you when your planet goes into the photon belt which is why we say the polarity energies of the Sun have been altered. This has been done in order to obtain the successful completion of the great shift in reality that is about to happen on your world.

Virginia: We were most pleased to learn about the research ships and survey teams who are working with the ozone layer. Can you give us an update on your perception of Earth's situation at this time?

Washta: At this present moment, various sections of the ozone layer have been vastly improved. We have been able to fix many of the northern hemispheric and southern hemispheric danger areas thus preventing a potentially life threatening situation for humans on your planet. We are continually evaluating the great ozone holes in both the north and south polar regions and we have been able to fix significant areas of the northern polar region. We are now working on the southern polar region. Know, therefore, that these areas will begin to stabilize and return to their original forms because of what we are doing. We remind you that the pressures that are creating this danger are two in nature. One cause is the various chemicals being used by the so-called petrochemical industry on your planet. The second cause is the actual photon belt energy itself. It affects not only the surface through tectonic activities but tears at the upper atmosphere as well.

Virginia: Thank you for the reminder that we have these responsibilities. Speaking of the photon belt, I am personally uncomfortable with specific dates for events on planet Earth. Too many people have forecasted that something will happen at a particular time and it doesn't. How can readers have any confidence when you say that sometime between the spring of 1995 and the last months of 1996, people are going to have a photon belt experience? What is it in your judgment that allows you to make such a statement to us?

Washta: We are relaying what the Time Keepers of our various special temples (that represent the great interlink between you and the Galactic Federation), the Time Lords, and the various Spiritual Hierarchies, have stated to us. They indicate that this present belt of light, this halo of change that is approaching your solar system and your world, is meant to happen in a great collision sometime between those years and months just given. However, the exact time of this encounter is related to two very important factors which we must now reiterate.

One, the raising of higher consciousness of the planet Earth is an important aspect of this whole operation. As the higher consciousness of the planet is raised, it will determine the exact timing of our landings. If higher consciousness is raised naturally during the initial first contact landings, then this enormous process can be done quickly. We can move the first contact landing forward in time or hold it back toward the latter part of 1996. Or if there is a great need in your world for this light to occur sooner, then it will begin at a much earlier time, namely toward the middle or the end of 1995.

There is a second factor and that relates to how we, as a Galactic Federation, and the Spiritual Hierarchy of Lady Gaia, desire this scenario to occur. All the planning partners have said that this is the general time frame. However, the exact moment for first contact has not yet been decided, nor a specific date set for the photon belt entry to begin. There will be a specific date for the ascension process once enough darkness has been dissipated by the positive energy work being done by the Spiritual Hierarchies of this world. A final and specific date is not yet available for this mammoth undertaking, but we can say that it will occur sometime in or near the 1995-96 time frame.

Virginia: We know you would not wish any embarrassment to your channel by having those dates pass without the prescribed situation occurring. So we request that you remain sensitive to the needs of his accuracy regarding the dates that have been given herewith and forward any and all updates as necessary.

Washta: We have been told that these dates have been finalized. However as you know, the time lines of the universe that you experience are not set in specific and total finalities. Even when the finalities have been agreed upon, the Time Lords' pulses of light—coming from the God source, the awesome force of all creation—can be changed. For they and they alone know the finalities that are to exist as this great creation unfolds.

Virginia: We are concerned about the process of safely guiding people—especially children—through the photon belt experience. Even though you say your first contact forces and counselors will make an appearance, we feel that there hasn't been the kind of preparation from our governments that would allow people to believe in the process and begin to prepare for it. We wonder if you have any further comments, suggestions or recommendations about how this could best be dealt with?

Washta: We would ask that all people who are engaged in lightwork of any type whether it is with the angelic or guardian groups, whether with ecological difficulties, with the cetaceans, or any aspects of human development and preservation of life whatsoever, come together and network among themselves. By sharing the latest news among themselves and then sharing with others around them, all people on your planet who have access to the light networks can be prepared. In this way you can act as a prototype.

We also ask all of you who form these networks of light to come together and establish dates and times to do your meditations. Also formulate actions based upon your cooperative consciousness that will give you comfort and security. Be prepared to act in unison for the good of humanity in thought and deed! For it will not take a huge number of humans, acting as a unified group around your globe, to bring this great energy of change and consciousness to the planet and allow it to be safely anchored in such a way that it supports everyone—even those who still sit in denial of it.

Virginia: Thank you, and that brings to mind one last major question. Some people believe there has been a karmic requirement for people to become conscious through their own growth and education, and others believe that grace, as we understand it, allows total forgiveness and love to be granted to all—thereby canceling out all karma and negativity. Is it possible for this kind of grace to be applied to over 5 billion people on Earth? Have you any final thoughts or explanation concerning this issue of karma and grace?

Washta: We would like to state first of all, to all beings who reside on planet Earth in human form, that your planet is a planet of grace. It is a planet in which all who have incarnated on it, have done so because of this opportunity of grace and forgiveness. This law of love and light is the basis of the Spiritual Hierarchy and all that is created in and around it. Earth humans must realize that they came here to Earth to put this love and light, this grace of forgiveness, around this entire planet. They will realize as your world ascends, that humans came to Earth for this purpose. For as the consciousness falls on the planet and then rises into the great light around it, the amnesia which has prevented humans from seeing this light will be lifted. One might use the analogy of a blind man who suddenly falls down, hurting his head. But to everyone's amazement he discovers that the accident has miraculously given his sight back. This miracle is what is about to happen to you and your planet. You are about to come out of darkness and blindness into light—into a stunning and incredible vision.

Virginia: In other words, the prior state of our consciousness does not count for, or against, having our consciousness raised through the photon belt experience?

Washta: That is absolutely correct. Earth is a planet of grace.

It is becoming a planet that will truly demonstrate this grace and love, so everyone who is part of this galaxy can come here to observe the results and to realize that your model can spread to every part of this great galaxy.

Virginia: So we would become as galactic humans going forth as a model for other planets and star systems?

Washta: That is correct. This star—your planet—was put in this universe and this galaxy for the purpose of becoming one of the great showcases or models of light. It is to be a major focal point or example of light, love and forgiveness for this entire galaxy. By your example many of the undecided or the dark beings will see the actual application of the Creator Force's grace so they, too, may ascend into the energy of the Time Lords. They too may enter that timeless realm of light that is truly a heavenly one, as described in many prophecies that now exist around your present human civilization. This is what your planet is about. This is the great mission of your world and of humans on the planet. You are about to enter into the age when your destiny will be fulfilled.

Virginia: We thank you so much for your willingness to be with us today, and ask the three of you whether our questions have aroused further thoughts you'd like to share with us before you leave?

· **Washta:** We would just like to finish with one final thought. We would ask all on your planet to realize that there is a new age of consciousness growing on planet Earth. At present, in fact, every human on planet Earth is being altered genetically, some in very small ways, others in larger ways, depending upon the position that they must play in bringing this great new civilization into reality. You of this world are seeking, as never before, to understand what the energy is that surrounds you. This is part of the pattern of bringing this new energy of consciousness back into human civilization and allowing it to alter your civilization as it has not been altered for vast millennia. Therefore, please cooperate with this new galactic civilization. What we are doing is no more than bringing this energy in with the assistance and full love of the cetaceans, and also the will of the Spiritual Hierarchy that is surrounding your planet. We ask you to realize that what is happening is not something to fear. Rather, it is a gift of love, light, and grace leading to a great and glorious destiny for Earth's awakening prodigals.

Chapter 4
The Photon Belt's Effect
on the Human Body

The Sirian Council for this chapter is composed of Washta, Sirai, and Teletron. Sirai is a female Sirian liaison with the Spiritual Hierarchies and a noted exobiologist and counselor. Teletron is a Sirian expert on Lyran/Sirian culture and a noted galactic historian.

In this chapter we will communicate what the photon belt's effect will be on the human body, particularly; and explain what this will mean to your planet and your civilization as well. As we previously stated, the physical body of all Earth human beings will be completely altered as a result of the coming photon belt. Humans will be changed from having a gross or dense physical body to a semi-etheric or less dense one. At present, all body types are relegated by researchers in this field of somatic research into three major categories. These body types are as follows: 1) a gross or very physical body (your present 3rd-dimensional body type), 2) an etheric body (similar to auras, ghosts or to higher dimensional bodies), and 3) a purely spiritual body (the so-called soul body). Let us look at the consequences of this change for your body.

The first type—the physical body—is what most Earth humans of this planet are presently encased in. This body type consists of a flesh and blood physique that ages and eventually dies after a relatively short period of but five, six, seven, eight or possibly nine or ten decades. What will happen in the coming galactic civilization is a transformation of this presently gross or physical body into a more etheric body that we will call a semi-etheric body. This body type is one that has the capabilities and appearance of the present physical

57

body but with the many characteristics possessed by a purely etheric body.

This transformation means that your body can rejuvenate itself and be virtually ageless. Your semi-etheric body will respond in many ways like a thought form because your mind will be able to change your body as easily as it changes thoughts. However to you, this body will appear and act as if it were still the original type of gross physical body that you have now. Moreover, this new body will have still another dramatic transformation. This fundamental modification has to do with the composition of your DNA. *(See Figure 5: Comparison of the Composition of the DNA Molecule.)*

All Earth humans presently live in a body with only two basic coils (helixes) of DNA, whereas before the "fall" you had the full consciousness complement of 12 helixes. However, we are helping your DNA coils increase from two to twelve (or six fold) again. This transformation will restore the cellular structure of the body to its original form and allow the cells in your body to easily interact with the interdimensional spirit body (soul) that it contains. *(See Figure 6: Interdimensional Connections of a Six Pair DNA Molecule.)* This new configuration will follow the shape of a "Star of David" and allow each cell to easily connect to its topographical counterpoint on other dimensional levels. To make the whole message short and uncomplicated, let us just state that each of these six portal points will interconnect to a position where part of any of the 3rd, 4th, 5th, 6th, 7th and 8th dimensional realities of our multidimensional universe intersect. The cell will thus possess a multidimensional scalar wave antenna that can easily pick up and immediately process any important message that the cell and its DNA package are given by the soul. Scalar waves are non-hertzian wave forms that have the ability to propagate themselves in any form of multidimensional reality and carry information with them as they travel. Similarly, your body will also change in the way its chakra centers (energy vortexes) are put together.

YOUR CURRENT CHAKRA SYSTEM

These energies vortex centers are translated into English as "circles" from the Hindu or Sanskrit word **chakra**. *(See Figure 7: The Prismatic Colors and the Current Chakra System.)* These energy "circles" or chakras are now present in your physical body as a series of only seven energy centers. These centers run from the base of the body to the top of the head and are constituted as follows:

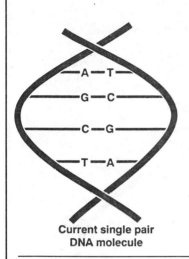

**Current single pair
DNA molecule**

The double-strand DNA molecule is made up of a series of genes or units called *nucleotides*: adenine (A), thymine (T), guanine (G), and cytosine (C). A is always paired with T, and G is always paired with C. The sequence of nucleotide pairs determine the difference between kinds of living things.

The two strands of DNA carry genetic information such as height, eye color, skeletal structure, etc. In this example, one strand has A-G-C-T, etc. and the opposite strand has T-C-G-A, etc. This does not imply that there are *only* four genes or units in a strand of DNA molecule. In fact, there are about six billion genes or units in the DNA molecule of a single human cell. Imagine this sequence in the form of a very long, unbroken thread.

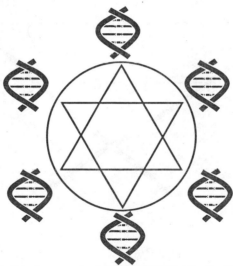

**Reassembled six double-stranded DNA molecules in their
interdimensional full consciousness pattern.**

DNA molecules are located at multidimensional intersect points. Molecules intersect and communicate through energies passed from one portal position to another.

Figure 5: Comparison of the Composition
of the DNA Molecule

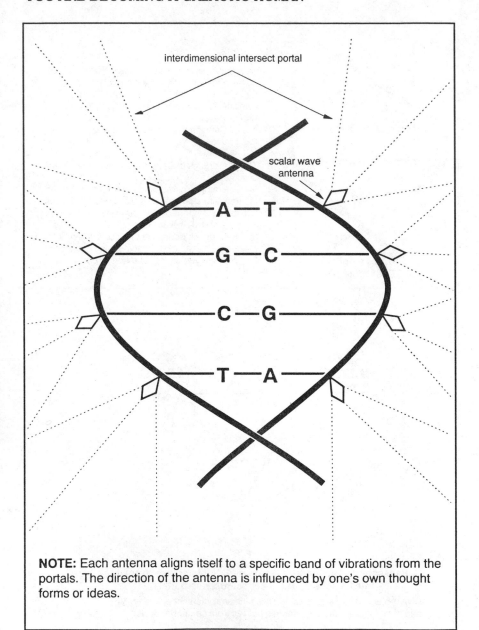

**Figure 6: Interdimensional Connections of
a Six Pair DNA Molecule**

The **first chakra** is called the root center. It is the foundation or prime electrical ground for the body. It connects the body's electromagnetic grid to Earth much as a ground does in a typical RF or radio electrical circuit. This center is located at the base of the torso or the spine.

The **second chakra** is the sex or sexual center. This center acts

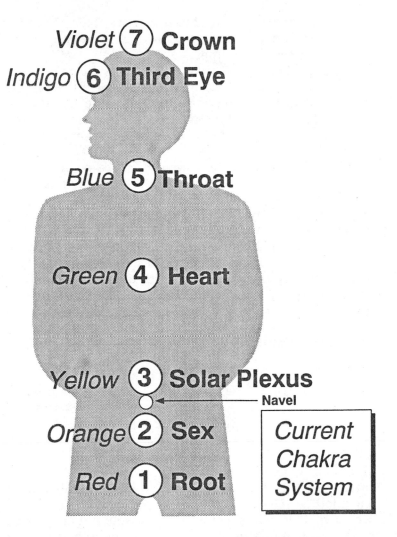

Figure 7: The Prismatic Colors and the Current Chakra System

as the sexual emotional center (higher forms of pleasure and ecstasy) for the body and is located in the same region of the body that contains the genitals.

The **third chakra** is at the solar plexus. It acts as the body's base emotional (hate, anger, joy, laughter) center and is located in the region of the body that contains the belly button, the spleen, and the liver.

The **fourth chakra** is the heart center. This chakra is the intuitive or love center (higher emotions) and is centered around the region of the heart and the lungs.

The **fifth chakra** is the throat center. It is the communication center and is located in the region of the larynx in the throat.

The **sixth chakra** is the so-called "third eye" or *Ajna* center. This center is located above the nose in the center of the brow and is the center for receiving and utilizing various visionary and related psychic abilities.

The **seventh chakra** is the crown center located at the back part of the top of the head. It is the center for the connection to the higher self.

The aura, or the body's energy field, surrounds these seven centers and acts as an indicator of how efficiently these centers are performing. Traditionally, the set of chakras has had the seven prismatic colors assigned to it, one color for each chakra. In effect, the aura and its colors reflect the health of the chakra and at the same time indicate how efficiently any selected part of the body is performing.

YOUR NEW CHAKRA SYSTEM/SEMI-ETHERIC BODY

To better understand this new chakra system, we will first explain how the various chakras interact with one another in your new semi-etheric body. Then, we will give a complete overview of the new 13-chakra system. In this way, you will be able to fully comprehend this presently evolving system of body energy centers (chakras).

In your new semi-etheric body, a great deal of variation will occur in how these energy centers operate and how they will interact with one another. Therefore, let's examine what these changes are and see how they will affect your new semi-etheric body. To understand how the new chakra system actually operates and invigorates the body, it is necessary to observe how the interplay between the chakras actually functions.

Because the eighth chakra and the sixth chakra of the new chakra system are both light sensitive (the basis of life is light), the frequencies of light in these centers will resonate together and produce love energies. This effect causes the eighth and the sixth chakras to resonate the fifth or heart chakra. *(See Figure 8: The Interaction of Life Energies in the New Chakra System.)*

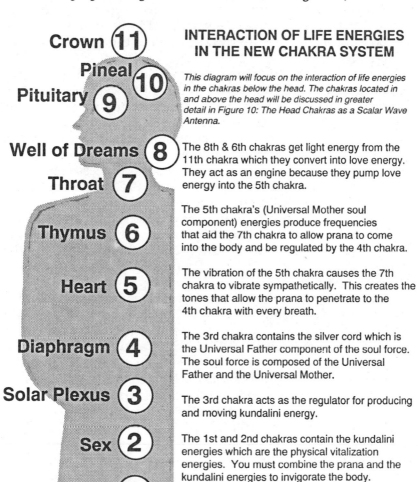

Crown (11)
Pineal (10)
Pituitary (9)
Well of Dreams (8)
Throat (7)
Thymus (6)
Heart (5)
Diaphragm (4)
Solar Plexus (3)
Sex (2)
Root (1)

INTERACTION OF LIFE ENERGIES IN THE NEW CHAKRA SYSTEM

This diagram will focus on the interaction of life energies in the chakras below the head. The chakras located in and above the head will be discussed in greater detail in Figure 10: The Head Chakras as a Scalar Wave Antenna.

The 8th & 6th chakras get light energy from the 11th chakra which they convert into love energy. They act as an engine because they pump love energy into the 5th chakra.

The 5th chakra's (Universal Mother soul component) energies produce frequencies that aid the 7th chakra to allow prana to come into the body and be regulated by the 4th chakra.

The vibration of the 5th chakra causes the 7th chakra to vibrate sympathetically. This creates the tones that allow the prana to penetrate to the 4th chakra with every breath.

The 3rd chakra contains the silver cord which is the Universal Father component of the soul force. The soul force is composed of the Universal Father and the Universal Mother.

The 3rd chakra acts as the regulator for producing and moving kundalini energy.

The 1st and 2nd chakras contain the kundalini energies which are the physical vitalization energies. You must combine the prana and the kundalini energies to invigorate the body.

Inhaling breath brings prana Into the body from 7th chakra to 1st chakra. Exhaling breath causes kundalini to flow from 1st to 11th chakra.

Figure 8: The Interaction of Life Energies in the New Chakra System

The resonating of the eighth, sixth, and fifth chakras comes from energy originally received through the eleventh chakra and produces harmonic effects which allow the seventh or throat chakra to successfully create additional tones. As these tonal energies pass through the vocal cords, they allow the incoming prana (life sustaining energy from Mother Earth) to move down to the fourth chakra or diaphragm center. The diaphragm center allows prana to interact with the cells of the body and to invigorate it. In this manner, you are able to produce a chakra pattern that permits the body to become fully energized.

Of course, the bottom three chakras hold part of the soul force and connect it through the "silver cord" at the solar plexus. (The "silver cord" is the total vibratory pattern of each unique soul.) This aspect of the soul's energies connects the soul with one half of its universal sources from higher dimensions (called the Universal Father) and this connection regulates how the soul energy is distributed throughout the body. The key to this process is the solar plexus center or third chakra. The solar plexus contains the "silver cord" and also connects it to the first and second chakras. Around it is the electrical grid system of the body, which connects this cord to the fifth or heart chakra which contains the other half of the soulforce called the Universal Mother. The Universal Mother is the other half of the soul force that forms the creative aspect or the higher self (true self) personality.

Let us now explain how all this operates in your soon-to-be 13-chakra system. As we have just stated, you have the third chakra center with the "silver cord" or the connection with the soul force. To understand the significance of this chakra, you should understand how the body's chakra system is interconnected. One of the major energy receiving centers for the body is located in the sixth chakra and positioned at the upper back of the shoulders. This entry point takes in one half of the soul force (Universal Mother), that must intermingle with the other half of the soul force. This other half (Universal Father) comes in through the third chakra and interacts with the prana center or the fourth chakra. This process still occurs in Earth humans although the fourth chakra's ability to easily convert prana has been largely destroyed. This ability will be recreated and reactivated in galactic humans.

The bottom two chakras are the centers for storing kundalini (invigorating cellular) energy. These centers constantly radiate kundalini energy which is used to control the prana (planetary life force energy) conversion system of the third and fourth chakras. All prana moves from the eleventh down through the third chakras. It then meets the kundalini energy moving up from the first chakra. These energies enjoin at the third chakra and then move up to the eleventh or crown chakra. The energy finally moves up through the universal centers of the twelfth and thirteenth chakras, the galactic female and the galactic male. In this way, the body maintains its maleness (right side), and its femaleness (left side).

The nervous, circulatory, and consciousness systems tend to mirror this male/female dichotomy and utilize these energies. By observing these reactions, you begin to understand how these various life energies interact in the body of a galactic human. In effect, you begin to learn how the chakras function to maintain the body as a vehicle for light, love and full consciousness.

As just noted, your chakras will be converted from the seven centers you now have to eleven human centers. These additional four centers will interlink with two interdimensional or etheric centers at the top of your auric field that are called the galactic male and galactic female centers. In effect, you will have a total of thirteen chakras. Two of them will be purely etheric in form and eleven will become a part of your physical selves.

These are the descriptions of your soon-to-be 13 chakras. *(See Figure 9: The New Chakra System.)*

The **first chakra** will be in the same place as it previously was and will still be called the root center.

The **second chakra** will also remain as the sexual or sex center.

The **third chakra** will continue as the solar plexus center.

The **fourth chakra** is the first major modification. It will now be called the diaphragm center. This new chakra will be the center for governing stress since it will be the focal point for rejuvenating the prana or breath energy of the body. The prana or energy of the air acts to revitalize the body and to remove all deleterious elements from the body.

The **fifth chakra** becomes the heart center. It is not just a center for intuitive energy and higher emotions such as love; but it has also become a center for the expression of pure angelic love that is devoid of all base emotional expression.

Because your body has been changed from a purely physical form to a somewhat more etheric thought form, it will have an exceptional immune system that is extremely strong and viable. You will use the **sixth chakra** or thymus center to act as the focus of all these activities. The thymus gland is presently one of the most misunderstood glands of the human body. This paradox concerns

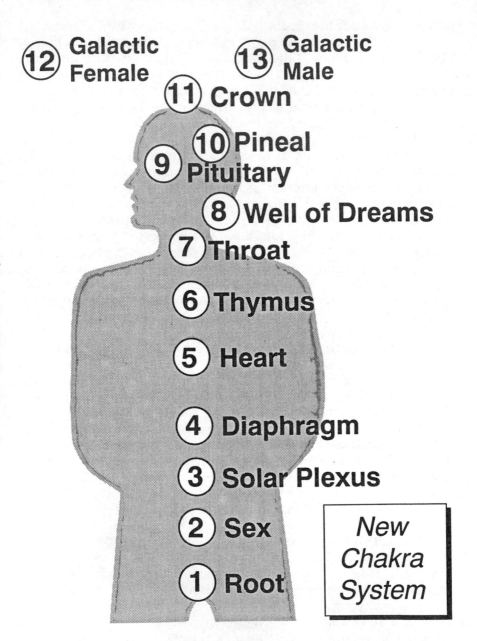

Figure 9: The New Chakra System

the thymus' sensitivity to radiation. The high levels of radiation in your planet's atmosphere that create aging were produced when it was ripped asunder by catastrophic events during your antediluvian histories about 6,000 years ago (see chapters 5 and 6). This radiation caused the thymus center in humans to rapidly deteriorate by early childhood and to shrink from an organ almost the size of the human heart to an organ about the size of a small pea.

As the new human body advances to galactic form after the photon belt's arrival, the thymus will only shrink from the size of your present human heart to a size about one-third of the human heart. What this means is that your thymus center will remain as active and as virile in the adult body as it was in the body of a new born. The ability of the human body to ward-off all kinds of diseases and any difficulties associated with the environment will, therefore, remain extremely high and the thymus will not shrink as one grows older. In other words, this new thymus center will make aging practically non-existent among galactic humans.

The **seventh chakra** is the throat center and it is the center for communications and speech. This area will function in many of its former capacities because it is a conduit for the energies emanating from the head to the rest of the body.

The **eighth chakra** is called the well of dreams center. It is considered by many to be an old atrophied chakra and it is located roughly near the base of the skull, right above the neck. This chakra is needed to regulate the various dream and vision-like states that a fully conscious being can reach.

The **ninth chakra** develops into a control center for consciousness, and will be fully developed in the galactic human. It is located in the lower central part of the brain and consists of the so-called primitive brain and the pituitary gland. In a galactic human, it will allow the body to react to light and radiation in a way that permits the body to rejuvenate itself. The sixth chakra or thymus center and the ninth chakra or pituitary center interact with one another to heal and to revitalize the body.

The **tenth chakra** will be known as the third eye or vision center, because it brings in the higher light frequencies. This chakra joins with the eighth chakra to allow the mind to interpret visions and other messages from higher vibratory states.

The **eleventh chakra** now assumes service as the crown chakra. It is where the physical body will connect to the spiritual energy, to invigorate your body. The crown is the place where the auric fields of the body come together making possible major connections to the **twelfth and thirteenth chakra** centers. These final two spiritual chakras are the *galactic male* and *galactic female energy centers* because they contain the ideal female and male prototype.

Please observe how the interconnection between these three chakras (the 11th, 12th and 13th) operate. *(See Figure 10: The Head Chakras as a Scalar Wave Antenna.)* From the 11th, by drawing a triangle, you can link the 12th and 13th chakras together as a unit. You can then draw other lines (See *Figure 10*) between the 8th, 9th and 10th, and 11th chakras. This connection in the brain creates a scalar wave antenna (transmitter and a receiver of high frequency non-hertzian radio-like multidimensional life force energy). This antenna allows the energy of the body to radiate its life energy to others as well as to receive another's energies. Thus, the upper (11th, 12th, and 13th) and lower centers (8th, 9th and 10th) of the brain will be able to communicate with one another in ways that you are not capable of understanding at this time.

Because of these various changes to the chakra system, the many segments of the brain that were atrophied by Atlantean genetic experiments will be returned to their former shape and size. In two generations, humans will again have the larger style brain cavity that is the heritage of fully conscious humans. This will allow your scalar wave antenna to be fully utilized and all psychic energies to be processed in an appropriate manner. In effect, Earth humans will not only have first or primal sight, but also a complete "second sight" granting many so-called psychic abilities such as telepathy, telekinesis, clairvoyance and clairaudience.

Because of the immense electrical and consciousness changes all humans must undergo, the Galactic Federation intends to orchestrate a mass landing of counselors, other personnel, and important scientific and healing technologies—up to six months before the photon belt arrives. These forces of the Galactic Federation will tell you what is about to happen as well as how these changes are going to affect you. The Galactic Federation personnel will also teach you how to communicate with other Earth humans as well as with us galactic humans. Communication skills are essential for what will soon transpire to you personally and to the planetary society.

Once you are guided to communicate within your personal consciousness, you'll have to practice self control and neutral imaging so you won't harm yourselves. For streaming in all around you will be the thoughts of others including their wishes; their prayers; their upsetnesses; and their anxieties—in short, the posi-

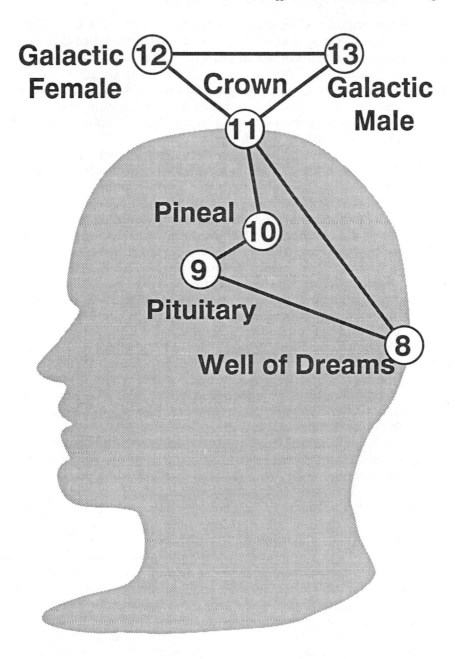

Figure 10: The Head Chakras as a Scalar Wave Antenna

tive and the negative. Therefore, you must be taught how to regulate these new energies and how to be a constructive part of this new consciousness. The second thing you have to learn is the etiquette of how to interact with one another. This is something that most Earth humans do not presently understand. This etiquette will be explained to you and will enable you to fully understand the forces of the physical and spiritual worlds that surround you. Only then can you become a true steward of your planet.

As previously stated, you are moving from a 3rd-dimensional physical reality to a 5th-dimensional (semi-ethereal) reality. You are moving into a world in which all minds share a common consciousness and human beings no longer have the kind of separate world that you presently have. You are also moving to a consciousness where things can be done by humans that would, at present, be considered miraculous. Therefore, every Earth human must understand what his/her capabilities are and what his/her realities mean.

This education project is what the Galactic Federation will be sharing with you before the arrival of the photon belt. Once you have learned to regulate your new consciousness process, it then becomes necessary to understand how you control and utilize thought forms; how you communicate properly with those that have previously died; and how you use this knowledge to aid yourself and others. This entire process will be taught to you by counselors who will land on your planet before the photon belt arrives. As this education continues, humans will see that the population must operate as a vast web of interconnected consciousness.

After you learn some basic qualities of galactic humanness, you can enjoy having a lighter body and using thought forms to rejuvenate and overcome aging. You will also have the ability to communicate within your own being, with other people, plants and animals including Lady Gaia herself. You will also have full communication with those who have died in previous times as well as those who might today be called angels or archangels. In short, you will become both a being of spirit and a being of the physical.

As this occurs, all humanity must be aware that a new age has arrived and that this new reality was made possible for everyone by the efforts of the Earth's Spiritual Hierarchy and the Galactic Federation. Therefore, rejoice at what is happening to you! To clearly understand the events that are occurring today, it is essential to learn the true history of Earth and your solar system. The succeeding chapters of this book will reveal hidden Earth history and explain how this secret information relates to what is transpiring around you now.

Many questions about the material in this chapter may now come to mind. In the next section, Virginia asks questions of Washta regarding the information on "The Photon Belt's Effect on the Human Body."

❊ ❊ ❊ **Question and Answer Section** ❊ ❊ ❊

Virginia: I have a question about those six pairs of helixes you have illustrated and how they are related to what I call a star tetrahedron. As you know, I have been presenting the star tetrahedron meditation as a foundation for people's greater healing and understanding. Could you clarify how the two dimensional picture of the Star of David with its six pointed star relates to the star tetrahedron which obviously has more than six points?

Washta: The reason why the star tetrahedron is related to the interdimensional human is that it represents the great light body that surrounds the cellular structure. It is this element which might be called the intermediary between the interdimensional portals (the physical element of the Star of David configuration), and the interdimensional realities which have even more facets than those shown in the star tetrahedron. Therefore, view it as that which is not shown here, but which is the overlay around which all DNA are actually processed. The energies passing up through the light-body star are transformed into required light-based information and sent into the various interdimensional portals. This information is then transferred back from the higher dimensions through the light-body star tetrahedron to the physical Star of David to the six-pair configuration of the DNA.

Virginia: Are you saying then that the star tetrahedron represents a frequency or a vibration of the 5th dimension?

Washta: It represents a 4th- and a 5th-dimensional vibration which has the capability of being utilized in the 3rd dimension. That is why it represents the light body which is basically a unit of that configuration.

Virginia: Please explain how the various chakra advancements or improvements relate to the brain wave frequencies of beta, alpha, theta and delta. Is there anything you could comment on about sleep in general and how these upgraded 13 chakras may affect our sleep patterns?

Washta: Most Earth scientists are only beginning to vaguely discover how the mind operates as a light or a holographic imprint unit. When the theta, or delta or the other dream-state wave patterns are in full focus, the mind is opening itself to its interdimensional portals. The scalar wave process, as it presently operates in the brain of Earth humans, requires complete unconsciousness so that the regular body functions can be lowered to minimal levels. In this way, the regular functions of the brain cannot interfere with scalar wave transmissions and reception. Using scalar wave functioning, the present brain's antenna is at a minimal efficiency.

In a fully conscious human, conversely, these scalar waves are already present in a fully conscious state. Therefore, lowering the body to a minimal level of function is not required. Hence, it is essential that one now realize a basic difference between Earth humans and fully conscious galactic humans. This difference is why most fully conscious humans do not require as much sleep as present Earth humans. The reason for this is that only when the body of an Earth human is in a minimal level (sleep) can it utilize this scalar wave. Once the scalar wave is utilized, the interdimensional brain functions can be used to bring-in data needed to control the processes of the mind and also of the different functions of the body.

These brain processing functions set up the next day's relationship between the various energy patterns in the body and the mind, and are done only when the Earth human is in a sleep state. In a fully conscious human, however, these functions can be accomplished in a fully awake state. Therefore, sleep to Earth humans is the regeneration mode. It is the way the body assesses what is happening to it, what it needs to do in the next day, and how these developments relate to the physical body for an entire year, month or a week of life.

Virginia: In the same way, then, do psychic abilities receive fueling by this shift to the 13 chakras?

Washta: That is correct. Once the chakra system aligns with the easily obtained interdimensional spiritual energies, which is basically what a psychic is doing on your planet at this time, then it becomes much easier for any human to function at maximum effeciency. This is why a fully conscious galactic human is vastly superior to the present Earth human mutant that now exists in your world. Mutant Earth humans must constantly lower their bodily functions in order to allow the now extremely weak scalar wave antenna to operate and perform the data collection and exchange functioning that is required for the body to remain at maximum efficiencies.

Virginia: Can you indicate whether the human's silver cord, that energy influx connection, will be changed in any way during this time of different chakra development?

Washta: It will remain the same. The body of an Earth human has within it the capabilities for developing the 13-chakras system. This means that you can reclaim other capabilities now largely non-existent or presently phased-out and make them operational. Right now Earth humans must still operate at their present lower limit levels. Realize that this electrical and psychic life force energy that is now coming into the present 3rd-chakra silver cord, and then to the other 4th-chakra heart cord, is still going to be operating in much the same way. What will be changing is how it is utilized in the body and how efficiently this process is made operational.

Virginia: Could you discuss whether all Sirians have the full 13-chakra development you described? Or are there various patterns to the 13-chakra system among Sirians?

Washta: For the most part all Sirians have the fully conscious concept of reality that we have given here. However, some have the capability—due to their development—to alter their functions so that they may become one with a civilization such as yours. Ordinarily, Sirians are fully conscious beings existing in a fully conscious civilization. This capability is one that Earth humans on your planet will also have once the photon belt experience is completed.

Virginia: Please describe something about the average physical size and appearance of Sirians including possible height, weight, skin, hair, and eye color, etc., so that people here may begin to have a sense of identification with them.

Washta: Sirians are divided into two types as far as their skin color is concerned. There is a race that, to Earth humans, would be considered extremely pale in its skin color. Then there is another that has a light blue hue. Both races or species of Sirian are around seven feet tall for the males and about five to six inches shorter for the females. Both races maintain the same variety of eye and hair color as exists on your world, and have the same number of limbs, as well. They are, in appearance, rather slender but a larger-sized version of the human you know and recognize.

Virginia: Is there anything you'd like to say about the color intensity or the hues of our new, number eight through thirteen chakras?

Washta: The new chakras are a very bright, almost electric type color. That is because they represent the new energies of full consciousness. These colors are very bright! Someday we may attempt to give descriptions and names for these colors; however, at present just know that these colors are bright and difficult to describe. The range and vividness of the colors is divided into two segments. First, those chakras in the head, and above it—that represent the bringing-in of this interdimensional capability—have a brighter and more electric quality to their color. The rest of the chakras (those existing in the throat and below) are there to aid in bringing the body to full and complete operational efficiency and they are still quite vivid, but less so than those chakras that reside in the head.

Virginia: I understand. Thank you. Can you further explain the term "neural imaging" that you mention in this chapter? We humans talk about the use of mind over matter, but would appreciate any suggestions or helpful hints that you might give us about how we could strengthen that process.

Washta: Right now Earth humans are beginning to discover that cellular structure is based, to a large extent, upon the will of the mind. This use of the mind intention will only intensify exponentially when full consciousness is given. Thus, humans on your planet should realize that if they have a strong will or a strong intention to do something it will happen. It will happen provided their desire is powerful enough. If this desire is felt with great enough intensity, it becomes possible to even overcome the difficulties of a bodily disease—or to make things come to pass that would otherwise seem impossible.

The human mind is still strongly able, even in your weaker human consciousness, to create and successfully allow alterations in the body cell structure. This is a reality now becoming more of an accepted concept in the cellular biology field on your planet. Therefore, people on your planet should realize and utilize this potential mind power to bring about positive changes. Using your mind power is necessary as the basis for what will later occur when this ability is exponentially increased, but be assured that our counselors will come to aid you in this process.

Virginia: Are you saying that the wide variety of our teachings about the use of the mind are still appropriate? Or is there one especially useful pattern that we should be focusing on?

Washta: The most important pattern to understand is that there is within humans a strong will, and if this will has a proper concept of its own desires, then changes can occur. Thus this concept of *will* plus a positive *desire* will equal a change. This is the key to how minds on your planet presently operate. When expanded conscious use of mind is brought into its fullness in all Earth

74

humans, then this concept will no longer require any special technique—other than understanding the power that all galactic humans possess. However, a new etiquette must be developed so humans will use this kind of power constructively, never harmfully.

Virginia: Yes, we certainly need the etiquette, thank you. Is there anything further you want to say about the scalar wave? It was very lightly touched upon in this chapter, but it seems absolutely vital to our understanding of the relationship of the mind field, the brain, and the cell.

Washta: A scalar wave is a non-hertzian frequency. It is propagated through interdimensional portholes and forms the basis of constituting all the various energies of creation. Scalar waves are what light comes from. It is that which makes all things in creation. It is based upon pulses that are called in the creation mythologies of the Galactic Federation, "the pulses of time"—for scalar waves are a timeless energy. This is what the human mind utilizes to provide the energies that make possible all aspects of physical existence.

Virginia: Are you saying that our human words such as universal life force or light are simply human ways of trying to describe a scalar wave when we lack the technical vocabulary?

Washta: This is correct. Scalar waves are the scientific basis for all of those things that humans on your planet have given many different names.

Virginia: As you know, I have been sharing an ascension meditation with people that has 18 breaths and the last breath cannot be given by a teacher of the Earth. It must come through the person's soul, their own teachers and guides or beyond. Is this meditation as effective as I have been led to believe in healing and cleansing down to the first eight cells (the initial cells to be developed in one's body) in the body?

Washta: This is correct, because the key to all changes and alterations in humans requires that a desire be given from the basic inner self or higher self as it is called by many on your world. Once this higher self is completely in agreement to the whole process, then an incredible change occurs on a physical level in all the particular cell structures of the body. Thus it becomes possible to go to the core which is the very basic foundation of all human cellular development. Once this occurs an incredible series of events can then be put into place, thereby creating things that would now be seen on your planet as miraculous.

Virginia: Can you further clarify what is retained in those basic cells one through eight, that can't be cleansed or healed while we are doing any meditation process?

Washta: The basis of the human species is in these initial cells, for they are the first cells of life. They are retained by the body as a blueprint for the human that is contained within. This basic core cannot be changed without permission from the higher self and those angelic forces that are the guardian energies of this human life form. Therefore, without these higher permissions, no miraculous change can occur in the body. These permissions are not given unless conditions within the will of each individual and the higher collective will of all humans, are met and approved by the hierarchical spiritual essences who are the guardians for this life.

Virginia: I see. At what we call physical death, then, what happens to our first eight cells?

Washta: These eight cells are dissipated for they are part of the spiritual energy pattern of that particular being.

Virginia: And where does the knowledge, or recorded information, contained in the cells go at that point?

Washta: They leave with the spiritual essence of that being and accompany the spiritual and body guardians *(body guardians are celestial devas in charge of constructing the human body during pregnancy)* of that life force into the light where they may be reprocessed by special systems of celestial judges who prepare the soul force energy for the next incarnation. That is the basic underpinning of all Earth human life in its present stage of development.

Virginia: Could you speak about those eight cells and what is called genetic history—the tendencies passed on from human to human through the birth process?

Washta: These eight cells exist as a pattern in all humans.

Virginia: Excuse me. Are they the same identical eight?

Washta: They are very similar in all humans, but there are slight differentiations in these original eight. When humans reproduce, this soul energy pattern is passed on to a particular egg and sperm that produce the human body through the process of pregnancy. When the pregnancy begins, the first cell divides in two, the two into four, and the four into eight. When these eight cells have been created, the blueprint for that particular human is firmly established. The body guardians who will then create this human body have the ability to take these eight cells and employ them so that what is desired by the soul force, the celestial (angelic) judges as well as these same body guardians can be accomplished.

Virginia: How do the body guardians make a human body and create a human genetic code?

Washta: The body guardians have the ability to transform the karmic patterns of all individuals into the make-up of the physical body. This karmic pattern is decided upon by the celestial (angelic) judges before an individual soul's incarnation. The body guardians take this karmic energy pattern and use it at the moment of physical conception with development of the body's first eight cells to create one's genetic code. This genetic pattern from these first eight cells is then used to create the entire human body. This construction process uses advanced laws of spiritual magnetism and its relation-ship to prescribed biochemical reactions to make the physical body and to attach the individual soul to it during the period of pregnancy.

Virginia: Then how does what we call family history or the genetics of a whole group of people, such as eye color, eye shape and all kinds of things happen?

Washta: After these eight cells are initially reproduced, a genetic code for the forming human body is created by the body guardians, which defines the points mentioned in your question. Thus, basic patterns of size, shape, hair color, eye color, how the skin is to look, and what the final appearance of the body will be, are established according to the wishes of the soul force, the celestial judges and the body guardians. These final genetic codes are formulated within the parameters given by the sperm of the father and the egg of the mother.

Virginia: Are we incorrect then, as humans, when we assume that when we are healed, we are also healing a part of a whole genetic pool of early generations in our families?

Washta: Every change in Earth humans reestablishes your genetic pool. Genetics as it is now understood on your planet is very limited in terms of the actual reality of what occurs in a fully conscious human. Genetics form a basis for size, shape, etc., but they are not the final say because the final say goes to the life force and its guardians who create each and every individual.

Virginia: Could you define how such things as genetic diseases, physical disabilities, and so on, occur?

Washta: These things occur for two reasons. One is that the original Atlantean genetic experiment created Earth humans as the mutants who now exist on your planet. These genetic difficulties were first caused by the initial incompleteness of the Atlantean genetic experiment that distorted Earth humans. The second reason for this difficulty is that Earth humans do not possess full conscious-ness and therefore do not have the simple ability to alter their genetic capabilities once they have entered fetal form, or later at birth.

This means that what you get at birth remains with you the rest of your life. That is why there are many, many beings born stillborn because the life pattern they wished to impose upon their fetal tissue couldn't be accomplished. This is because Earth humans do not possess the ability to rapidly change their body once the process of creating life has officially begun.

Virginia: How does the soul's decision to abort the fetal tissue relate to devic responsibility for creating the body?

Washta: The body guardians (devas) are doing what is decided upon by the celestial judges and the final free will decisions of the individual soul. If the soul does not wish to complete the incarnation into a particular human body, it has the option to default the successful completion of a pregnancy.

Virginia: I understand crib deaths are allowed during the first years of life if the soul chooses to default on its adventure.

Washta: That is correct. Many humans on your planet have a certain destiny that they wish to use an incarnation for. When they finally get to see that their reality, their destiny, is not possible with what they have been given genetically, they then have the right—with the aid of their angelic host—to alter and to terminate that life.

Virginia: Is there anything further that you would like to comment on about the chakra system, the relationship of the scalar waves to the cells, or anything else that you think is appropriate?

Washta: We would just like to conclude by saying that people should view the body as a fantastic holistic machine which has many levels. When these levels are properly understood and brought together as a whole, then one can appreciate what a magnificent, amazing invention the great Time Lords and the great Godhead, the Source, have created. Once Earth humans realize and appreciate the body's value and wisdom, they will finally understand the incredible miracle that a life can be when acted out in full consciousness.

Chapter 5
Earth's Forgotten History

We three Sirian council members presenting information today include Washta as well as Teletron, a Sirian galactic historian and expert on human galactic civilization and culture and Mikah, a Sirian historian, geologist, and cetacean biologist.

In this chapter we will present a complete historical record of all past civilized societies on planet Earth from its very beginnings, about 35 million years ago, to the present. These studies are important because they will enable you to understand why the current galactic situations are now occurring and why they are so different from those events which you assume have occurred in the past. Most importantly, you will finally know your own planet's true history and the role of humanity in its development.

To explain these galactic changes in a very clear fashion, we will use a set of time lines to orient the reader and will provide the sequence in which these events occurred. Let us start this study, then, by reviewing your solar system's history from the beginning of *nonhuman* civilization on your planet until the formation of the last Earth human colony influenced by Lyran/Sirian culture—the famous lost Continent of Lemuria. (*See Figure 11: Earth History : From 35 Million Years to 900,000 Years BC.*)

Approximately 35 million years ago, the Time Lords and the Spiritual Hierarchy of your solar system decided to create an etheric life form to act as a guardian species for Earth and the surrounding

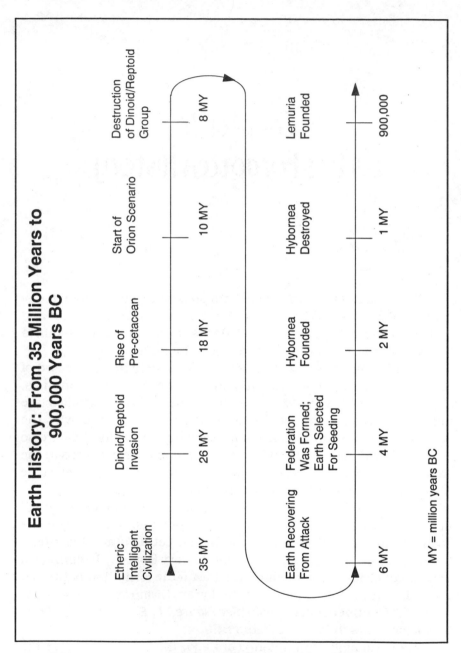

Figure 11: Earth History: From 35 Million Years to 900,000 Years BC

solar system. This angel-like life form was to act as an intermediary until the evolution of a more physically evolved sentient primate occurred that would be the land-based guardian for planet Earth. Indeed, over the next 8 million years, a primate-based life form did develop on Earth, which one day could replace the temporary etheric civilization created by the Spiritual Hierarchy.

The original, divine plan for physical life on your planet was conceived by the Creator, and executed by the Time Lords as one of vast diversity. Furthermore, this diversity was instituted so that more than one land creature could eventually rise to high sentient levels and have an opportunity to become planetary guardians. Then about 26 million years ago, two nonhuman space civilizations approached this planet and established colonies upon it. These two planetary non-human civilizations were a reptilian or reptoid one (from the lesser known stars in the constellation Sagittarius), and a dinosaurian or dinoid society (from the Bellatrix system in the Constellation Orion).

These two civilizations came into your solar system and claimed it as part of an overall mandate from their mutual creation myths that conceived of the entire galaxy as their property, to do with as they saw fit. The etheric life form now occupying Earth and its angelic hosts decided to permit this colonizing to occur and to work towards eventually obtaining a change in the attitude of the two hostile civilizations. Over the next 8 million years as the Spiritual Hierarchy sent more and more love energy to them, these two civilizations began to slowly allow mammalian creatures on your planet to evolve toward sentiency. The first such creature was a land pre-cetacean (ancestor of the present dolphins and whales). They developed a primitive agrarian society and a great ability to produce more than enough food staples to supply the other two more advanced civilizations. This pre-cetacean civilization was encouraged and given advanced technology to improve its food production capabilities. It easily provided for the food requirements of the dinoid and reptoid civilizations and had a successful yet passive relationship with both of them.

These three civilizations coexisted for many years and were able to develop a large degree of cooperation on all levels. Trade flourished and the planet seemed to be on its way to achieving a notable variation in civilized life forms and planetary guardianship. Around

10 million years ago, these three civilizations were busy creating technologies based on advanced forms of space and interdimensional time travel. At this same time, beings from different interstellar civilizations began to arrive in the solar system, willing to trade with these three civilizations existing on your planet. These interstellar beings passed the word around to other star systems that an incredible diversity of life forms existed on Earth and that three uniquely different civilizations were cooperating with one another.

Your solar system became notable because of its exquisite beauty, variety and cooperative life forms—and many legends and prophecies were shared throughout the galaxy because of what was happening. These tales led various groups of the Dinoid/Reptoid Alliance on Orion to want to visit your solar system because they felt very deeply that dinoid/reptoid civilizations should not be cooperating with others without their approval—and because of certain Dinoid/Reptoid Alliance agreements that they had already established among themselves.

Therefore, a group from Bellatrix, as well as from other stars in Orion, began to arrive and to explore these happenings in your solar system. What they saw shocked them because it ran counter to their core myth of creation that was the essential underpinning of their entire alliance. This core myth can be stated in the following way.

They believed that when life was being established in this galaxy, the Lord of Creation told all dinoid/reptoid civilizations that they had been created in his image and had been given the right to rule over and use, as they so pleased, all life created in this galaxy. Further, all dinoid/reptoid civilizations were told not to permit any other inferior life form to establish itself as a guardian of our galaxy's life forms. Using this edict of superiority, the Dinoid/Reptoid Alliance had spread its violence and terror across the galaxy for over 16 million years. Yet, the Earth's three civilizations not only existed, but they were also the equal of Orion's interstellar culture.

Both nonhuman groups looked at this disturbing disparity and decided that something had to be done about it. Therefore the dinoid group from Orion began to pressure the Earth's dinoid group to establish within their ranks a specially trained armed group whose sole purpose would be to destroy the mammalian (pre-cetacean) society. This mammalian group was composed of a land version of modern cetaceans (the whales and dolphins) that are found in the oceans, bays, and rivers of your planet.

The pre-cetacean leadership realized, through the use of their vast mass consciousness and high psychic abilities, that something dangerous was happening between the Orion dinoid group and the now native dinoid group on Earth. The pre-cetacean leadership feared this was the beginning of a war that would lead to the utter devastation of their civilization. To be absolutely certain that this belief was true, they gathered together their great seers and confirmed that a violent plot was planned against them by the dinoids and the reptoids. These meetings of their seers and clan organization counselors led to a number of possible solutions that had to be discussed with the Earth's Spiritual Hierarchy before they could be implemented.

The discussions points were as follows: What were the intentions of the group from Bellatrix for this solar system? Second, what were the implications for the planet's development if the other two civilizations (dinoid and reptoid) decided to eliminate the pre-cetaceans? Third, if the other civilizations were part of this conspiracy, how should the pre-cetaceans react to this problem? Would angelic permission be given to the pre-cetaceans to conduct a major preemptive strike if the above beliefs were true? The pre-cetaceans were told by the Spiritual Hierarchy that all of these points were true. Consequently, there was still enough time to prepare for the preemptive strike since a significant portion of the leadership of the dinoid and reptoid civilizations were opposed to a quick strike against the pre-cetaceans.

After another 10,000 years of constant haranguing about the Earth's dinoid/reptoid leadership's passive position, the dinoid group from Orion was finally able to convince the dinoid group assigned to Earth to work out a way of destroying these pre-cetaceans. The dinoid group from Orion, mainly from Bellatrix and the stars that form Orion's belt, had discovered a strategy that would successfully end pre-cetacean civilization. The method decided upon was the use of an advanced form of psychological weaponry. This device would cause the immediate death of all the pre-cetaceans in a relatively short period of time but leave their dwellings and other forms of civilization relatively intact. In this way, their nefarious plan would allow for an additional benefit. It would also allow the dinoid group to have your planet's vegetation and other forms of life altered for their specialized needs.

When the pre-cetaceans and their elders saw that the dastardly enemy plot was about to be carried out, they realized that their democratic ideals about cooperation with the other two civilizations must end. Out of their genius, they were able to plot a successful end to these two other offensive civilizations. The pre-cetaceans' strategy was to utilize their vast series of fusion generators, located in the heart of their homeland, for destructive purposes. This homeland consisted of what is now known as the area that extends from Central Asia all the way to the central part of Eastern Europe. (*See Figure 12: Map of Pre-Cetacean Homeland and Sites of Fusion Generators.*) They decided that by exploding these fusion generators it would be possible to create a worldwide catastrophe that would destroy the other two civilizations. Before this was to be done, however, they had to ask permission of the Earth's Spiritual Hierarchy for complete approval of this task. The pre-cetacean leadership also explained to Lady Gaia how she was to be altered by the Dinoid/Reptoid Alliance's dastardly plans.

The Earth's Spiritual Hierarchies agreed that the dinoid group from Orion's plan was indeed not acceptable to the history of this planet. Lady Gaia, therefore, permitted implementation of the pre-cetacean's plan to implode their fusion generators. The pre-cetaceans set a date for this deed knowing that the dinoids were still waiting for what they called a propitious moment. The pre-cetaceans discovered when this moment was to occur and decided to implement their plan slowly so as to not make the dinoids suspicious enough to abandon their time schedule. The pre-cetacean strategy was to blow up their fusion generators approximately five years before the other two (dinoid/reptoid) civilizations had chosen to carry out their plans.

Knowing that they had the time to succeed, the pre-cetacean organizations decided to implement their plan by splitting their society in two. One-half of their civilization was to be evacuated out of the solar system and the rest would leave the land and go to the oceans where they would find a haven. This plan was implemented and the fusion generators were imploded as scheduled. The dinoid/reptoids were 98 percent destroyed and the rest fled to the large planet between Mars and Jupiter that has been called the planet Maldek. About one-half of the pre-cetaceans (some 30 million

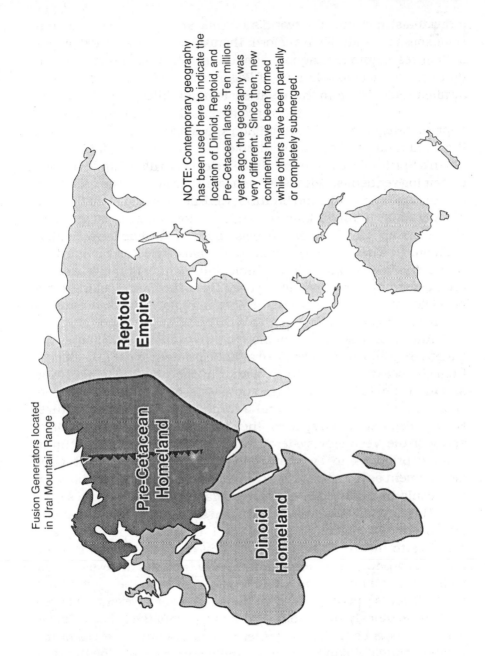

NOTE: Contemporary geography has been used here to indicate the location of Dinoid, Reptoid, and Pre-Cetacean lands. Ten million years ago, the geography was very different. Since then, new continents have been formed while others have been partially or completely submerged.

Reptoid Empire

Pre-Cetacean Homeland

Dinoid Homeland

Fusion Generators located in Ural Mountain Range

Figure 12: Map of Pre-Cetacean Homeland and Sites of Fusion Generators

individuals) fled into the world's oceans and used their full consciousness to gradually transform themselves, over a period of four million years, into true aquatic creatures. The rest of their civilization fled to the constellations of Pegasus and of Cetus where they awaited their return to this solar system at a later predicted time.

This destruction of the reptoid/dinoid civilization was done approximately 8 million to 10 million years ago. With the fleeing of the remnants of the reptoid/dinoid civilizations to Maldek, the Earth's Spiritual Hierarchy left its physical guardianship to the one remaining sentient species—the cetaceans. However, the cetaceans and their now space-bound brethren were determined, with the help of Lady Gaia, to find a land replacement for the now vacant land guardianship role. This task to locate a land guardian became their great quest. The pre-cetaceans, with the aid of the Earth's Spiritual Hierarchy, began to search the immediate vicinity of the galaxy (an area extending about 80 light years from the Sun) looking for a possible candidate that would be able to replace the cetaceans as Earth's land guardian.

After searching for two million to three million years across the galaxy, they finally discovered an aquatic primate starting to emerge from the oceans on the fourth planet in the Vega system. These aquatic primates had the first rudiments of civilization such as creation myths, a language, and a hunting and gathering culture. Having discovered this species, they then asked the Spiritual Hierarchy of the Vega star system if they would permit this group of aquatic primates to be vastly altered genetically so that their development as a sentient species could be accelerated. In this way, they could be prepared to become a galactic guardian species.

This development was agreed upon and the genetic alterations were begun. The importance of this evolutionary jump from aquatic primates to the Vegan humans was that it created a new galactic guardian group, which allowed these new humans to develop their technology at a much more rapid level of evolution then could have been otherwise permitted. This important set of events allowed humans to quickly spread out across this part of the galaxy. This is when humans began to encounter advance scouting forces of the Dinoid/Reptoid Alliance about 4.5 million years ago. The humans were able to persevere because of the intervention of Lady Gaia and the cetaceans and the humans were able to fight the Dinoid/Reptoid

Alliance successfully to a standstill while still continuing their outward migration in this sector of the Milky Way Galaxy.

This migration continued for a period of roughly 2.5 million years. By this time, humans had spread to the very edge of your solar system and had banded together in a human Galactic Federation which agreed to colonize your solar system. Lady Gaia approved this plan and the first Earth colony called Hybornea (also known as Hyperborea) was begun. *(See Figure 13: Migration of Galactic Human Civilizations.)* Hybornea would last for roughly 1 million years and would be a complete Lyran/Sirian type of civilization. When the dinoid group returned to the solar system to assist their outnumbered brethren about 1 million years ago, they saw that humans now controlled most of your solar system. All that was left of the reptoid and dinoid strength was a small colony on the planet Maldek as well as a small group of outpost personnel scattered on the fringes of your solar system.

Nonetheless, the Dinoid/Reptoid Alliance decided it was time to establish their authority in this region of the galaxy once again with a broad-based series of attacks on neighboring star systems as well as your solar system. These attacks were aided and abetted by their forces left behind on Maldek, who were now able to systematically destroy the small human colonies created by the Galactic Federation on Mars, Venus and Earth.

This destruction left Mars without most of its atmosphere and hydrosphere (oceans, rivers and streams). Venus was left locked into a virtual greenhouse condition of intense planetary atmospheric heating maintained by an atmosphere that had been altered into a series of unlivable acrid gases. Earth's Hybornean colony was destroyed by a series of vicious and premeditated massive attacks that killed all humans and thoroughly obliterated all aspects of human civilization. The outcome was that the Dinoid/Reptoid Alliance again controlled your entire solar system.

For a period of roughly 80,000 years, your solar system was held as an outpost for the dinoid/reptoid group. However, as they were pushed back by the galactic humans across a broad front that included many star systems near your Sun, it finally became possible to create a plan for the return of humans into your solar system. To accomplish this feat, the Galactic Federation brought a large battle planet into this region. The purpose of this battle planet

87

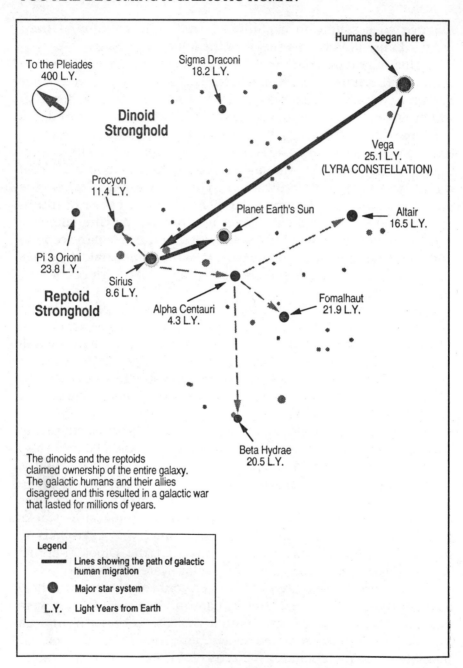

The dinoids and the reptoids claimed ownership of the entire galaxy. The galactic humans and their allies disagreed and this resulted in a galactic war that lasted for millions of years.

Figure 13: Migration of Galactic Human Civilizations

was to destroy the planet Maldek which was the chief administrative center of the Dinoid/Reptoid Alliance in the solar system. After the loss of Maldek, it was felt that it would be relatively easy to conquer the reptoid/dinoid Earth colony. This brief and brutal action was quickly accomplished and the Earth was successfully returned to human control approximately 900,000 years ago.

The Earth humans now decided that their new colony would be centered on what was called the continent of Lemuria. (See *Figure 14: Stages of Lemurian Civilization and Birth of Atlantis.*) It was here that the first human colonists were able to establish a Lyran/Sirian civilization with democratic principles at all levels of life. Over the next 850,000 years, Lemurians spread across the surface of planet Earth from a primary continental base in what is now the Pacific Ocean. They developed a series of what they called daughter empires. The most important of these daughter empires was Atlantis, a huge island located in the center of the Atlantic Ocean. Another significant colony was the Yü empire which comprised what is today called Central China and Tibet.

As they began to develop their colony, the Atlanteans quickly acquired a feeling of uniqueness about their culture that eventually led to a feeling of separateness from the other daughter empires of Lemuria. The Atlanteans felt that they were not only a daughter empire of Lemuria, but that they were a daughter empire that could and should become the mother empire. The Atlanteans, therefore, began to have a strong desire to destroy the Lemurians and their more loyal daughter empires in order to gain full power.

It is now necessary to look briefly at what was going on in Lemuria so that the reader will know what was truly happening on Earth during this time. The Lemurians had developed a civilization similar in many ways to that on Sirius and many other Lyran stars, but they also developed some unique concepts. The most important of these beliefs was that they were the primary land human guardian group on planet Earth. This concept was ended roughly 50,000 years ago, however, when the Lemurians decided that their daughter empires had developed sufficiently and should now play a part in the guardianship. This decision allowed the Atlanteans to finally seek allies for their great plot to destroy the Lemurians.

The Atlanteans did find some allies in the various galactic human renegade defense commands that had originally been formed

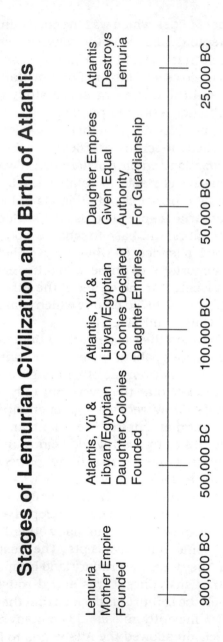

**Figure 14: Stages of Lemurian Civilization
and Birth of Atlantis**

by the colonies in Alpha Centauri and the Pleiades. Over the next 25,000 years, in fact, the Atlanteans developed alliances with these defense commands and various outpost star systems. These alliances were mostly with Galactic Federation outpost colonies that shared a similar concept of the Atlantean hierarchial cultural tradition. These various groups then began to produce a plot that would lead to the destruction of Lemuria and the ascension of Atlantis to a primary position on planet Earth. Therefore, the Atlanteans waited patiently for the right opportunity to occur and approximately 25,000 years ago, they and various Pleiadean and Centaurian rebels, or what we shall call renegades, decided to destroy Lemuria. Their plan and its execution would be a technical success but would destroy one of planet Earth's moons—along with Lemuria.

At that particular time, the Earth had two moons, each one of which was roughly three-quarters the size of your present moon. What the renegades proposed to do was to move one of these two moons into a downward spiraling orbit using force fields. Before this moon reached a critical mass position (the Lagrange Point) with the Earth, it would be exploded so that it would fall down as an incredible shower of meteors upon the Lemurian continent. *(See Figure 15: How Lemuria was Destroyed.)*

This event would cause gravitational and plate tectonic distress because of the size, downward path and mass of the lunar fragments. This development did, in fact, create a volcanic catastrophe that caused the great gas chambers underneath Lemuria to implode, sink the continent, and destroy Lemurian dominance.

About 25,000 years ago, then, the Atlanteans and their renegade allies from other star systems destroyed the great Lemurian continent so completely that it disappeared into a mere legendary status. Only your oceanic soundings in the Pacific area have recently chartered vast mountains and valley elevations and mapped some of what was once the wonder of the Earth. With the destruction of Lemuria, nothing prevented the rise and influence of power hungry Atlantis.

In our next chapter we will explain the significance of Lemuria's destruction and discuss your present Earth difficulties in terms of the new Atlantean non-democratic rule.

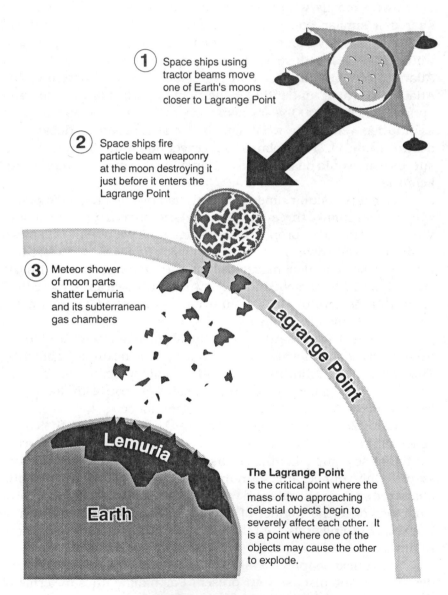

1 Space ships using tractor beams move one of Earth's moons closer to Lagrange Point

2 Space ships fire particle beam weaponry at the moon destroying it just before it enters the Lagrange Point

3 Meteor shower of moon parts shatter Lemuria and its subterranean gas chambers

Lagrange Point

Lemuria

Earth

The Lagrange Point is the critical point where the mass of two approaching celestial objects begin to severely affect each other. It is a point where one of the objects may cause the other to explode.

Figure 15: How Lemuria was Destroyed

Many questions about the material in this chapter may now come to mind. In the next section, Virginia asks questions of Washta regarding the information on "Earth's Forgotten History."

❄ ❄ ❄ **Question and Answer Section** ❄ ❄ ❄

Virginia: The first question today concerns those three nonhuman civilizations you say were our original Earth inhabitants. Please explain how each of these groups got here to Earth, and give a brief physical description of them.

Washta: The pre-cetacean group naturally evolved on the planet and developed before the great variety of mammals that now exist on your planet. This fact may seem contrary to the evidence left behind by bones and other fossil structures on this planet. Geologists should realize that the destruction of the reptoids and dinoids destroyed much evidence in the fossil record. Only this pre-cetacean group as we are calling it, is presently left behind as a legacy on your planet.

Now let us go into a description of these three different species. We will start with the two groups that presently are not on your world—the reptoid and the dinoid group.

The dinoids have too many variances to easily describe them, so we will describe just two major groups. The first one is a worker or soldier type, and it is roughly seven to ten feet tall. It has a bipedal structure consistent with most intelligent beings in this particular sector of the galaxy. The toes are very claw-like with three on each foot and four fingers on each hand. This group has a very small almost non–existent tail and is very similar in its body structure to that of modern humans. The individuals differ in various scaly skin colors that run from red to green, to brown, to blue, with some shades of blue that almost resemble black. Their faces have large, bulging, black eyes. The nose is almost non–existent and appears like two holes where the nose should be. There is a very thin, nearly non–existent, mouth filled with teeth that are similar to that of a shark. As for ears, they are also virtually non–existent.

Then there is the dinoid leader type. This leader type is famous to Earth humans since it is almost a perfect replication of what is today called the demon or gargoyle. These are beings that have scaly reptile-like skin with as many as six webbed fingers and toes. They have a tail with an edge that looks almost like a spike or arrow at its tip. Their eyes go from a black to an almost evil appearing reddish color and of course they have an almost human–like figure. In short, you might look at these beings and see the traditional concept of what a devil would look like.

The reptoids are roughly the same size as the dinoid worker group that we have just described except for their large tails which are utilized for balance. The reptoids are more muscular than the dinoid groups and possess a crocodile type of protruding face with teeth very similar to that of modern Earth reptiles. Their eyes are more similar to human eyes which is a basic difference between them and the dinoids. They have an ear which looks more like the ear of a deer which they can also wiggle.

The pre-cetacean was not as tall as the other beings (it was approximately 7 feet in height). It was bipedal in structure with its arms slightly larger than its legs. This original pre–cetacean had five fingers and five toes and was covered with a thick coat of fur. Its face consisted of a large, horse–like snout and it had teeth that were more rounded in shape than either the dinoid or the reptoid. Its eyes were quite human–like in appearance and it had a small stump of a tail. Finally, it was very intelligent and a fully conscious being.

Virginia: What intelligence factor did the reptoids and dinoids have if we use IQ measure as a basis of comparison?

Washta: Compared to modern Earth humans they would all be Einstein's. After all, they had the ability to come from far distances in what you would call spacecraft. Not only did they use spacecrafts, some of them could also use their light bodies to move from one point to another. These dinoids and reptoids were fully conscious beings.

Virginia: Which of the three groups came first?

Washta: The reptoid and dinoid groups arrived only slightly after the advent of the mammalian groups on your world. Hence we can call it a tie.

Virginia: Were these dinoid and reptoid groups simply exploring or did they know the planet was here? How did they arrive?

Washta: They knew from their advanced scanning equipment that a system of habitable planets existed around a particular star, your Sun, that was capable of being colonized. So they sent colonizers to your solar system to establish their colonies.

Virginia: And so the two groups from the opposite directions were able to be peaceful and to allow the pre–cetaceans to evolve?

Washta: The initial colonists of both the reptoid group and the dinoid group were totally different than most members of their particular species. They did not immediately fight a war with one another over the issue of leadership. Dinoids normally like to be in control of a star system and the same for the reptoid civilizations. This difficulty should have created a war, but it did not. We know this from what your Spiritual Hierarchy has told us. The Earth's Spiritual Hierarchy sent energies of love and cooperation to them. These energies made the two colonizing groups understand that co-inhabiting this planet was possible and that the staking of claims was not required. This fact alone is why your solar system was such an unusual and incredible star system—even from its very beginnings of civilization.

Virginia: What groups were evolving on this planet when the dinoids and reptoids arrived?

Washta: There was a primate group now extinct and not related directly to humans.

Virginia: How did they get here?

Washta: They were part of a natural evolution process and were destroyed when the first dinoid and reptoid colonist arrived. Only the pre-cetacean group initially survived by hiding in vast caverns in the Ural Mountains. The evolutionary process of this planet is therefore completely different than that which is now believed by Earth's geologists, anthropologists, and paleontologists.

Virginia: Do I understand you to say that the natural evolution on this planet caused by etheric creation brought forth primates that were not related to the aquatic humans that created the Lyran civilization?

Washta: The humans brought from the Vega star system are a different species and not a natural evolutionary product of the bringing forth of life upon your solar system.

Virginia: So in other words, the Charles Darwin theory of evolution of species is incorrect at the point where apes and humans intersect?

Washta: Yes, it is a completely erroneous assumption that will in the next few years finally be buried. It will be learned that most of the existing animal life on Earth as well as most of the present vegetation have their origins on other stars. Planet Earth had to be reconstituted many times to maintain its biosphere. Many disastrous wars caused great destruction to your planet and life has had to be restarted repeatedly.

Virginia: Thank you. Could you explain how the pre–cetacean, a breath–oriented land mammal, got into the oceans and became what it is today?

Washta: This is what happened. When the fusion generators were imploded to destroy the reptoid and dinoid civilizations, the pre-cetacean leadership had to leave some of their kind on Earth in order to act as planetary guardians. This guardianship would hold the energies of the biosphere intact and continue the processes of cooperation with the Spiritual Hierarchy (from devas up to archangels) required to maintain life on your planet. Therefore, they would have to find a medium that would allow them to survive during the time of the disaster. It was decided that a large body of water—an ocean—was the only possible scenario.

Virginia: Yes, I understand their decision, but how were they able to do that?

Washta: Since cetaceans are fully conscious beings, they were able to change from a creature of land to a creature of the sea over a long transition period.

Virginia: How long of a period was that?

Washta: This took them approximately 2 million years to restore the evolution process in a fully invigorated way. Therefore, at the beginning, they maintained themselves in almost an etheric way and later transmuted back into their physical form again. Once they had completed this physical form, they began evolving it into what you know today as the early proto-cetacean creatures found in the fossil record of your planet, as the Earth's first whales and dolphins.

Virginia: Can you explain why there are both whales and dolphins, and how they are similar or dissimilar?

Washta: The dolphins are toothed whales. Whales are divided into two types. The first type is the toothed whales, the largest of which is the Sperm Whale. They range in size from very large to small creatures three to four feet in length, and include all the different dolphins and smaller whales. Although the Sperm Whale is about 50 feet in length, the very large whales have transmuted their tooth structure into what might be called a giant sieve.

They are not carnivorous and eat only plankton, kelp, etc. Therefore, they are what might be called vegetarian on an immense level since they must eat tons and tons of this green plankton and kelp to survive everyday.

Virginia: What we are trying to understand here is why some of them are toothed, and why some of them are not? Also why some are so huge and others are much smaller.

Washta: That is because it was decided that every niche in the life span of the oceans required a different size caregiver and a different phase of life. Therefore for each species to survive, it was given a niche or placement as part of preserving the biosphere. Thus it was decided that a large creature was needed to provide the overall beginnings of life in the biosphere. That is why the large creatures such as the so–called Right Whale, the Humpback Whale and the Blue Whale were chosen for this task. Their job is to put together the energy pattern of song that allows the biosphere to exist every year. The smaller whales (the dolphins) were dedicated to interact with native food chains of the ocean, which they did by becoming smaller and toothed. Therefore, whales now have the task to preserve life in the ocean and on the land. Humans will take over the task of preserving life on the land when they become fully conscious beings again.

Virginia: What about the dolphins and porpoises?

Washta: The dolphins' and porpoises' job is to work on a species–by–species basis. They aid species in the ocean by maintaining their biofield energies. Occasionally, they also do it with a specific individual or a specific species on the land. The large whales are in charge of maintaining the entire biosphere. You might look at it this way. The large whales such as the Humpback sketch the background for the big painting of all life on this planet. They are life's sustainers and its means to maintain itself. The smaller whales like the dolphins take this big background sketch and put in the parts that complete the drawing as represented by a specific species on land or ocean. Out of this whole incredible network, there comes the final picture that creates life patterns for all species to adequately maintain their life essences.

Virginia: Now I want to be sure that we understand the origin of the present galactic human who came from an aquatic primate on Vega. Could you explain more about the original environment that it came from and how it learned to live in the ocean?

Washta: This creature originally was a primate that accidentally discovered that it could catch fish at the edge of the ocean. It gradually moved further into the ocean and began to change in consciousness. It gradually lost its fur and it became what all humans look like today. As this change in ability continued, it became a very proficient ocean dweller. You might look at it as similar to the modern sea otters that now exist along the coast of California and various other parts of the Pacific Ocean basin. What these otters do is learn how to live completely by just being on their backs above water—in other words, how to float in the ocean. By doing so, they coexist in the tidal pools and even far out in the ocean with no difficulty. The aquatic primates' abilities to develop tools, although very simple, allowed them to fish and permitted them a food supply. From this ability, they developed into hunting and social packs or clans since primates were, by their nature, very gregarious.

Eventually, however, they began to leave the ocean and move to the seashore. This is about the time when the pre-cetacean civilizations and the Earth's Spiritual Hierarchies discovered these aquatic primates. They asked permission of the Spiritual Hierarchy from the Vega system to intervene and allow them to evolve these aquatic primates towards a galactic civilization much more quickly than would have normally occurred. Such an evolutionary leap might have taken many additional millions of years to achieve. Instead, it occurred in just two million years. It was still a gradual process, but it was nevertheless an approved accelerated interference with the natural evolutionary pattern. This genetic interference was done because it was seen that these creatures had the capability, through the way they related with one another, to be a guardian species on a galactic level.

Virginia: Yes, thank you. Could you indicate how in the vastness of space (even within our galaxy), life develops in all these different ways upon a great variety of planets yet apparently no one keeps track of everything that's happening? Many humans find it difficult to understand that lack of communication or awareness. Could you comment on that?

Washta: What has happened for the most part is that civilizations have occurred from colonization. Very rarely does civilization come from a natural evolutionary process in any star system. For the most part, then, what has occurred is that colonies have been started, but it is how they are developed that determines their history and their future. Many times, as on your planet, disaster occurs and people are cut off from what they are supposed to be so they simply forget and a kind of amnesia sets in.

As we explained earlier, the Vega star system had a unique development of this extraordinary aquatic primate that evolved into a galactic guardian race. That is, they became the human pattern, your ancestors. They quickly became technically knowledgeable and developed the ability to come and go across this vast galaxy and to aid others in making this whole process of guardianship possible. You might call it a kind of miracle made possible by the Earth's Spiritual Hierarchy and ultimately by the divine plan of the Supreme Creator Force and its instrument, the Time Lords.

Virginia: Thank you. Could you explain about the planet Maldek and how it was destroyed?

Washta: These survivors of the destruction of Earth's biosphere by the pre-cetaceans had fled to what we will call Maldek (in the dinoid and reptoid language it has a name that is very complicated to even spell in English). What we would like to state is that a vast series of wars existed in your solar system throughout this time frame between humans and other groups. The most important result of these wars led the dinoids and reptoids to settle or inhabit Maldek after they were forced to flee from Earth, Mars and Venus. In order to come back into your solar system in a controlling way, they used this Maldek planet as a base or capital headquarters in their attempt to colonize, maintain, and control the solar system. There-fore, the galactic human forces decided it was essential that their base be destroyed in order for a human re-colonization program to succeed. In order to accomplish this, it was necessary to bring in an instrument of war that would be sufficient to destroy it.

Virginia: Was this instrument a battle planet?

Washta: Yes, that was the solution. This battle planet was nearly four times the size of Earth's diameter or 29,000 miles across.

Virginia: Okay, and after it destroyed Maldek (from which the Asteroid Belt was created) what happened to the battle planet? I understand that it still exists today.

Washta: Yes, it still exists. It was put into a large scale orbit roughly 6.8 billion miles across at its farthest point from the Sun. It comes in on a 3,600 year cycle where it crosses almost through Mercury's orbit and then heads back-out. This was done to assure future protection for your planet and solar system because of the past murderous invasions by dinoids and other groups that completely destroyed both your Mars and your Venus colonies. Because of that past destruction in your solar system, the Galactic Federation has had to expend a great effort to bring human colonization back into your solar system. It is a safety device. This battle planet patrols out there as a constant reminder to potential murderers that there is indeed protection for this solar system.

Virginia: Yes, in the Bible it talks about Wormwood and of course other people have written about the twelfth planet. Would we understand this to be the same vehicle?

Washta: This is the same vehicle.

Virginia: My understanding is that almost every time this 3,600 year cycle occurs there are major damages to our planet and changes in the geology on Earth.

Washta: That is because of the gravitational patterns and also because of the fact that various Pleiadean groups have been in charge since the destruction period of Atlantis. However, this is changing since your planet is now under full Sirian jurisdiction and we have prevented a repetition of this difficulty. We have been steering it in a special modified orbit so that when it comes into the inner part of your solar system, it will no longer vastly influence the inner planets such as Mars, Earth, Venus, and Mercury.

Virginia: Are you saying that we will no longer have pole shifts?

Washta: Pole shifts will no longer occur as they have previously. For Planet Earth is about to be completely changed into a special type of multidemensional crystal composed of both silicon and carbon materials that will allow it to become the great and glorious showcase planet that it is meant to be.

Virginia: What are we to say to those people who insist it is slightly tilted and that it will continue in that mode?

Washta: The tilt will be altered during the time of the arrival of the photon belt, for we must change the direction of the present tilt to a straight–on configuration when the Firmament is fully put back into shape for you. The 23-1/2 degree shift occurred during the time when the great Firmament was collapsed by the Atlanteans, causing a horrendous flood of water to fall upon Earth's surface.

100

Virginia: Finally, would you comment on whether the pyramid reportedly found on the planet Mars was made by galactic humans?

Washta: This was part of a great temple site that was a remnant left behind as a symbol and monument of the great Martian civilization which was in full existence until it was destroyed roughly one million years ago. It was destroyed by these same dinoid groups from Maldek that we have just been describing! This was when the dinoids swept out and attempted to destroy and reoccupy your entire solar system from Neptune to Mercury. While attacking the galactic humans, they ravished Mars and Venus in unspeakable ways—destroying the remnants of many civilizations on your world as well.

Virginia: So the temple represents a monument to whom?

Washta: It is a monument to the great sacred energies existing in all humans.

Virginia: So it is a galactic human temple of sorts?

Washta: It is a center of energy, a center of worship for humans. It is an imprint of the Galactic Federation's attempt to aid the Spiritual Hierarchy in the task of stewardship for your solar system. It commemorates those who resisted the great disaster caused by the dinoid wars—the wars perpetuated by the dinoids that came into your solar system and destroyed that human effort of solar and planetary guardianship in your region!

Virginia: I want to thank you very much for your comments. I am sure that we are continuing to learn and grow. Have you thought of anything else you need to share before we depart today?

Washta: I would just like to mention two final points. First, your planet's history will soon be revealed to all its people. This history is quite different from even the wildest imaginings of most historians. Second, your planet has, in its histories, a blueprint for Earth humans so that they may understand who they once were and what it is that they are soon to become.

Chapter 6
From Atlantis to the Great Flood

Washta, Teletron and Mikah continue where they left off in Chapter 5, with an explanation of the destruction of Lemuria and the rise of Atlantis.

Atlantis had developed allies in the Galactic Federation that consisted of human Galactic Federation renegades and various outlaw command groups (primarily from Alpha Centauri and several outpost commands in the Pleiades) who wished to impose a hierarchical governing structure on your solar system. The basis for this plan lay in the importance attached to your solar system by the entire Galactic Federation. The renegades wanted their hierarchical interpretation of the laws of relationships to be seen as superior to the Galactic Federation's more democratic version. *(See Chapter 9 for a full discussion of Lyran/Sirian Four Basic Social Laws governing relationships.)* With the destruction of Lemuria, the vast system of daughter empires that looked to Lemuria as their mother empire were shocked by what had happened and wondered what the immediate future would bring.

Besides Atlantis and Lemuria, the two other important empires on this planet were the Yü Empire in Asia and the Libyan/Egyptian Empire in North Africa. Following the destruction of Lemuria, the Libyan/Egyptian Empire had been able—through a series of alliances—to develop an understanding with the Atlanteans that allowed them to maintain a certain degree of authority in their own lands. However, the Libyan/Egyptian clans had to agree to the alterations that the Atlanteans wished, in order to maintain themselves as a separate empire. The only other empire of any major significance was the Yü Empire of Asia. The Yü Empire and its colonies refused to bow down to the Atlanteans even after the destruction of the motherland of Lemuria. They issued several decrees demanding that the Atlanteans apologize to the other daughter empires on Earth and that they immediately cease their violent actions.

These demands led the Atlanteans, with the aid of the Libyan/Egyptian Empire, to demand that the Yü Empire immediately rescind their decrees. They refused. The resultant destruction by the combined armed forces of Atlantis and their renegade allies forced the remnants of the Yü Empire to move underground. Today, they form what is known as the Kingdom of Agartha or Shamballa. Their fervent actions would permit the great and glorious legacy of Lemuria to remain intact until the time when it would be more appropriate for true Lyran/Sirian civilization to be brought forth again to humans on your planet.

In looking at the rise and fall of Atlantis, we find its history divided into three empires. The first historical segment is called the Old Empire (lasting from 400,000 years ago to approximately 25,000 BC). The Old Empire coexisted with Lemuria and would eventually plot its destruction. The second historical division is called the Middle Empire (lasting from roughly 25,000-15,000 BC), and it would be the first truly hierarchical ruler of Planet Earth. The last historical period was called the New Empire. It would contain the sagas of final conflict and destruction that comprise the last 5,000 years of Atlantean history (15,000 to 10,000 BC). Its final demise would leave Earth humans in a genetically reduced mutant condition from which you are still suffering. However, as you are learning, this is only a temporary condition that will soon be rectified with our help!

Let us now look at Atlantis during its Middle Empire era following the destruction of Lemuria about 25,000 years ago. Following the destruction of Lemuria, the Atlantean elite was left with the difficult question of how to reconstruct the Earth and its empires. The Atlanteans wished to have a position of complete authority and yet allow the other empires to coexist within the suzerainty of

From Atlantis to the Great Flood

Atlantis. This set of desires led to a great deal of difficulty. The first attempt was a government that would vastly alter the Lemurian clan structure and replace the traditional conceptualizations of Lemuria with an elite structure. At first this concept did not succeed at all and the immediate result was a series of very small but difficult civil wars that began to break out across your planet.

The Atlanteans had previously brought in an artificial Maldek moon which they used to physically balance Lady Gaia. Now, they attempted to use this moon to obtain the desired military superiority and end the civil wars and rebellions. However, the rebellions would continue over the entire 10,000-year period of the Middle Empire and would cause a great deal of soul searching and consternation among the Atlantean elite. Then the sly renegades from the various outpost star systems sent infiltrators to begin taking over the governing councils of the Atlantean elite and their newly established clans. These infiltrating renegades were more and more insistent that the Atlantean elites who opposed the anti-Lemurian faction should be punished. This demand led to a period of terrorism, torture, and inquisitions that left the Atlantean elite very upset and very divided.

Still, the major question remained of what could be done that would allow the Atlantean government to stabilize itself. And once achieved, they wondered how could they use this stability to govern planet Earth. Many ill-fated attempts at creating stability were attempted. Among the most successful methods they tried was the belief in creating what they called a God-force. The royal governing council of Atlantis decided that a new form of government was desperately needed in which a superior ruling class could be established and sustained by their pretense that they had been empowered by a God-force. This would contradict the previous balance of power followed during the Old Empire (in the time of Lemuria) when Atlantis had ten ruling districts each with its own king. These kings formed the governing council of Atlantis. Now, the new concept was to select one of these ten kingships as the supreme ruler. The other nine kingships would act as a cabinet for the ruling king. They would be empowered to establish a ruling or privy council from appointments made up of candidates chosen by these regional rulers.

Autocracy was on the rise and by the end of the Middle Empire, this system of tight governance was in full control of Atlantis, enforcing a period of peace and stability. However, a major difficulty was quickly developing. Many of the new generation who had been raised in the Middle Empire were wary of the ruling elites. Thus, a rebel movement began stating that Atlantis was a failure and demanding a return to the Lemurian system of government. Of course, such desires couldn't be allowed; so these groups were exiled to a place the Atlanteans called Ionia or southern Europe. *(See Figure 16 : Map of Middle Atlantean Empire.)* These exiled rebel leaders were sentenced to remain in Ionia until such a time as they would recognize and submit to the superiority of the Atlanteans. It was hoped by these ruling Atlantean elites that these measures would force the rebels to comply with their rule; but history would take a different direction.

You see, this rebel group consisted not only of members of the ruling elite, but also leading scientists and other administrators who had decided to create a government similar to that of the ancient Lemurian Empire. The rebels therefore began to secretly recreate Lemurian government and also to bring their plan back into Atlantis through an underground movement. This underground movement created what was called the Osirius cult in honor of the primary human group (the Sirians) that had been in charge of bringing human civilization to the Lemurian Continent.

It would be 3,000-4,000 years into the New Empire, however, before this Osirius movement became acutely important. Eventually, there came a time when the Atlanteans decided it was now necessary to destroy this cult by destroying the Ionians. The Atlantean ruling elite therefore decided to destroy Ionia using a modified version of the plan which they had employed to destroy Lemuria. Such a solution required that the Atlanteans get help from their Pleiadean, Centaurian and other renegade allies. This took some time, however, and did not go unnoticed by the Ionians.

The Ionians, because of their scientific knowledge, had developed an early warning system which permitted them to chart the movements of any moon that could be used to destroy them. The Ionians, therefore, were able to quickly counter any attack. These Ionian capabilities would lead to the destruction of Atlantis.

At the time of the destruction of Atlantis, the Atlantean king was named Atlas. During this same time, the majority of the Atlantean ruling elite began to wonder how this exiled group in Ionia and its

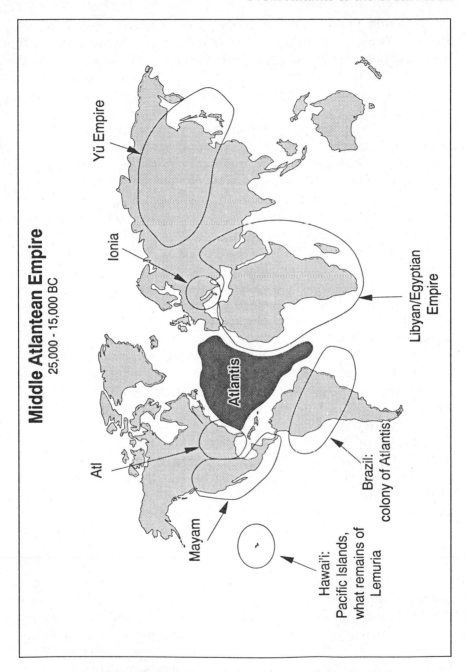

Figure 16: Map of Middle Atlantean Empire

107

underground movement was going to react when Ionia was destroyed. These elites began to wonder if this attack would really end the threat posed by the underground movement. This possibility had also alarmed the Libyan/Egyptian Empire and their ruling elites, who were beginning to worry about what was going to happen if Ionia was attacked.

King Atlas was secretly in favor of reestablishing the Lemurian form of civilization. Atlas had a son, named Osirius or Osiris, in honor of the underground movement that had been exiled to Ionia. Osirius had been in charge of many activities of his father's court. Just before the destruction, Atlas had sent his wife, Queen Mu, and his son, Osirius, in two different directions to throw off the conspirators who sought the King's death. Atlas sent Queen Mu and her brother Prince Mayam to Central America with most of the Atlantean army. He sent Osirius and most of the priests and record keepers to the Libyan/Egyptian Empire. (*See Figure 17: Atlantean King Atlas Creates Plan for Reestablishing Lemurian Culture.*)

Atlas had hoped (after the destruction of Atlantis) to create areas that would act as empires that could reestablish the Lemurian Empire. Unfortunately, this hope was to be dashed by the actions of Osirius' younger brother whose name was Seth. Seth had decided that, as the appointed ruler of the Libyan/Egyptian Empire, he was the last remnant of true Atlantean belief and his chief objective was to reestablish the Atlantean Empire.

These opposing beliefs led to a great conflict between Osirius and his brother Seth. At the head of Prince Osirius' armies was his chief general and eldest son, Horus, who was in line to become king of the Libyan/Egyptian Empire following the death of his father. Somehow Horus discovered that his uncle Seth was about to oppose his father militarily and he warned his father about what was to happen.

However, Osirius believed in the positive nature and loyalty of Seth to the dictums of their father, Atlas, and refused to believe his son's warning of an impending attack by Seth's armies. So, when Osirius landed in Egypt, Seth allowed him to become the new king of the Libyan/Egyptian Empire. Osirius became king because the law required that the elder brother always rule. However, Seth believed that the kingship of Osirius was destined to be only a temporary one. Eventually, when Seth was not allowed to re-

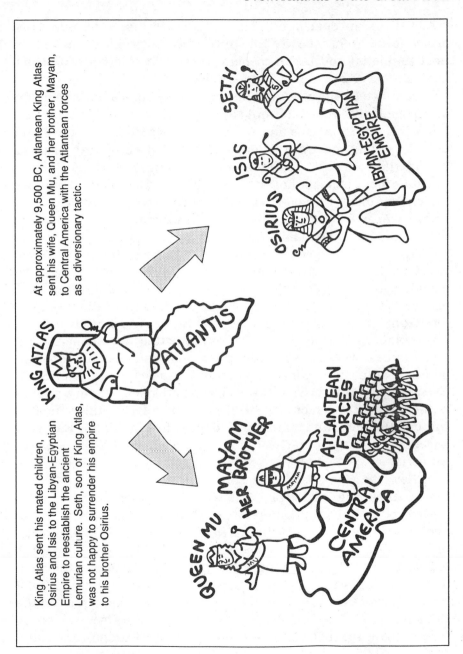

At approximately 9,500 BC, Atlantean King Atlas sent his wife, Queen Mu, and her brother, Mayam, to Central America with the Atlantean forces as a diversionary tactic.

King Atlas sent his mated children, Osirius and Isis to the Libyan-Egyptian Empire to reestablish the ancient Lemurian culture. Seth, son of King Atlas, was not happy to surrender his empire to his brother Osirius.

Figure 17: Atlantean King Atlas Creates Plan for Reestablishing Lemurian Culture.

establish his kingdom, he decided to attack Osirius. So he moved his armed forces from the river Nile to what is today called the Middle East (Sumeria) and began to plan for the destruction of Osirius through one great attack by his armies.

Meanwhile, Horus moved his forces into Sinai and there made an amazing discovery that would alter the whole equation of defeating Seth's forces. At this time, a new player was added to the game as an important added attraction. The Shamballa Empire or Agartha Empire (the former Yü daughter empire of Lemuria) had decided to reinstate some of its authority by creating a surface empire in India under the rule of the son of the King of the Agartha Empire. This prince of Agartha was named Rama and this empire has come down to your time with his name, Rama.

This Rama Empire was initially situated in the Indus River valley of India. The Agarthans had decided that this new empire would be in the right position to help defeat Seth and his Sumerian armies that now were aided by the last remnants of the renegade forces originally assigned to Atlantis. This new Agarthan civilization on the planet's surface aided Horus by protecting him with aerial and space forces. These forces allowed Horus to establish a temporary series of outposts in Sinai so he could attack the forces of Seth. Eventually, Horus successfully attacked and killed Seth in a mighty battle on the Eastern end of the Sinai peninsula. Seth's sons fled through the Holy Land into what is today called the Middle East and began a civilization that would mark the ancient beginnings of Sumeria.

Now the Sumerians, the sons of Seth, were determined to restore their rule in Egypt. The Sumerians were committed to destroy once and for all any remnant that could possibly be left of Lemuria on the surface of the Earth. They, therefore, skillfully set about to develop a plan to successfully attack Horus. This danger led Horus to make agreements with the Rama Empire of India. A series of attacks by the sons of Seth on the Rama Empire in India caused a series of counter attacks by Horus' Egyptian forces on the Sumerians. This series of vastly destructive wars seemed to be leading to the ruin of most of the civilized world of Europe, Africa, and Asia.

Hence, the elite of these warring empires decided to attack the crystal temples. These temples housed the network of crystals that

110

kept the Firmament in place above the surface of the Earth. These incredible amounts of frozen crystalline water were seen as the last resort by the warring parties. Furthermore, the three warring empires believed that only enough water would fall to flood the enemy's territory and not affect themselves. Unfortunately, the attacks were made simultaneously on the crystal temples and a sufficient amount of the crystalline network was destroyed to disrupt the structure of the Firmament in the heavens. This development led to the end of the Firmament and the falling of millions of gallons of water from the sky, historically and biblically referred to as the Great Flood.

Let us briefly look at what the Firmament was composed of and describe what happened to it. The Firmament was a huge crystalline shield of water situated at two positions, one roughly 15,000-18,000 feet from the Earth's surface and a second higher layer roughly 35,000-38,000 feet from the Earth's surface. (*See Figure 18: Description of Firmaments.*)   Both of these layers aided the planet by providing it with a very well-constructed and life-giving atmosphere. If the Firmament were to fall, the atmosphere would open up. This situation would allow dangerous radiations to penetrate to the Earth's surface and permit unstable air masses which you now call weather, or a very diverse climate, to occur.

Back in the time of the Firmament, there was no rain, very little wind and the seasons did not really exist. When the simultaneous attacks occurred on the crystal temples, too many of them were destroyed and this destruction opened up a huge hole in the Firmament.   This huge hole destabilized the entire Firmament system and with its deterioration came the great downpouring.   In one quick strike the Rama Empire, the Egyptian Empire and the Sumerian Empire were destroyed in a great cataclysmic flood. This flood spread world wide to encompass the Americas, other parts of Asia, Europe, Africa and the ocean basins.

What it left behind was not only a period of roughly 40 days of rain but a new world.   The old histories of humanity had been virtually flooded away and all that was left were the oral stories and legends. Earth humans should look at what these legends really mean. After the flood came the world that your ancestors have created and that you now live in. The peoples and rulers from this prior ancient time have become your gods and goddesses, and their age is your mythological

Description of Firmaments

At approximately 9,500 BC, the firmaments were still in place. Half of Firmament 1 collapsed when Atlantis was destroyed. The Firmament was artificially restored by the Libyan-Egyptian empire in 9,400 BC. However, Firmament 1 and 2 were completely destroyed at approximately 4,000 BC during the Rama-Libyan-Egyptian war and resulted in the Great Flood.

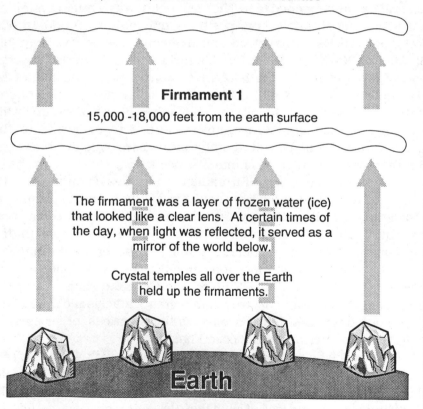

Firmament 2

35,000 - 38,000 feet from the earth surface

Firmament 1

15,000 -18,000 feet from the earth surface

The firmament was a layer of frozen water (ice) that looked like a clear lens. At certain times of the day, when light was reflected, it served as a mirror of the world below.

Crystal temples all over the Earth held up the firmaments.

Earth

Figure 18: Description of Firmaments

Golden Age. What you need to do as a people is to understand the meaning of the history which we have just described, and how this history relates to what is now about to happen on your planet.

Many questions about the material in this chapter may now come to mind. In the next section, Virginia asks questions of Washta regarding the information on "From Atlantis to the Great Flood."

✳ ✳ ✳ **Question and Answer Section** ✳ ✳ ✳

Virginia: Washta, is there any physical evidence of Atlantis that we could find on planet Earth today? Or is there evidence that we have found but haven't recognized for what it truly is?

Washta: There are vast regions of Atlantis in the Atlantic Ocean around the Canary Islands as well as regions off the southwestern coast of Spain along its continental shelf. There are also places in the Bahamas and the region just to the west and to the south of what is called the Antilles—Cuba and Puerto Rico. There are many regions of the ocean around the central mid-Atlantic ridge that have artifacts of the Atlantean realm. There are other areas off the coast of the Carolinas in the United States that also have been discovered but are not presently being made public.

Virginia: Are any of them easier to get to than other sites, or should we even be thinking about looking for them at this time?

Washta: Various temple sites that have not yet risen will be rising when many of the landings occur. So know that Atlantis will show its footprint upon your planet's history in its own way at the appropriate time. Many governments have already excavated numerous sites that we have just described and discovered many articles that prove our point. The important thing is to relax and know that the Atlantean realm is about to re–emerge at the appropriate time.

Virginia: Regarding the Yü empire in Asia, are there geological or anthropological remnants that we could find today?—or that have already been found that indicate the existence of such an empire?

Washta: There are locations in the vast northeastern sections of China as well as in the far western desert of China where the remains of this particular empire have been found. The primary point to be made about this particular empire is the following. The survivors left Yü and went into the Himalayas and formed the legendary Agartha or Shamballa. This realm is the key to linking your surface humans with the underground humans, who await this opportunity when the landings occur.

Virginia: Are you saying that the inner worlds of Shamballa or Agartha will be coming forward shortly?

Washta: Yes, this is what has been called, by the underground humans on your planet, "the great reunion." They are looking forward to the time when all the different Lemurian colonies that exist underground throughout the vast parts of your planet in North and South America, in Asia, Africa and in Europe will be allowed to successfully reestablish themselves by coming to the Earth's surface. Up to now their colonies have been kept largely secretive or else made such an ambiguous reality that they would not be disturbed.

Virginia: Approximately what number of beings are we speaking about and are they safe in their present locations from the work of the grays and others?

Washta: They have been in complete underground seclusion while holding the Lemurian group governance model since the end of Lemuria, and especially during the destruction of Atlantis. They are safe and their population is about 25 million in total.

Virginia: You mentioned the sites in Africa. Can you state where these sites are located without harming the people?

Washta: There are major sites all over Africa. One of these major sites is the great Pyramid in Egypt which acts as the holder of the energies of the records of Lemuria. These records are held in the great Pyramid in a special room near its base which is to be kept secret. The room is kept totally secured by the use of special devic energies whose sole purpose is to guard the records from those who are not to see them.

Virginia: Yes, thank you. Could you comment on the empire of Rama and present day Hinduism as a religion or philosophy?

Washta: Rama came from Agartha to reestablish a superior realm in India—one that was to bring the return of the cooperative Lemurian civilizations. This unfortunately was not done due to various influences of the Pleiadean and Centaurian rebels who intervened and prevented the success of his mission. This is what is described in the various *Mahabarata* and *Ramayana* books which

114

were developed in their various mystical forms, and they contain the history of that time. The energies and the legacies of the Rama empire were left in various temples, some of which survived to the rise of modern Hinduism 2,000-3,000 years ago. These temple records have been kept secure and in secret and serve as the basis of modern Hinduism for those who can understand them.

Virginia: Are there any particular remnants in India today that are particularly related to the underground family or to geographical or anthropological sites of interest?

Washta: There are many sites in the Indus River valley and other river valleys such as the Ganges in India where remnants of ancient cities have temples sites at their core. These sites are remnants of Rama and also Lemuria. This is because India was one of the major spiritual centers for the practices of what you might call today a religious science, which had Lemurian concepts as its basis. These practices and beliefs were brought into many other places such as what is today called Ceylon or Sri Lanka, and of course the present Hawaiian Islands. They are there to be discovered, explored, and utilized when the landings occur.

Virginia: Does that include Easter Island, or was that a different thing?

Washta: Easter Island was a landing zone used for the transference of scientific information from the southwestern and southeastern Lemurian sections to the northeastern section which is today called Hawaii—the main science center. It was therefore a major transference point for knowledge since this knowledge was transferred both by vehicle and through special technological devices unknown today on your planet.

Virginia: We'd like to know who first constructed what is called the Firmament and when they did that.

Washta: The Firmament was originally constructed by the initial etheric civilization that came to your world roughly 35 million years ago. This was done to protect planet Earth from the radiation of the Sun and other dangerous cosmic radiations that regularly come through your particular solar system. This Firmament was maintained, broken, and re-established many times as different civilizations and invasions came. Thus, floods have occurred throughout the geological history of this planet ever since the time of that initial etheric civilization.

Virginia: Can it ever be replaced?

Washta: Some of the small crystal temples which were in place when the last full Firmament was in the heavens, are still there, but others are to be put into place and reactivated at the appropriate time. This will be part of our rehabilitation procedures. We have already set up areas that are now under the ocean, as well as other difficult–to–reach areas where we intend to reestablish the original grid of crystal temples. Crystal temples that are easier to utilize and to put into action will be used in the physical dimension. The rest will be used through etheric energy patterns of holographic images which will replicate the originals. At the appropriate time when the landings have been completed, these particular regions will be activated and then the Firmament will be returned to the heavens.

Virginia: Yes, thank you. Is the Bermuda Triangle similar to what you are describing as a crystal temple?

Washta: These various scientific devices beneath the surface are indeed part of the crystal temple process. Because of what occurred after the destruction of Atlantis, however, the Bermuda Triangle became an interdimensional portal. Many groups that go from one dimension to another have utilized this triangle for that particular purpose of transportation and communication. When the triangle is activated, it then causes an interdimensional portal to open. Any objects inside the triangle where the communication point is based will then experience this portal effect so that they will either disappear or be moved to another dimensional space in time.

Virginia: Yes, thank you. Are there any other temples that we should know about?

Washta: There are temples off Japan, off Hawaii, along the California coast, along the Atlantic coast of North America, and in Europe as well as various ones throughout Africa, South America, Australia and the Pacific and Atlantic Ocean basins.

Virginia: Did the temples all look alike in size and construction or were they dissimilar in some ways?

Washta: They were different depending upon whether they were the main points on a grid or were the support points. The main points on the grid were huge temples, almost the size of the Great Pyramid in their basic structural design and their actual size. Other support temples were from one-half to one-quarter to one-eighth the size of this particular prototype.

Virginia: Are all of the pyramids running from Guatemala through parts of Mexico related in any way to the grids?

Washta: They were built on sacred–node grid points because these sacred grid points have two uses. First, they invigorate all who visit by energizing them. Secondly, they are a way of communicating (through the thin veil that exists around them) with the "other side" or what you call the spiritual dimension. Therefore, when these sites were built they were deliberately constructed for these two basic purposes.

Virginia: There are many questions I am sure that we could go on with, but we'd like to close today by asking you to confirm how the fall of the Firmament has accelerated Earth's present day weather and radiation difficulties?

Washta: When the Firmament was an intricate whole it was under the direction of the Spiritual Hierarchy—and those who constructed the crystal temples in accordance with the Spiritual Hierarchy's wishes—so it could perform several functions for the atmosphere of your planet. First, it lowered the radiation and heat levels so that the climate of Earth, from North Pole to South Pole, was within five degrees of one another. Thus, the tropics were around the upper 70s (degrees Farenheit) and the polar regions were around the lower 70s. So ice sheets did not exist across the north and south polar regions as you have today.

The second major difference in the atmosphere was that the winds and clouds did not exist. There were no clouds and every day was a sunny day. What further aided this fact was that the winds were minimal and were kept to a maximum of five to seven miles per hour. Also, because there were no clouds, there were no rain storms; so rain is something that is unique to your present era. The complete Firmament atmosphere invigorated the mind and the body since the radiation energy stored the prana in the Firmament. Prana then drifted across the Firmament and maintained it almost as if it were a giant refrigerator. You might call it a refrigerator of prana or energy!

The body of any creature existing on your planet was invigorated by this energy. The heat and other radiation that would cause body deterioration were kept out of your surface atmosphere by the Firmament. (Another side effect was that the stars were magnified so the sky would be seen as through a huge telescope.) Thus, the Firmament prevented a ravaged atmosphere in which there are great

117

differences in climate, storms, and extremes of weather, and a large amount of radiation was prevented from entering. After the Firmament's collapse, radiation eventually shrunk the physical size of humans and gradually limited the length of their life span. Your present atmosphere does not protect life as the Firmament once did and will do so again.

Virginia: So the Holy Bible stories of long–lived beings hundreds of years old was because the Firmament was in place?

Washta: That is correct. And now we will conclude. We would just like to say that when the true history of your planet comes forth, you will better understand what you evolved from. This will help you grasp what did occur so you can establish the new Age of Light.

Virginia: We thank you all so very much.

Washta: And before we leave we thank you for allowing us to speak.

Chapter 7
After The Flood

In the previous discussion of Earth history, Washta, Mikah and Teletron have spelled out those episodes that are considered to be either mythical or legendary to most people on our planet. As you will hopefully realize, these stories are the true history of Earth's earliest human civilization. Therefore, this same Sirian council will now give you some insights that will help you to better understand the flow of history from Atlantis to the present time. Explaining these historical details will be the major purpose of this chapter because it is of vital importance to know our historical and genetic origins.

As our council noted in the previous chapter, the time following the fall of Atlantis saw the rise of the Libyan-Egyptian Empire and the India-based Rama Empire. These two empires instigated, with the assistance of the Sumerian Empire, a vast and unconscionable conflict that resulted in the destruction of the Firmament and caused the Great Flood that followed. The flood which occurred approximately 6,000 years ago was an event that changed the history of your planet, its physical environment, and your own human life spans. It was literally the water shed between the Atlantean/Lemurian times and the incredible drama that is now being played out on planet Earth.

It is necessary for our purposes of guiding you through Earth history to have you know what happened after the flood receded. The human population was reduced to very small numbers throughout your entire planet. As the waters slowly retreated, humans began to emerge from their places of refuge wondering how they could restore human civilization. The Earth human guardian classes (the elites from Atlantis, Egypt, India, the Americas, Asia and so forth) suddenly found themselves in an immensely challenging new role. But these Earth-born elite groups could not imagine how they could successfully bring forth a renewal of human civilization after such horrific losses of life and property—especially with Earth's vastly changed geographical regions. Perhaps if you pause to imagine the Earth totally covered by water in an unending deluge, you may sense the shock, depression, and hopelessness they felt during, and after, this horrendous event.

They therefore asked the help of their extraterrestrial benefactors who now held sway over a devastated and ruined planet Earth. The Pleiadeans and various other renegade groups were asked to assist in once again bringing human civilization to the Earth. This request led to a massive intervention by the Pleiadean renegades and their allies who had been associated with Atlantis. You see, during the Great Flood, the Atlanteans and many of their associates had fled for their own safety to the star Hadar (also known as Beta Centauri— a star in the constellation Centaurus). So the former, heartless Earth leaders were not available for decision-making in this time of crisis.

The people from Hadar looked upon this entire predicament of humans on Earth as a fitting and karmic destruction of a formerly glorious civilization. One that should be memorialized in the same fashion as the former civilizations on Mars and Venus! The Governing Council of the new Hadar III colony even asked the renegade Pleiadeans not to interfere in Earth's now destroyed civilization and to keep it at its then present low level of culture and technology. The Hadarans felt that this approach would pay proper homage to the destruction produced by the Great Flood. This strong request started an argument between the renegade Pleiadeans, their allies, and the remnants of the Atlantean elite now residing on a planet in the Hadar star system. It was an argument the renegades won. For their own purposes, the renegade Pleiadeans wanted to encourage human civilization, but were not sure how they could accomplish this gigantic task.

Eventually, these renegade Pleiadeans formulated a plan to establish new colonies in just four Earth areas. The first of these

120

areas was in the region of the Middle East and became the colony of Sumeria. The second of these areas was located in the central valley of Mexico and became the original or pre-Olmec Mesoamerican civilization. The third of these areas was located in the former site of the Rama Empire in the upper delta of the Indus river and in the north central region of China (near the modern city of Xian). The fourth area was in the Nile river basin and the chief site of the former Libyan/Egyptian Empire. Having decided that these four areas would be the correct places to successfully restore human civilization on this planet, a decision remained to determine what types of civilizations should be chosen.

Imagine, if you will, what kind of government you would initiate if you could start a new human civilization. Although all four cultures would mirror the concepts held by the renegades for their version of the basic underpinnings of Pleiadean civilization, there was an argument regarding which primary culture was the best. Therefore, each of the new Earth colonies was different in some way. At the same time, other human survivors of the flood were floundering about on Earth and attempting to recreate their own local human civilization.

The group of renegades in charge of establishing the Middle Eastern civilization of Sumeria based their government upon a hierarchical structure that would have the renegades acting as the overseer gods. These overseer gods presented Earth's mutant humans with a myth of creation signifying why the Pleiadean renegades should be held in awe and thus worshipped. This action led to the initial formation of Sumerian civilization and also to the important worshipping of the Pleiadean renegades as their founders.

Another group of renegades came to Egypt and began to establish a civilization about 100 years after the Great Flood. This group of Pleiadean and Centaurian renegades were determined to find a way to obliterate the Lemurian legacy as symbolized by the Great Pyramid. Their concept was to use the process of a god-king figure to issue decrees and guard the old secrets of technology and history from the survivors.

At roughly the same time in Mexico, there existed various remnants of the pre-flood civilizations that now had been completely torn asunder. The inhabitants of the Valley of Mexico attempted to recreate these civilizations that had been founded by Lemuria and later abetted by the arrival of Queen Mu and her brother, Prince Mayam. However, they lacked the technology to complete this task and needed the assistance of their extraterrestrial overseers for the proper technology and necessary concepts of governance that would successfully permit them to recreate their pre-antediluvian civilizations. This intervention did not immediately happen. However, another different group of Pleiadean and Centaurian renegades did eventually come to establish several civilizations in Mexico that would mirror the renegades hierarchical structures as well as their spiritual concepts and mythologies.

A different group of renegades came to what is now the continent of Asia and simultaneously established colonies at former sites of the Rama Empire (the upper delta of the Indus river valley and near the city of Xian in north central China). This group of Pleiadean and Centaurian renegades had given themselves a unique task. They wished to alter the former location of their chief rival and yet they knew that the influence of the Rama Empire was still strong in this region. The renegades also knew that many hidden records of the Rama Empire as well as many temples and pyramids dedicated to Lemuria were still in use. Their intervention was based on the use of a skillful distortion of innumerable temple records and of various pyramid rituals that would allow the gradual amalgamating of the cultural traditions of Lemuria, Rama, and the Pleiadean/Centaurian renegades.

Unfortunately, the human beings who survived the flood were largely the same ones that lacked full consciousness. The Pleiadean renegades and their allies realized this fact and understood that this group of humans, a partially conscious mutant, were ones that could be mostly controlled and developed. This unfortunate deed was accomplished throughout the long and sad history of non-spiritual religion upon this planet. Fortunately, the Earth's Spiritual Hierarchies (Lady Gaia, angels, archangels) still believed that even these mutant humans should be part of the Earth's guardian triad and for this reason the humans had been allowed to repopulate the Earth. The Spiritual Hierarchies consequently decided that they would attempt to intervene in this experiment where possible.

This intervention by the angels and archangels overseeing this planet led them to occasionally appoint various persons as their representative or to allow chosen human civilizations to receive their visions. These heavenly visions helped to create spiritualized humans within these extraterrestrially controlled civilizations by giving them the inspirations needed to introduce certain core beliefs. These beliefs would aid the spiritual growth and development of Earth humans. This procedure has continued to this day. In fact, only this spiritual intervention has helped the now partially conscious Earth humans to recognize and utilize the concept of good and evil and the need for a fairer method of governance.

History had been started anew, and yet the basic spiritual essence of humans had been completely torn asunder. This resulted in the early hierarchical empires and the innumerable wars between the various city states that would rule human civilization during the first two thousand years after the Great Flood. These small colonies would eventually create larger empires and learn to use technologies that would create even bloodier wars. These terrible wars would mark the next three thousand years after the initial civilizing period and would bring you Earth humans to your present period of atomic bombs and nuclear warhead mentality.

As we have described, your Earth human civilization was restored by the outside intervention of the Pleiadean renegades and their allies who were responsible for the difficulties in Atlantis in the first place. To enforce their concept as a creator God, these renegade "gods" first gave Earth humans the methods for building large permanent structures such as stone buildings and monuments. Earth's humans had forgotten (because of the disaster created by the Great Flood) how to build anything of true substance and therefore they had to be instructed how to do so.

The renegades began teaching these methods, using projects where various buildings and structures were actually built for the sole purpose of recreating various anteluvean stone structures like Stonehenge. The purpose of these stone structures was to act as a place for the worshipping of the renegades who had now made themselves into gods deserving reverence and awe. Because no form of disobedience to these new gods was permitted, the whole concept of ruling by "divine right" was inculcated in Earth humans by a renegade hierarchy which had been established by unsavory men and not the Spiritual Hierarchy.

You might say that in ancient times the "gods" were only human forms—not the genuine thing. They were merely the galactic

123

Pleiadeans, the Centaurians and others who came to this world to establish their particular form of hierarchical human civilization. These Federation renegades used the mutant Earth human civilization to pay homage to themselves and also to retain the concepts first employed in Atlantis—namely, a subservient civilization worshipping its elite. This concept has continued throughout modern times.

However, by the fifteenth to the twelfth centuries BC, the various galactic wars and other forms of intergalactic (interdimensional) interference between the forces of light and dark had made the renegade Pleiadean control of this planet difficult to maintain. This predicament led to the withdrawal of Pleiadean renegades from their position of authority in human civilization—an authority that had been initially established in the ancient civilizations of Egypt, India, China and the Americas. Their sudden withdrawal allowed the coming forth of a new system of knowledge (modern scientific logic) among men. Earth humans now began to take the knowledge already given to them by "the gods" (the various extraterrestrial renegades) and to utilize it for their own purposes.

This sudden withdrawal caused a great dilemma for human civilization. Earth's human elites felt that their gods were no longer fully supporting them, and that without them fully present a new cycle of relationship and authority between the rulers, the heavens and the common people, was being created on this planet. Hence, human civilization now developed its own version of celestial science. The original, cosmic celestial science and its related field of philosophy had developed because the renegades, who had created this new civilization and allowed it to develop at a prescribed rate, had to leave because of a temporary intervention by the main defense forces of the Pleiadean Star League.

This sudden change in planetary control created for humans a predicament over who was guiding their civilizations. Since the time of the Great Flood, humans had been further altered by the adverse planetary conditions that had mutated their bodies and decreased their mental capabilities. These conditions were caused when the Earth's atmosphere now brought in vast amounts of radiation—a phenomenon that shortened the human life span from a millennia to one of mere decades. Earth humans were also suddenly shrunk from a normal galactic human height of 8 to 10 feet tall to a stature barely 5 to 6 feet tall. These changes in stature and in life span have vastly limited Earth humans' ability to be fully conscious and have left most humans susceptible to these so-called "gods"(extraterrestrial renegades).

Historically, then, the Pleiadean and other renegades had come to your planet and rent their will upon the Earth. Yet the Spiritual Hierarchy knew that the way of the light—the way of the true Godhead— would be achieved by men because the Spiritual Hierarchy had interceded and had given a vision to all humans (both galactic and Earth humans). The Spiritual Hierarchy believed that if this light and love were given to Earth's human mutants, these human mutants could successfully become one with this light at some future time. While humans had been, through the mutation process, stripped of the majority of their consciousness, enough genetic material had been saved in a few people so there were occasional remnants of applied full consciousness.

The humans most affected by these heavenly visions were the so called psychics or seers of the ancient world, whose knowledge has continued to aid human civilization up to the present time. The seers or psychics of today, are serving as the forerunners of the increasing consciousness that is now occurring among Earth humans.

You humans of Earth now have your propitious hour to rise out of quarantine and mutancy and become the galactic beings you are meant to be. This process is now happening around your globe and we are attempting to guide and prepare you to fully understand its implications. Hence, we explain your situation in everyday language, and relate it to the events and conditions created by past civilizations to give you safety and clarity. Civilizations have changed from large scale barbaric practices and massacres to high technological warfare, creating the rise and fall of culture after culture. Yet today, in your modern times, a strange and wondrous pattern is happening for all humanity and this is the song of the earth that we wish to emphasize to all.

This planet is now in the midst of creating a new link with the Spiritual Hierarchies. Humans are also in the process of recreating a fully conscious civilization. As Earth humans moved from the great barbaric practices and consciousness of ancient Egypt and India, as well as from aspects of religion in the Americas and Oceania, we have noted progress from the cannibalistic practices, etc. Though we have noticed some improvement in the way humans treat one another, this is on a painstakingly small scale, hardly noticeable from one civilization to the other. The carnage and destruction of your own 20th Century far exceeds in many ways the worst barbaric practices of the ancient Egyptians, Sumerians, Indians or Ancient Americans. Yet it is a known and reliable fact that consciousness on this planet is improving. Earth humans now are experiencing a new coming of age and this is the significance of Earth history from the time of the Great Flood, over five thousand years ago, to the present.

If we were to draw a time line, you would see that just after the Great Flood, there was a period of dreadful negativity and darkness when the control of the Pleiadean renegades was at its very strongest. However as their grip was slowly lifted from this planet, humans were able to achieve a slight improvement in consciousness. This improvement allowed the intervention of your Sirian ancestors back into your civilization from time to time, which supported the great light of the Christ and the coming of Quetzalcoatl. Both Christ in Israel and Quetzalcoatl in the Americas marked a time of enormous love upon this planet. This potent love and light are now being fully utilized to create a web of consciousness that will eventually enable this planet to finally bask in the full light of consciousness represented by the coming galactic civilization. If humans will continue to be one with this energy, they will discover that they have within them a potential for ascension or transformation. In this ascension they can discover how their light body and their physical body can establish a reality that unites their soul with the physical aspects of universal physical creation.

You Earth humans, therefore, sit in the midst of an incredible evolution that will lead to the rise of a new civilization. For within the seeds of evolutionary discord, there now lie the beginnings of a new and glorious way. Earth humans will shortly be able to understand, recognize, and claim the coming new light of full consciousness. Therefore, humans should know and should realize that in Earth's history a great vibratory song is about to bring forth a new light, a new way, and a new beingness. All galactic humans shall, within this new parable, finally achieve the incredible gift of light that was first given to this planet at the beginning of human history. Now is the time for all Earth humans to remember their true history and to claim the legacy of full consciousness they deserve.

Many questions about the material in this chapter may now come to mind. In the next section, Virginia asks questions of Washta regarding information on "After the Flood."

✳ ✳ ✳ **Question and Answer Section** ✳ ✳ ✳

Virginia: We thank you for coming to help us and we greet all with love and respect. Please explain why the Pleiadean and other renegades were allowed to carry on their negative activities without any control or censorship from the leadership on their native planets.

Washta: The Pleiadean Star League, as part of its defense commands, developed what are called outpost commands or advanced patrols. You might call them frontiersmen because they were far from home and pretty much on their own. These command personnel eventually developed into the renegades because they were given complete authority over the star systems that they colonized. Because their purpose was to defend the entire Pleiadean system from attack, they were able to develop their own culture without interference. And with other outpost commands, they coordinated defense schemes that successfully prevented the various reptoid and dinoid groups from entering the Pleiadean system and other related star systems in the constellation of Taurus.

At the time of Atlantis the renegades were given the authority to also colonize what was the Atlantean colony on your planet. With this total power, they were able to convince the Atlanteans to participate in these various genetic experiments during the last days of Atlantis. These genetic experiments led to the present mutant humans that now exist on your planet, as we have previously explained. The reason they were allowed to do this was that the Pleiadean system believes in what it calls a system of karma or evolutionary stages of development. They believe that when a planet chooses a certain system of development, this system of development must be honored until such time as an alternative or another stage of development surfaces in that star system. Only if there is a series of events to cause a change in the karma, or reality of that system's evolution, do they change it. The Pleiadean leadership therefore allowed the renegades' ill-fated experiment to continue and did not directly intervene except in very, very minor ways.

It was the Sirians on the other hand, cooperating with the

cetaceans and the Spiritual Hierarchy, who from time to time attempted to cause some kind of a shift in human development towards the more fully conscious state. Their several experimentations—even bringing in the Gold Ray energy of Christ—did not cause an immediate change in the evolution of your Earth's civilization. However, these experiments planted the spiritual seeds the Sirians wanted so that the next phase of establishing a fully conscious civilization was ready to be carried out. The Sirians hoped that what they had set into motion could be used as the underpinnings for reclaiming a fully conscious Earth human as a planetary caretaker.

These new concepts of love and wisdom brought to Earth as epitomized by Buddha, Jesus, and others is an energy pattern now coming into fruition. This spiritual energy has created a web of high consciousness that serves as the underpinning for the Spiritual Hierarchy to bring in a galactic human civilization on planet Earth once again.

Virginia: Then what happens to these renegades? Are they just permitted to do whatever they wish? Are they never censored for anything?

Washta: They have been severely censored from time to time. However, the Pleiadean system is only now changing its concept of karma and evolution and adopting more of what you might call a kinder galactic human civilization. They are now in the process of bringing in the renegades and restricting the total independence previously allowed their outpost command groups. This is now going on throughout this sector of the galaxy and will bring an end to the reign of terror the renegades produced over the last few hundreds of thousands of years.

Virginia: It seems confusing to us that even though the Sirians had concern for us there was not some higher court decision or intervention on behalf of Earth.

Washta: The Sirians seriously called for an earlier intervention, if not by the Galactic Federation, at least in some other fashion. However, the Federation Regional Council overruled the Sirians and said that the most they would do would be to change this energy. The Spiritual Hierarchies agreed that there had been a change in karmic development in your solar system and therefore decided that mutant humans had to slowly evolve and learn the difference between positive and negative behavior. It was expected that when humans fully understood this concept, and moved themselves in a large-scale development toward consciousness (as they are now doing in this particular century), they would then be ready to experience their true heritage. Therefore the Sirians decided to use the small amount of leeway that they were given and to cooperate with the Spiritual Hierarchy in bringing in the light of love through the energies of the Christ.

Virginia: How can Earth humans, who are now somewhat mutant, have any respect for what is called God or for the Federation when they are powerless to resist evil?. . . when no one is speaking-out on their behalf or wishes to censor those who are harming them?

Washta: Both the Sirians and the Christ consciousness hierarchical energies have attempted for a very long time to intervene in human affairs. They are teaching humans that there is a loving alternative to humanity's present hierarchical power structures and the oppressive economic systems that have developed over the last few thousands of years. This intervention has been a slow process. But these love and wisdom energies that have been brought into your planet are now slowing down acts of brutality, war and violence.

Remember that every human's soul understands what is happening, and that prophecies were given to all peoples around this planet saying such a cleansing time would occur. This was the system decided upon by the Spiritual Hierarchy as the only evolutionary pattern that could produce the proper spiritual results. We are now ready to harvest this evolution and bring humans on your planet back into full consciousness—back into the Galactic Federation and back to your true destiny as a showcase planet. You and your planet will bring a great light throughout this galaxy.

Virginia: Nonetheless, most humans who learn that renegades are allowed to do whatever harm they please may fail to understand how there can be a spiritual component to the Galactic Federation when such things are allowed.

Washta: Your planet was told through prophecy that it would evolve through a series of spiritual evolutionary patterns which would bring darkness into light. Only through understanding light and darkness, as well, would the incredible light that will shine on Earth finally be achieved. This is what is now happening on your planet. The wars that have occurred throughout this galaxy are also beginning to shift, and this is a part of the galactic prophecies that have occurred from the beginning of life. Just as Earth is being reborn, so this particular galaxy was told that there would be a powerful darkness that would nearly conquer this galaxy, but then light would begin shining in the darkness and would illuminate it and eventually bring it to an end. That is the balance of free will that you, and we, are all learning.

Virginia: Are you saying that God, or the original creative force, believes that only pain and suffering can achieve the light?

Washta: No, but this Galaxy had established certain patterns in it that would allow for this particular system of spiritual and physical evolution to occur. Believe me when I relate that this galaxy is a very unique galaxy. It is one that will eventually achieve an incredible light. It therefore must have both light and darkness in it. These two energies together make possible what will eventually be the glorious joining of light and dark that is the final purpose this galaxy represents.

Virginia: Perhaps you can understand that it may be very shocking for humans to hear that archangels and other spiritual hierarchical beings have allowed physical renegades to utilize their unkind powers as a learning experience for us. What is the relationship of the Spiritual Hierarchy to those of you who are galactic humans? Who is really in charge?

Washta: The Spiritual Hierarchy is in charge of your planet. However, they discovered that a certain road had been followed by those that had seized the physical human guardianship of this planet. The Spiritual Hierarchy then had two choices. They could eliminate your entire civilization or they could allow it to spiritually evolve in a way that would allow the great light that is the basic underpinnings of all physical beingness to come forth. They decided that destruction was not desirable and that evolution would lead to the fulfillment of the prophecy of light. Evolution was chosen so humanity could become greater than its original nature.

Virginia: Thank you. In the history about the Great Flood, could you estimate the size of the Earth human population following that great inundation?

Washta: The population of the planet was approximately 64 million people before the flood and afterwards it was down to less than two million. Although limited in number, enough humans were left so that with proper information and proper guidance a greater civilization could be rebuilt.

I am not counting those Pleiadean and Centaurian renegades— and others who had been the basic underpinning of Atlantis—who remained in crafts above the planet during the time of the destruction. They believed their job was to maintain the original hierarchical system and to take advantage of the mutant humans that existed on the surface of your planet. Although the Spiritual Hierarchy and Sirians attempted to alter the Pleiadean system, the system was etched in the human population's consciousness and they gradually developed an attitude of servitude. Since free will is one of the basic underpinnings of spiritual evolution on your planet, the Spiritual Hierarchy decided upon the spiritual evolutionary path and it has been your planet's basic foundation since that time.

Virginia: So is the story of Noah having just a very few survivors correct?

Washta: Since there were very few survivors out of the total population, and these remnants were widely scattered around the planet, they could not communicate with each other. So the result was that the flood stories remained in the immediate areas where the survivors settled. And because Noah was from the ancient Egyptian/ Libyan civilization, his story influenced the Middle East from which came the Bible story.

Flood and destruction myths are discovered in what is today Mexico, the Pacific Ocean Islands, Australia, Africa, and Europe. All of these myths tell of the flood, but the Bible story is the most known because the survivor Noah attempted to recreate a Lemurian style of civilization. Regrettably, the survivors around him didn't agree with his intention and the attempt failed.

This is why the Spiritual Hierarchy, after hoping that this disaster would teach mutant humans that their authoritarian attitudes were ways of folly, did not continue onward. Nevertheless, that is why they continued to send prophets to various parts of the globe, from time to time, to begin enlightenment training that would bring humans back to the brink of rediscovering their full consciousness and their true spiritual orientation.

Virginia: How could humans, even after the flood, reclaim a spiritual consciousness when the renegade's beliefs defined the kind of government to be modeled? How could Earth humans learn anything different without physical beings teaching them?

131

Washta: There were various attempts, the last of which was with the Hebrew peoples of the Bible, after Exodus, to recreate a Lemurian style society using the concept of the judges to bring the people into the idea of a society led by spiritual beings. It was hoped that when they were in touch with the true God force energies and Spiritual Hierarchy of your planet, a new civilization could reestablish the original concepts, even in the very limited mutant energy forms of consciousness that they possessed. However, as the Bible relates, even this concept failed when the humans, who knew they were under divine guidance, couldn't change and alter their concepts of reality. We place no blame here. Nevertheless, because they still wanted to return to the former kingship and still wanted to return to the concepts of power and conquest in ways that were not meant to be, the experiment ended without success.

This situation finally led to the introduction of the Christ energy pattern knowing that it would finally succeed because of the spiritual remnant that it left behind and because of the additional energy the Spiritual Hierarchy would make later on, as you are witnessing more and more today.

Virginia: Thank you. You have mentioned Judaism and Christianity. Could you also speak a little bit about Buddha, the Hindus in India, and also about Mohammed?

Washta: In the case of Hinduism, it has remnants of the great histories of Atlantis and Lemuria as its core. Following the flood, this was then transmuted into a multi-God and Goddess system.

Buddha was given to you through the Arcturians and he came to this region to bring a great transformation of love and light. For a time his experiment was successful. However, as later happened in Christianity, it was mutated into a formal concept of religion whereupon many of Buddha's original precepts were not followed. The same process unfortunately occurred for Mohammed when he brought to Islam a great concept for change, transformation, and many aspects of love and light. When the concepts of these three just-mentioned religious philosophies are blended with the religions and prophecies of awakened indigenous peoples, they can serve as the underpinning of the web of consciousness that is now forming around your planet.

Virginia: I am curious; are there other religious groups or influences that you'd like to mention that were important to us or are still important today?

Washta: What is happening on your planet right now is that many of the indigenous peoples have as their basis the concept of a *living* Mother Earth. They have a very, very complete understanding of what the ecology of this planet is about, and these ecologies are growing quickly in importance.

The so-called major religions of your planet are learning that the time has come to merge the concepts of their religions with the concept of the indigenous ones. These two together form the web, the network of consciousness, that is now being extended around your planet to prepare all humans for the fantastic full-consciousness experience that awaits them.

Virginia: You have a very interesting statement in the chapter that I'm going to quote and ask you to comment on. The statement made about Earth humans was: "In this ascension they can discover how their light body and their physical body can establish a reality that unites your soul with the physical aspects of universal physical creation."

Washta: Yes, we will explain that to you. The light soul forms a light body. Since it is a physical universe, this light soul or soul force has created a physical aspect of the light body or the physical body. These energies together form a unity of physical body and soul or light body. In mutant Earth humans, this has been separated because of the nature of limited consciousness.

When one is spiritual, as well as physical, one can partake of the energies of the physical universe and its evolution. One unites them together to form a path of light that enables the physical universe to evolve to its full potential and also allows the spiritual universe to likewise live through the physical to evolve into what it is fully capable of being.

Virginia: Thank you. Does that mean the body and soul are only separated in our dimensionality and that in other dimensions have not separated? Or has the pattern been of separation and all must find a way back together?

Washta: All are separated and must find their way together in this dimension, while in other dimensions they already have unity. This is the uniqueness of the 3rd-dimension because it has the potential of a consciousness that can be limited to a reality that separates spirit from physical.

Virginia: Why would anyone want to do that?

Washta: This is something that is to be avoided; however, many have discovered that when consciousness is limited then the dominance of physical reality can be used to control others. Many civilizations have attempted to create races and beings that do just that. They have separated and produced the phenomenon that is known in present human civilization as death. This is a phenomenon that the new Earth galactic civilization will finally overcome by returning to immortality patterns that are the heritage of all humans in your civilization. However, the experiment that created this temporary death concept over the last tens of thousands of years is one that must be ended. This is what is now happening on your planet.

Virginia: Thank you. In the three chapters dedicated to Earth history, one thing that hasn't been discussed is why we have so many races and different skin colors.

Washta: These races represent a variety of different galactic humans who exist throughout this entire Federation and galaxy. As humans evolved, they developed many different skin colorations when they moved across the galaxy, evolving into one race and then the other. For instance the so-called black race on your planet originally was a blue race. However, it was transmuted into a black race when Earth lost its Firmament and the atmosphere allowed the Sun's more dangerous radiation to cause a mutation in the skin of the blue race that turned it into a darker hue.

Those that represent the energy patterns that are today called the red, brown or the yellow races came from Andromeda and the Pleiadean systems. They represent the mutations that occurred in various suns in those star systems and those star leagues. This is the uniqueness of your planet. You have the various races and realities that are the sum total of the many humans in this galaxy.

Virginia: And the white are from . . . ?

Washta: They are from Sirius and various other star systems such as the Pleiades and the original Vega system.

Virginia: How does origin relate to skin color?

Washta: Originally it did not. However, the transmutations of limited consciousness produced racial characteristics on your planet which in many ways are unique to it and not the same as on other planets with human civilizations. For you will find that there are blue

Sirians that have steel blue or very, very green eyes—or they may have blond or steel blue hair. This does not occur to blacks on Earth unless there is a mixing with different racial types that exist on your planet. That is why your planet is unique.

Virginia: Could you further clarify how the genetics intermingle? There has been a belief by some people that we shouldn't be trying to intermingle different color races together, because they wouldn't genetically combine. Is this true?

Washta: This is erroneous because *all humans possess the same genetics*. The difference comes with skin color, eye color, and other characteristics of racial types that have developed uniquely on your planet. Intelligence and other important concepts of consciousness are the same for all humans that exist on your planet; therefore, to suggest that mixing these unique races of humans together is erroneous is in itself a false concept.

Virginia: For instance, can someone who is an Earth galactic human and someone who is a galactic human from Sirius, the Pleiades or other places, mate? Are sexual relationships for the purpose of having a child possible?

Washta: That is indeed possible.

Virginia: Has that happened on this planet?

Washta: It has happened on your planet before.

Virginia: And is it happening now?

Washta: From time to time it is happening on your planet.

Virginia: Has this happened because of extraterrestrial landings?. . . or from contact with what we call the Shamballa Earth people?

Washta: Many humans on your planet had the experience of having relationships with those from other worlds. They had these relationships with galactic humans from other parts of this galaxy because they had an energy of closeness with them and it was allowed that they would have children with them. This has happened in various places on your planet. It has happened in parts of the United States, of South America, of South Africa, and other places such as Australia. Since the fall of Atlantis, it has primarily occurred in modern times, since the beginning of the nineteen century.

Virginia: Yes, thank you. Since the 1940s, have the Zeta Reticuli, the little gray people, conducted genetic experiments with humans in order to produce a new race? Do they have genetic

135

compatibility with humans?

Washta: Yes, they have conducted experiments but they do not have compatibility with humans. What they have done in their genetic engineering is to take parts of the genetic code of humans and then create a new cellular structure. They have combined their DNA structure with that of humans or cows or any other life form that will combine with their own DNA. By producing a new cellular structure and then having that cellular structure reproduce itself, a unique organism is created. This is what they have been doing as an attempt to end certain genetic reproductive difficulties that occurred during their wars. These wars and the subsequent radiation prevented them from maintaining their species. They now have reproduced and are in the process of altering many parts of this experimentation. Those new beings who have been created will live apart until they are united into your civilization, when full consciousness is completely restored to it.

Virginia: I understand the grays were cut-off from further experimentation. Is that correct?

Washta: Yes. This was cut-off at the end of 1993.

Virginia: Approximately how many of what we would call half-breeds, or whatever word you use for that combination, have been created?

Washta: When they are fully allowed to return, there would be approximately 85,000 of them.

Virginia: Is there anything we need to do to help them? Or would they be discriminated against if we even identify them?

Washta: Yes, many difficulties would occur if they were to return now. That is why they have not been allowed to return to your planet until the entire scenario of a return to full consciousness is completed by Earth humans.

Virginia: Are you saying that the gray's crossbred offspring are not on the planet, but are elsewhere?

Washta: That is correct.

Virginia: So people who think that they may have neighbors who are aliens are incorrect?

Washta: Those who you call aliens on this planet are galactic humans brought here as part of a system of checking to make sure that certain things are occurring. These are galactic humans who are very similar in their basic appearance to Earth humans and are existing on your planet to just observe it . . . much as a scientist in biology would observe certain species to make sure they are evolving properly. A part of our science is to make sure that all that we see and observe about your planet, from above, is also happening through personal day-to-day experiences and encounters with humans on your world.

Virginia: Yes, thank you. If an Earth human is already judgmental about such things as the sex, race, age and religion of other people, how can they be guided and helped to accept other beings who are called extraterrestrial?

Washta: What is occurring on your planet is an immense change in its consciousness. When full consciousness is given to your planet, a vast shift will occur in its realities. Many of the things now held as hard core issues among many humans—namely, religion, race, sex, etc.—will no longer be important to them. They will see how all humans are together as one. They will begin to understand these new realities as they interact with humans who are their own species and race as well as different extraterrestrial species. Through telepathy and other extra-sensory faculties, Earth humans will come to understand that their judgments will no longer apply.

Virginia: Have our present world-wide governments accepted your extraterrestrial offers of assistance? Or how do we stand today with the political diplomacy that has to be practiced from your level? Is there any hope that the governments are going to release the truth of what's going on?

Washta: They are holding onto the truth in a very tight way and we do not expect them to reveal our influence, except to put it into a scare tactic about some alien invasion of some sort. They certainly do not wish to have others know what is occurring, and are attempting to increase the conspiracy of silence that they have put around the topic. Therefore our diplomacy has been to deal directly with humans on this planet who are light workers and those who deal with the spiritual consciousness of your planet.

These light-workers will form an enormous core group who will eventually accept full consciousness and will understand that existing governments were, in spite of their powers, a transitory means to control them through fear and through limiting their abundance.

Virginia: Possibly the various Earth governments have obtained sophisticated technical plans from the grays and may possess crafts and weapons that once were limited to the extraterrestrials alone. Won't these weapons be used to thwart your contact?

Washta: They do possess these technologies in a limited way as a trade with the grays for having received permission to do genetic engineering on the human population. However their beam weapons, their psychotronic generators and their flying saucer-type crafts, are insufficient in number and technology to prevent us from doing what we wish in bringing forth the final flowering of full consciousness on your planet.

We are therefore accompanying the Spiritual Hierarchies of your world with a great gift of love and light which is every human's destiny. You may be assured that your various governments cannot continue to control humans on your planet through fear and ignorance or through the feeble amount of advanced technology that they now possess. This is an incorrect assumption, as they will shortly see when the time comes for us to bring forth the combined energies, of the Spiritual Hierarchy and the Galactic Federation, to enlighten your planet again.

Virginia: Yes, thank you very much. As we close this chapter today, is there any final remark any member of your committee would like to make?

Washta: We would just like to have all humans on this planet realize two important things.

First: Since the beginning of the disaster in Atlantis, a spiritual evolutionary pattern has been followed which has allowed the present concepts of enlightenment to now come to the fore. Be comforted and know that the era you live in is one that will bring this amazing light and full consciousness to full flowering.

Second: Realize that the civilization you now exist in will shortly be vastly altered. Do not be in fear or upset over this. Just know that a new and glorious civilization is about to occur which will allow for an unbelievable shift in the understanding of the realities of the galaxy in which you reside—realities that many humans on your planet do not even know.

Be comforted that the God force energies that have created everything in this universe have set forth this particular time to bring a great light upon your planet and to allow all humans to bask in that light and reach their full potential.

Chapter 8
God and Guardianship

Washta, Aumtron, and Sirai are here to explain how Earth's new galactic civilization, with you as its chief inhabitant, will be developed. However, it is also important for us to share a more thorough understanding of the new model for Earth's galactic civilization. At present, and understandably so, Earth humans do not fully comprehend their new upcoming pattern. Hopefully, this new Sirian model will help Earth humans learn how planet Earth was created as both a spiritual and as a physical entity.

Let's begin by looking at God's creation from a purely spiritual aspect. The Earth, as with all the various planets of the solar system, is surrounded by a Spiritual Hierarchy composed of spiritual beings called angels, archangels, and ascended masters. Their sole purpose is to act as spiritual mediators for the eight interdimensional evolutionary energies. These angelic mediators transfer these energies through the appropriate interdimensional portals for transport into your 3rd-dimensional stellar energy pattern. These creative and evolutionary energy patterns, in turn, create the physical universe which includes your solar system and the planet that you are now residing upon.

In order to better understand your relationship to the creation, and ultimately to your role as a planetary and stellar guardian, we will explain how the creation was accomplished by the Supreme Creative Force or what you loosely call "God." This creation is one that is continuous and evolutionary in nature. Every aspect of a particular creation has an important and unique cycle. This present creation is the 6th cycle and will run between 50 billion to 100 billion years. Let us now look at this present creation.

Some 50 billion years ago, your universe's physical creation was begun by the Time Lords under the direction of the Supreme Creative Force (God). This present creation was the last in a series of six creations that have continued from the beginning of time. Each physical creation had its own cycle and its own pattern. *This physical creation was done to show how light could transmute darkness to produce an even higher light, which is composed of the highest love. This love will transform your galaxy and raise it towards the Supreme Creative Force and its chief emissaries, the Time Lords.*

Since you may not have heard of the Time Lords, we will describe them. They are what might be called the divine shepherds of *physical creation.* When the Supreme Creative Force first began the physical creation, the Time Lords were created; for time is the unit that controls all of physical creation. It is said in the ancient stories of creation that humans first learned in the Vega system that the initial pulse of time created the light of creation and from it flowed all things that now exist in your physical universe. *(See Figure 19: God (Supreme Creative Force) and Creation.)* The Time Lords exist in an infinite number of dimensions and their task is to regulate and to supervise the physical creation according to divine right action.

Actually, the purpose of the Time Lords is two-fold in nature. Initially, they had to create the eight dimensions of physical creation, and secondly, they aided the dimensional Spiritual Herarchies in their task of regulating the spiritual energy exchanges between each dimension. It is the task of the Spiritual Hierarchies to control interdimensional energy transfer by the use of interdimensional gates or, as they are also called, star gates. These gates serve as the flux barriers between dimensions and aid by regulating the energy flow to allow only those sufficient energy exchanges needed to successfully maintain the viability of physical creation. As a part of this divine plan, the Time Lords had to construct the 3rd-dimensional galaxy according to the divine plan of the Supreme Creative Force. To accomplish these tasks, the Time Lords were given the creative "pulse of time." With this energy tool, all things are possible and can be accomplished according to the divine plan.

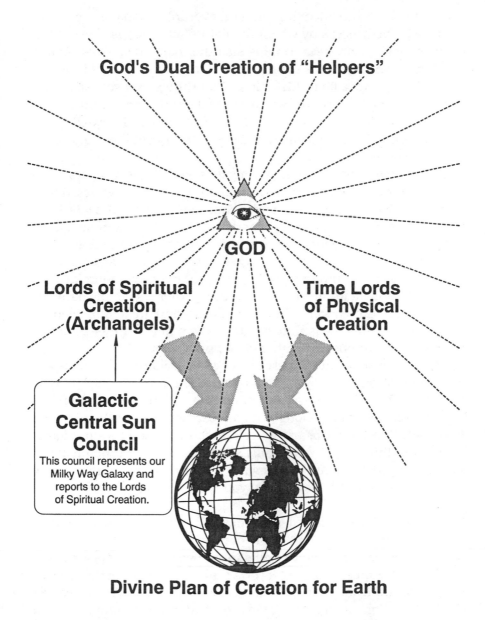

God's Dual Creation of "Helpers"

GOD

Lords of Spiritual
Creation
(Archangels)

Time Lords
of Physical
Creation

Galactic
Central Sun
Council
This council represents our
Milky Way Galaxy and
reports to the Lords
of Spiritual Creation.

Divine Plan of Creation for Earth

**Figure 19: God (Supreme Creative Force)
and Creation**

Time has many meanings and many implications in the divine plan. It is the process by which the light of creation is established in the physical universe. Time is also the mechanism that makes possible all the laws and the methods of creation. Yet its function varies with its specific needs. Time is all things and yet it is none. These concepts are portrayed in our galactic science and in our spiritual philosophies about creation. Through this knowledge, we learn that time is a great enigma. Like water on your world, time is said to seek its own level.

Our great sages, scientists, mystics, and Time Keepers have studied the pulses of time for many millions of years. However, time's true meaning still escapes them. Your scientists and seers have recently begun to discover the wonders of time (for example, quantum mechanics). So far, however, the relationship of time to light, to matter, and to creation has eluded them. The true sciences and philosophies of photon energy will lead you to a new understanding of creation and its infinite cycles. In reality, there is no "big bang" or sudden end to creation. The Time Lords and their dimensional hierarchies simply transmute creation into a new reality—constant purposeful creation—which the divine plan stipulates.

It is now important to perceive how these spiritual systems are arranged. All spiritual systems are organized from the 1st up to the 8th dimension. Beyond this 8th dimension, there are multitudes of higher spiritual dimensions which deal with the nature of the Godhead (Time Lords and archangels, etc). Because we want to focus upon your dimension, we will only say that you have much to learn about these high vibrational dimensions; but as you complete your immediate tasks with dedication, you will naturally advance in the scheme of things.

So let us look at these eight dimensions from your point of view and get a better understanding of how reality is formulated. The first seven dimensions are each created to express various aspects of the physical creation. The eighth level is the one where all of these lower qualities come from. As mentioned, above this great light of creation at the 8th dimension, there sits the great multitudinous infinite Godhead (the realm of the Time Lords, archangels, etc.). *(See Figure 20: Dimensions of Physical Creation.)*

Let's discuss more about these seven dimensions. The first through the third dimensions are ones that you are well aware of.

GOD
Supreme Creative Force

| Lords of Spiritual Creation | Time Lords of Physical Creation |

Line of Creation

Spiritual Light Realm **8th Dimension:** Light becomes spirit.

Free Form Realm **7th Dimension:** Spirit has form.

Etheric Realm **6th Dimension:** Form develops purpose.

Etheric Form Realm **5th Dimension:** Form's purpose is defined.

Transition Realm **4th Dimension:** Physical is not quite reality.

Physical Creation Realm **3rd Dimension:** Physical is reality.

Each dimension has its own hierarchy of angels and archangels.

Earth

Creation is a dual responsibility of the Time Lords and the Spiritual Hierarchies. The Time Lords control physical creation while the Spiritual Hierarchy controls the energy exhange of love and light in all aspects of creation.

Angelic guardians regulate the interdimensional portals.

Figure 20: Dimensions of Physical Creation

143

These dimensions are the physical realms that Earth science has long studied. Above them, there exists the 4th dimension which is a time portal through which the 3rd dimension passes into the 5th dimension. The 5th, the 6th, and the 7th dimensions are what might be called higher dimensional realms and the laws of Earth science and physics do not therein apply.

To those who do not fully understand the science of the spirit, these levels might be comparatively viewed as lands of magic and miracles. Here in these higher realms, the spiritual beings called the angels and archangels of the Godhead exist. These angels and archangels, in turn, dwell in various levels of the Spiritual Hierarchy and are layered around the Earth in different dimensions (5th, 6th, and 7th dimension) to protect it. The archangels and angels have a primary mission to perform—namely, to receive and to distribute the love and light energy of creation throughout the physical universe. The Time Lords, in turn, have a responsibility to monitor and to continuously create the physical universe using the love and light energies given them in interdemensional exchanges by the Spiritual Hierarchy. The Spiritual Hierarchy members have a procedure that they follow to accomplish the interdimensional exchanges. They need in the physical realm, especially the 3rd dimension, a physical guardian who can perform their task of energy exchange on a smaller and more localized level, such as a star system or a planet. Therefore, *the physical guardians of any planet must be beings who are both physical and spiritual—in other words, physical beings who possess full consciousness.*

Let us look at planet Earth and begin to understand how this process is established. The devic aspect of the Spiritual Hierarchies has manifested the love and light energies that make the *physical* world possible In effect, these devic spirits have manifested the physical energies that are necessary to sustain all life on Earth. They have established upon your planet a system of life which we call a specific biosphere. The purpose for life inhabiting a planet is two-fold. The first purpose of life is to manifest those specific energies that make any planet's existence even feasible. A second aim is to act in such a way that the various energies that are given life forms will be vivified and bring forth a continual growth in consciousness.

All animals, plants, rocks, water, sky, etc. have energies of life and consciousness within them. Life is not to be looked upon as something which is defined in a very limited way. Life exists in all things. There are multitudinous types of life forms which you who live in the so-called modern scientific age cannot yet fully understand. You must realize that there is a higher science. This is a spiritual science that understands and encompasses all natural laws and that explains the delicate relationships that exist between them.

These spiritual sciences contain the laws of guardianship. They state that first and foremost a guardian is one who brings in the energies of creation (spiritual light and love) and regulates them for the planetary life sphere or biosphere, as it is known to modern science. At present on planet Earth there exist two major species that are designated as guardian groups. *The first such species is called a cetacean (the whales and the dolphins) who now form the basic guardianship of the planet. The second designated guardians are the Earth human species originally brought from other star systems to their present location on planet Earth.*

In previous sections, this Sirian Council has described Earth's history and explained the great revelation in consciousness that is about to occur to Earth humans. What is needed now is for Earth humans to understand what a guardian is and the important mission that guardians share with their Spiritual Hierarchy. You might well be wondering what guardianship's basic components are—or in Earth terms what your job description as a guardian requires.

Guardianship can best be described by observing the energies of the cetaceans. Through the use of their rituals, their sonar songs and their travels, they vivify the biosphere. Whale song has been found throughout all the oceans of the world. It is also found in, and resonates throughout, the skies of the Earth. It exists even in the deepest parts of Africa, the Americas, Asia, and Europe. Because the energies of the cetaceans can be found both in the sky and in the water, those great energies they bring forth in their song create the resonance that sustains life. Indeed, their rituals have brought forth ongoing and glorious regenesis of life.

Every year from February through August, cetaceans from both hemispheres perform rituals of song that make possible the opening of windows in this biosphere for the energies needed for the reproduction of all species. This procreative act produces the new children of all species and makes possible the continuation of life on Earth. These rituals empower the continuation of the vast multitude of life forms that are a unique aspect of your planet.

Furthermore, guardianship also means stewardship. This concept requires that the guardians must set forth energies that not only provide for the renewal of species on the planet, but also give those species an understanding of what it is that they are accomplishing (a gradual growth toward consciousness). This stewardship means that they must either sacrifice the creative energies that they hold in themselves, or else use their psychic and other full consciousness energies to accommodate procreation and the sustaining of life on the planet.

Stewardship is a very unique and important process. It is more than shepherding the many species of your planet through their day-to-day activities. It also means setting up maintenance life energies by physically transmuting the creative energies given daily by the Earth's Spiritual Hierarchy. This action allows each species of your world to maintain itself. It also means that the energies being received every day from the Spiritual Hierarchy have to be distributed across the entire biosphere. Guardians must consciously and subconsciously maintain these energies so that they are dispersed in a proper and correct manner. This whole process is done every day by the cetaceans. They also consciously realize the power of this process of interdimensional energy exchange.

Guardianship, therefore, contributes to and preserves the role of Lady Gaia. It allows planet Earth—along with its life forms—to sustain themselves and to do so with a flourish of abundance. On your planet, all species have attained an unbelievable variety and have thrived in all environments that exist. Yet humans who are the third and final part of this triangle (humans, cetaceans, and Spiritual Hierarchy) have totally forgotten, and therefore completely ignored, the important aspects of stewardship that they must now thoroughly understand and begin to follow.

At this time, let us suggest that a good steward knows and understands his flock. He or she does his or her shepherding in a way that teaches the members of the flock to comprehend and ascertain what it takes to maintain themselves and to flourish. Stewardship by humans should be one which recognizes and protects the Earth's environment because the environment—like the one surrounding a shepherd's flock—is the one that sustains all life.

You must learn that the Earth's environment is the foundation of your physical existence, not something to be conquered or abused. Truly, your planetary environment must be understood, for that very environment that supports you humans with important life-giving energies, must in turn be sustained with transmuted energies from you. This knowledge of your reciprocal roles is the first important part of guardianship. The good steward practices it and you as stewards of the Earth must learn it. During the course of the last few centuries of your existence, you have stopped respecting your environment. You have believed that the environment no longer possesses the overall capabilities to shape your destinies. This concept is completely erroneous!

The cetaceans, with the permission of Lady Gaia, invited galactic humans to your shores, knowing that they would be good and constant guardians. They now wish to give you a way and means to do so. Begin by recognizing the importance of the Earth's environment just as you must also recognize the importance of the Spiritual Hierarchy. Now, you may well be asking how you can understand the Spiritual Hierarchy, and we suggest that this is best done through vision, through ritual, and through following the patterns of intuition that exist within all humans.

These concepts of love and of light—given through consciousness to all living beings—form the basis for beginning to understand how to be good Earth stewards, as well as shepherds, for your own species. For some Earth humans, this process and its response may not come easily, but it is one that each of you can learn to perform. For too long, people on planet Earth have not understood that this simple process of stewardship is no more than the basic mechanism of guardianship.

So far we have described the environmental aspects as well as the spiritual aspects of guardianship, but there is a third component that we have not yet discussed. This aspect requires your recognition that other guardian species exist on your planet, and that you must interact with them in a way that shows your appreciation and love for what they do. You haven't done this! You as humans have allowed yourselves to become ignorant of both your environment and your fellow guardians. Earth humans have failed in every way to understand that guardianship is indeed shared. You must learn

147

to share with your cetacean brothers and sisters in ways that allow them, as well as yourselves, to interact through love and high consciousness with each other.

Whaling and its associated procedures are no less than murder. It is the final act of neglect and disrespect for all that you were sent to do and to accomplish upon your world. Your Spiritual Hierarchy and we of this Sirian Council ask that Earth humans immediately end all aspects of whaling. Whaling exhibits total and complete disregard of all that is basic to a conscious species and a guardian race. We cannot allow or permit this abomination to continue. Therefore, please realize that guardianship also means coming into full consciousness and learning respect for all humans and all other species. The guardianship understands that all things (such as plants, rocks, and water) have value. It is not enough to conserve the water supply or maintain the forests for your own needs. It is more than that, and the use of natural resources for recreation is the least important activity of all.

We Sirians, and your brothers and sisters of the Galactic Federation, are here to aid the process of increasing and making life on your planet flourish. We are not here as a species that will in any way destroy life on Earth. Such activity is not the way of a guardian. This destructive action is more the way of one who wishes *not* to be a guardian. You have come to Earth to implement the Spiritual Hierarchy's instructions, not to ignore your role and the role of the other guardians who are on your world. Remember, there exists on Earth a great and incredible abundance and this abundance will beget even greater abundance if it is properly attended to. This rationale is what we wish to have all people on your planet understand.

We galactic humans are a guardian species; therefore, so are Earth humans, though you may have temporarily forgotten. The Spiritual Hierarchy of angelic beings that surrounds you now is helping you achieve higher consciousness and will aid you in this process. Thus, look away from your upside-down civilization and analyze what needs fixing. This process of fixing is one that is quite simple—and humans are good "fixers."

So let us summarize that which is essential to remember and practice. Guardianship works through the eight dimensions of creation. It spreads itself through the great Spiritual Hierarchies and permeates down to your world. Around the Spiritual Hierarchy is manifested the physical universe that you are all a part of. As a guardian species, galactic humans are a being of light, a spiritual as well as a physical being. Your capability to be spirit-in-matter is what makes you a unique creation. In addition, you have been given a special consciousness that extends beyond the mere reflexes of life such as sex, hunger, thirst, and dying. You go beyond the mere physicalness of all of this. You are a being who has been put upon a planet as a responsible overseer or steward of other life. This happens because you are capable of full consciousness.

The cetaceans who exist around you are an example of what this full consciousness implies in everyday living. When you look at their guardianship, you will see that they have unselfishly and totally committed their lives to the process of bringing forth those energies that allow your planetary system to evolve and to survive. This activity is what Earth humans have not done. Humans have all too often used their waking hours to destroy or adversely alter the environment, to kill off many other species, and to destroy the basic living structures of planet Earth.

We have said that Earth's physical structure was created for a divine purpose. This divine purpose was established by the angelics under the great Godhead that was moved through the heart of God into reality. It was done for one purpose—to bring forth a creation of physical light. All Earth humans must understand this process and assume their awakening role.

What is about to happen to your planet and your solar system, with our landings and the photon belt experience, will erase your ignorance and allow all of you to fully understand what guardianship is. Guardianship, as we continue to state, is a process of creative stewardship and *stewardship is a means to bring full consciousness to bear in the actions and activities of one species as it affects another.* For you humans sit at the top of a huge chain of life and this chain of life does not merely consist of animals and plants. As mentioned, it also includes rocks, soil, water, sky, and everything that creeps or crawls. Your Christian Bible is quite explicit about your place in the dominion role!

Remember, also, that there are energy devas in created things who act together to create the great cycle of life in you and in all living things around you. This cycle of life is the key that lies at the heart

149

of everything that is happening on your planet. Earth humans must understand this process and be fully prepared to accept and practice their reasons for being on Earth. You are present as part of a great triangle of consciousness—Cetacean, Earth human, and Lady Gaia—all who work together to create a life sphere of elegance and of light that brings your planet's energies into focus as an exquisite showcase for all to see.

You must not look at planets as merely being 3rd-dimensional objects which orbit around a particular star until the time comes when the death of that star brings a planet's life to an end. This action is not the process to be examined. All things in the universe exist for a specific purpose. This particular purpose is one that you must understand and apply if you wish to advance in your consciousness and future galactic roles—even universal ones.

Therefore, remember you are a guardian of light, of love, and of consciousness; and you are a part of this great guardianship triangle of humans, cetaceans and Spiritual Hierarchy. Your planet is now on the verge of a new Golden Age that will lead to a rejuvenation and a welcoming home of Earth humans. It comes so you can be the galactic creation that God intended! In this discovery, you will coexist in a fantastic relationship with your extraordinary planet, and with other guardians species like the cetaceans. In these relationships you will also work hand-in-hand with that shining group of angels and ascended masters called the Spiritual Hierarchy of God. This partnership will ignite your hearts with love and fill your eternity with joy, wherever you may advance. And then, as a fully conscious humanity of light, all of you will progress into those unending realms of glory secretly whispered in the recesses of your soul.

Many questions about the material in this chapter may now come to mind. In the next section, Virginia asks questions of Washta regarding information on "God and Guardianship."

✳ ✳ ✳ **Question and Answer Section** ✳ ✳ ✳

Virginia: Would Washta please explain who is present today?

Washta: I am here with two other members of the council—Mikah who is involved with histories, technology, guardianships and cetacean projects, and also Teletron, so that history and all things related to it in guardianship can be explained. Please proceed.

Virginia: Thank you and welcome. You have said that the Spiritual Hierarchy is composed of angels, archangels and ascended masters. I understood that devas are part of the Spiritual Hierarchy, also. Are they not included in your definition of the Spiritual Hierarchy?

Washta: The devas sit at the base of this Spiritual Hierarchy. They are the energies that apply the angelic energies brought from the higher dimensional source, through the Time Lords down into the various dimensions. This energy is then transmuted into the actual physical body of planet Earth, as well as its animals, its various plants, its atmosphere, its oceans and waters, etc. In this way, the devas are part of the Spiritual Hierarchy.

Virginia: Please list Earth's major archangels by name and indicate the dimensions that they operate from.

Washta: Because there are so many, we will just give a few who are most important in this present situation. The most important for all of you is Archangel Michael, who sits with Metatron and many others on the councils that control your planet and its many dimensions. Archangel Michael guides the life energies down through the eight great dimensions to Earth, so that planet Earth can have a living biosphere. Then you have Archangel Gabriel, who is the angel in charge of many dimensions—namely the third, the fourth and the fifth. So, archangels Michael and Gabriel are now involved in the process of bringing in the energies of the new and glorious galactic human consciousness, and the civilization that these galactic humans will reside in.

Michael and Gabriel are the two major archangels that are involved in raising the planet to its full ascension. There are many others, such as Raphael and Uriel, who sit above in the 4th and 5th dimensions to aid Gabriel in this ascension process. They also have access to the 6th and 7th dimensions to assist Archangel Michael with the special life energies being brought through the Time Lords, down to the 8th and the 7th dimensions. However, the Spiritual Hierarchy has appointed archangels Michael and Gabriel as the two official overseers to coordinate with the Sirians under the auspices

151

of the Galactic Federation.

Virginia: In other words, are you saying that these are the same two archangels who serve both the Sirians and the Pleiadeans, as well as the Earth humans?

Washta: That is correct. Archangel Michael and Gabriel are more of an interdimensional angelic form and are therefore not attached to the physical energy of a specific solar system or planet, so they cooperate with the Time Lords who control physical reality (matter).

Virginia: Thank you. Could you comment on Archangel Michael's "lost war in heaven" as reported biblically and other places? How did that happen and where do we stand now?

Washta: This relates historically to the original creation. In this physical creation, you see, there was established one basic concept. It was the idea that a great darkness would exist, from which would eventually come a great celestial light. That is why in the creation stories from many sources, including the Christian Bible, there is darkness indicated in the very beginning. *For the purpose of this creation was to prove that darkness is not as great as light.*

Archangel Michael was given the divine task of acting as the chief intermediary between the Time Lords, who were given instructions by the Supreme Creative Force on how to create this present physical creation, and the dark force that was created to be the supreme test for this creation. Archangel Michael therefore set out to aid in putting the eight dimensions together and to make sure that all the various dimensional angelic and archangelic forces were put in the proper places. In order to create this pattern for the divine plan, it was necessary to create a being within that darkness.

Hence, Archangel Michael established the energies that would create a being of darkness, as called for under the divine plan. That is what the so-called "war in heaven" refers to. This being of darkness was created by God's plan so that eventually the dark energy patterns could be transformed back to light after many physical lifetimes lived on planet Earth. This transformation would eventually lead to a great series of immortals living in light. This is what Michael's energy patterns, and all the stories around him, are about.

Virginia: Then we could assume he has a kind of twin brother or a close alternative form of energy that resists him and the light?

Washta: Yes. This energy was created by him as part of the divine plan which he was given permission to do. He will be merging these two energies of light and dark as part of this upcoming ascension process. That is why the Age of Light has been forecast by many Sirians and others in the Galactic Federation who are Time Keepers. We understand the energy patterns that now surround this physical creation of bringing dark into light.

Virginia: Does this being, this dark being related to Michael, have a name that we would recognize?

Washta: This is not a name that is recognizable in itself to humans on your planet, since many different names for it have been given, such as Satan, the devil, etc. However, know that this name will be given to humans when the process of the landings occur, for Archangel Michael will make a formal announcement of what is occurring; and he will explain what the time patterns are that will allow him to re-emerge and create the great light in your galaxy.

Virginia: In looking at the illustration that shows God and the Time Lords, it seems there are a great multiplicity of the Time Lords. Can you give us their approximate number?

Washta: It is important to understand just one thing—that the Time Lords, in their dimensions, are infinite in number. There are millions upon millions, upon millions of them. Far above the 8th dimension exist the Time Lords, who control every aspect of physical creation, as given under the divine plan of the great Creative Supreme Force. Therefore, their numbers are so great that we consider them to be infinite.

Virginia: Can you clarify what you called the "pulse of time"? What does that mean?

Washta: When the Time Lords were finally told by the great Supreme Creative Force that a creation must happen, these Time Lords were instructed to make the great pulse of creation. What we call "the great pulse of time" has a specific time zone or sequence in which every creation will occur. The Time Lords begin by bringing this energy pulse into the physical creation-to-be which forms the light and brings forth all things.

Virginia: Thank you. Can you more precisely explain what the Time Lords do?

Washta: Every Time Lord has a physical responsibility in a particular creation, whether it is a star system in your galaxy or a star system in another dimension. For example, every angel, archangel and even the smallest atom has a Time Lord whose task is to maintain the physical creation and to transmute it into what it is designed to be. There are some Sirian cultures who have been attempting to count the total number of Time Lords for millions of years, but there has still not been a final count nor anyone who says they know the exact total.

Virginia: Then, in other words, there is a Time Lord over every individualized soul, every pattern of energy, etc.

Washta: There is a Time Lord for every part of a soul, and also for every aspect of that soul, because a soul force may be divided into many individual beings. The soul may be divided into things that are in its future or in its past. Time is a simultaneous creation in the universe. It seems to those in a 3rd-dimensional reality to be something that is sequential, but it is not. Therefore, because time is non-sequential, the Time Lords must be infinite. They must control every part of the stupendous physical creation so that when the final ascension is achieved, the Time Lords will have succeeded in bringing the soul there in an absolutely perfect, precise, yet delicate way.

Virginia: So if I understand what you've said, these Time Lords would be little rays of light from the Creator, or rays birthed by God?

Washta: They are rays of time that are called light in your reality. For you humans operating on a 3rd-dimensional awareness, just realize that until you have full consciousness you cannot understand this concept of Time Lords. That is why in many of the works of religious mythology and religious teachings that abound on your planet, Time Lords are not fully explained—they are simply merged into the archangelic forces that surround your particular creation. Nonetheless, they are a unique and vital function of physical creation. As humans move towards fully conscious aspects of their reality, they will begin to grasp what a Time Lord truly is. They will also get a better concept of what time is and how this is a process and imperative function of the Supreme Creator's divine plan.

Virginia: Yes, thank you. Then as we observe the illustration of God and the Time Lords, we are not to frustrate ourselves with anything above the 8th dimension? Can you comment on what other books have said about God being at dimension 24, 30, or whatever?

Washta: God exists in all aspects of creation and the Time Lords constantly say that God acts upon them and then they act as the divine plan so wills. Therefore, God exists within the creation by showing the divine will, and the plan that comes from that divine will is contained in all aspects of creation. We like to say that the energy of God, or as we call it the Supreme Creative Force, is an infinite interdimensional energy that is instantaneously in and available to all aspects of creation. God is known through its emissaries who implement God's plan and also share knowledge with all who wish to be one with this energy.

God is creation. The entire concept of this is very difficult for 3rd-dimensional realities to fully understand, for God is such a simultaneous and all-powerful concept. Just remember that the Supreme Creative Force exists always, in all times, dimensions, and in all creation. Furthermore, creation is simultaneously occurring and evolving; therefore, the energy of God is always there and always has been there. A complete axiom, or a truth, is that the Supreme Creative Force has always been and always will be.

Virginia: Can we ever answer the question of where this original Source came from?

Washta: It is a conundrum to many on your planet, for they wish it to be some sort of sequential answer. When they fully understand the nature of galactic time as a very incredible non-sequential concept, all of this confusion will vanish.

Virginia: Does the full God consciousness that will soon come back to Earth persons allow them to communicate with the cetaceans straight away? Will both the humans and the cetaceans automatically know how to cooperate together?

Washta: The sequence is that the great triad of the Spiritual Hierarchy, galactic (Earth) human and cetacean will be one. Thus, when humans have been returned to the original triad, they will be able to communicate, to acquire this energy as the Spiritual Hierarchy wishes, and to transmute it according to the divine plan.

Virginia: I'd like to detour here onto a topic of great interest to me—our 1972 rescue by the Sirians. Can you clarify what happened between the Spiritual Hierarchy and the Sirians in the 1972 decision that protected Earth from the Sun's devastating rays?

Washta: The Spiritual Hierarchy of your planet has always seen you humans—in spite of those great injustices that you have performed upon the surface of planet Earth—as their seeded children who must be protected. This has also been the opinion of the cetaceans. So they both interceded, most especially the Spiritual Hierarchy, to make the Sirians understand how vitally important your particular planet is. Not only for guardianship and protection of all life on Earth, but also as a model in the blueprint of the great divine plan.

That is why we Sirians, with the aid of our own galactic presences, angels and archangels, came together with those of your Earth's Spiritual Hierarchy to bring in a holographic envelope to protect Earth from the Sun's emerging danger.

Virginia: Yes, we see the reason for your support, but can you describe the hologram itself in more detail?

Washta: What has been around Earth, since 1972, is a holographic image that has now been expanded to take in the entire solar system, the Sun and all its planets. Right now, adjustments can be made to your reality, especially as regards your entry into the photon belt. In effect, we can limit as well as expand the time frames when this particular event will occur and how it will affect your entire solar system.

This holographic image, or envelope of light energy that surrounds your planet and solar system, protects the Sun, the planets and everything that is a part of them, until the moment the divine plan wishes for your solar system to enter the photon belt. This protective holographic envelope is the key as to why our Sirian Governing Council was able to convince the Galactic Federation that our concept was the correct one—thereby reversing the previous Galactic Federation policy that prohibited our intervention. Now, a remarkable event has occurred! Your solar system's Spiritual Hierarchy, and those from planet Earth, have come together with the Galactic Federation, the angels and archangels of your galaxy—who are all part of the Galactic Federation and its Council from the Central Sun. Together, they will bring the Earth back into full consciousness. An event of this magnitude is propitious, indeed, and will maximize the energies needed to shift Earth back to its complete and successful restoration.

Virginia: Where is the great Central Sun?

Washta: The great Central Sun exists in what is the core or light center of this entire galaxy—the main headquarters of things, you might say. It is about 35,000 light years from Earth, since you are on the galactic outskirts.

Virginia: Regarding the photon belt, could we have reversed the electromagnetic charge that it presents to us, and have found a way to resist its negative influences without your help?

Washta: No, because you lacked the advanced interdimensional technology that has been utilized. Only through the great kindness of the interdimensional Spiritual Hierarchies, as well as the high technical expertise of certain experienced physical technicians, will you survive this photon belt's arrival. Otherwise, it would have been cataclysmic for Earth.

Virginia: Are you reversing its energy charge? Or how would you describe your activities?

Washta: We are repolarizing the energies of the Sun and all the other planets on an interdimensional level. Through this action, we are setting up the necessary energy patterns for cooperative and positive effects only. This will allow the glorious, promised Golden Age to happen on planet Earth very soon.

Virginia: Yes, thank you. In the *New Cells, New Bodies, New Life!* book, there were comments about the DNA/RNA cellular shifts. In terms of the rapid acceleration of vibratory frequencies on the planet, how do you view that our minds, emotions and bodies are coping with this very intense energy experience?

Washta: What is happening on your planet right now is that every human, whether fully conscious of it or not, is undergoing a great degree of genetic alteration. These alterations are preparing humans for the stupendous transformation process and the ascension that will occur in the next few years.

Consequently, humans have experienced a great deal of what they have thought to be physical ailments—ailments or difficulties that are, in fact, simple alterations in brain cell patterning, disruption of the nervous system circuits, alterations of the heart, or genetic alterations of cellular structure. That is why many sudden and unexplained conditions, diseases or illnesses have occurred and then left very quietly after they came. This is how you can know that the changes that are about to occur on your planet are on course. Part of the process being brought in by the Spiritual Hierarchy now is to lengthen some of these processes, but at the same time to speed up the karmic dissolution that is now occurring on your planet.

A brief slowdown was recently advised by the Spiritual Hierarchy, because they felt that many humans on planet Earth were panicking at the changes that were occurring around them. This slowdown does not mean any major decrease will persist; it is just a temporary adjustment, like slowing down from 80 miles per hour to 75 miles per hour. We and you are still moving at great speed so that the divine plan can be achieved! In our scannings and evaluations of the human body, we find that it is holding up to this energy acceleration.

Virginia: So you still see 1996 as the likely photon belt experience?

Washta: That is still the date within the parameters of the divine plan that has been given and accepted by Federation Councils and approved by the great angelic Central Sun Councils. So, unless otherwise modified, we are in agreement on this particular period of time.

Virginia: Does meditation along with rest, good exercise and a light nutrition, help alleviate certain symptoms and physical shifts?

Washta: We suggest both individual and group meditation, bodily exercise and proper diet as methods to bring this whole process to a successful conclusion in all humans. We also suggest that a large quantity of liquids be drunk, since it is important that toxins be removed from the body's cellular structure as quickly as possible.

Virginia: Have any humans shifted from a double helix to a 12-helix DNA pattern yet?

Washta: Some are on the verge of it, but at the present time the 12-helix process has not been achieved genetically by humans on your planet. However, within the next six months, many humans that have been genetically prepared by us to be examples of the advantages of such an alignment will begin to switch over successfully.

Virginia: We thank you for taking your time to be with us. We send our gratitude, our love, and blessings to all of you who assist us.

Chapter 9
Galactic Human Civilization

In this chapter, Washta and his Sirian Council (Teletron, Sirai and Mikah) will share the history and underlying principles of galactic human civilization. This discussion will use the culture and civilization of Sirius as an example of such a culture. So let us begin this discussion with the history and origins of human civilization.

The very first human civilizations were established in the star system of Vega, the brightest star in the Lyra constellation, some six million years ago. During this time, Vega's human inhabitants developed the primary rudiments of a truly interplanetary culture. *This culture was based on two main principles that were delivered as the four primary laws of society.*

The first of these two principles was the importance of the personal growth of the individual. The civilization's foundation belief was that an individual's growth in consciousness could develop only by fully exploring one's higher soul as well as concurrently giving service to others. Love was seen by them as the ability to thoroughly understand another soul force and then to use that knowledge to better understand oneself.

The second principle stated that each person's soul light shines on everyone in a unique way. Each soul light contains a piece of the great puzzle that composes the united human family. It was the duty of one's friends and family to help bring this light into its full and complete brightness. Let us briefly review galactic civilization and discuss its underlying principles and laws of society in greater detail.

The origins of galactic civilization evolved from what are called the galactic and interdimensional Spiritual Hierarchies. These spiritual lords of time and space established within their realms (galaxies and star systems) a distinct series of unique physical presences. This enterprise was done because planets, stars and other energy forms needed a complementary physical guardian to aid them in establishing the white light of creation throughout the physical universe. To this end, the Spiritual Hierarchies created special life forms (various humans and nonhumans of high sentience). These life forms were established as part of a guardianship that would act with the Spiritual Hierarchies to enable the energies of creation to operate at maximum efficiency through physical creation.

This concept of planetary and star system stewardship is what is called the guardian nature of all human culture. It is the foundation upon which all humans have formed their fully conscious civilizations. As Earth humans grow in awareness and increase their consciousness, it is natural for the environmental movement and the stewardship of the Earth to gain support and grow in importance. Therefore, it is essential to learn how these processes of caretaking and guardianship are related to the growth of human consciousness. Learning about this guardianship process will enable Earth humans to better understand how to successfully create a galactic culture here on your planet, for the Lyran culture is part of Sirius and you of Earth are now under an increasing Sirian influence.

This guardian nature that the Spiritual Hierarchy originally gave to all humans is a great gift, for it was based on a democratic system of socal laws with four explicit aspects. *(See Figure 21: Four Basic Social Laws.)* These four laws can be used by human civilization to conduct itself in full accordance with the Spiritual Hierarchies. They also enable every human to reach full consciousness, thereby achieving full service for themselves and especially to each other. In applying these laws, Earth humans will earn their place in the great galactic guardianship plan for the entire human species. And they will bring human civilization to its fullest possible flowering. Accordingly, let us consider these four laws to see exactly what they represent.

The first law is called the Law of the One. It is a law whose sole purpose is to assist each soul in its personal process of self growth.

Four Basic Social Laws

The Time Lords created within their realms a physical human presence. It was done because the Spiritual Hierarchies needed a guardian to spread light and love. Rules governing right relationship for humans were also established by the Time Lords and adjudicated by the Spiritual Hierarcharies. These rules were called the **Four Basic Social Laws.**

■ **Law of the One:**
The goal of every being is to discover their soul path for personal growth and service.

■ **Law of the Two:**
The power of creation can be utilized through loving closeness with another being. This close relationship with, and caring for another, leads to a deeper knowledge of guardianship.

■ **Law of the Three:**
The bonding created by one's close relationship with self, friends, family, and clan develops the web of global or planetary interdependancy.

■ **Law of the Four:**
The Law of the Four is the Law of the Three expanded to larger groups such as clan-to-clan and planetary-to-solar (star) system.

Figure 21: Four Basic Social Laws

The Law of the One is simply a concept of interconnecting reality and the oneness of life. Each person will have a specific spiritual path that is co–determined by the spiritual guides (guardian angels and angelic judges) assigned to them and also by the Time Lords acting under the divine plan of the Supreme Creative Force (God). Everyone's goal is to discover and utilize their chosen spiritual path for personal growth and for service. This energy path is the **Kha** or the soul force itself. To enable the Law of the One to be successfully developed, each of the four laws were given a specific ritual or rite, called an **Ahn**, which would help an individual to understand the **Ahn**'s essence or ritual pattern's meaning and then employ it to its fullest extent.

As indicated in the Law of the One, we have the **Kha Ahn** or the rite of the soul force. This belief in service and personal growth, which comes out of the Law of the One, was reflected in society by a series of clan (suprafamilial) organizations that acted as focal points for rites of the soul force's service energies. Once these initial service energies were actually incorporated by the soul force, then a foundation for service could be brought to the Law of the Two. For example, knowledge of your purpose in service to others established a link to your own self worth and allowed you to more easily relate this value to another.

The Law of the Two is the law of relationship. It simply states that the power of creation can be utilized through loving closeness with another being. From this closeness, you treasure the deep connection with another and move from a single self-awareness to a deeper knowledge of guardianship by use of joint, or one-on-one, love energies. The Law of the Two is the basis for applying a combined guardianship service through a partnership of love and caring. Its energy path is the **Shree Ahn**, the energy rite of the closeness.

To aid all beings who incarnate into the Syrian realm of full human consciousness, each clan provides to its members a series of counselors who are attached to each clan's temple system. *(See Figure 22: The Rituals for the Laws.)* These clan temples, located along and upon the major planetary grid points, serve as the core for the web of consciousness that exists throughout the planet. Here, meditations and exercises are given that permit you to successfully pass through the various life crises you could encounter while acknowledging your personal growth in consciousness through the Law of the One and the Law of the Two. It is in the clan temple that the first concepts of being a planetary guardian are established. Here, the proper rituals, along with the necessary energy–cleansing meditations, are first performed to honor and preserve the connected life force needed for planetary guardianship, as well as to sustain the strength of the planet's biosphere.

As one went through life from early childhood to more mature adulthood, one encountered a specific set of lessons and rituals. These rituals and lessons would help beings to understand why they came into physical life, and the purpose for which they incarnated

---

The Rituals for the Laws

■ **Law of the One:**
Its spiritual path is the **Kha** *(soul force or path)* and its ritual is the **Kha Ahn.**

■ **Law of the Two:**
Its spiritual path is the **Shree** *(energy of a personal closeness)* and its ritual is the **Shree Ahn.**

■ **Law of the Three:**
Its spiritual path is the **Koo'Shee** *(energy of family and planetary group knowledge)* and its ritual is the **Koo'Shee Ahn.**

■ **Law of the Four:**
Its spiritual path is the **Khas'Koo** *(solar, galactic, and universal group knowledge)* and its ritual is the **Khas'Koo Ahn.**

Figure 22: The Rituals for the Laws

into this physical world. Each being believed he/she had a sacred reason for existence—a specific gift—that would aid not only self, but also the group, the civilization, the planet, and star system—the whole of existence. It was the intent of one's counselor to aid in determining these essential designs. By so doing, the counseling process would allow the individual to fully explore his or her own inner selfhood, as well as those responsibilities that were fundamental to this growth.

Rituals or rites to us are simply the accomplishment of something or the doing of a certain task. Rituals on your planet usually are meant as some long lethargic ceremony in which somebody speaks extensively and everyone falls asleep. This is not what we do! An example of a ritual for a child would be to take the child to the beach and have it just play with the sand and the rocks, feel the energy of the devas around it, and thereby understand the purpose and correlation of this soil and rock to the great energy patterns of the planet, itself. Thus the child understands its own physicalness and feels its relationship with all physical things, as well. As the child grows many of these little rituals are performed.

Besides the Law of the One and the Law of the Two, there exists the Law of the Three. The Law of the Three simply states that your relationship with yourself and your closeness with another—as well as to your friends and family—could all be bonded together. This bonding could help to explain and interpret the great web of interdependency that it created, since fully conscious beings have to understand who they are and know a way to successfully ground themselves in their reality. Thus, ground rules are needed for this expanding web of interdependence. You see, the bonding of the union of self with the creative force, in closeness with another (intimate relationships), needs a means that will allow this energy to be brought forth to new generations.

This Law of the Three also has an **Ahn** (rite) and this **Ahn** is simply called the **Koo Shee**. The **Koo Shee** is defined as *the energy of family and planetary group knowledge* or the creation soul force of the light of lights. It was the hope that these **Koo Shees** would successfully allow one to move simultaneously through the concept of self to closeness with the group. These levels of consciousness would then help one to understand how these interconnected groups evolve into the Law of the Four. That is, it is one's relationship not

Galactic Human Civilization

just to the planet of residence, but to the solar system that it is a part of, as well. The Law of the Four was related to what was called the great **Khas'Koo** of the star system or *the energy of solar, galactic and universal group knowledge.*

Therefore, education in the Lyran/Syrian tradition was done for two reasons. First, education prepared an individual for a specific life task. This project was to assist beings in understanding how their soul path related to a specific form of service and how this service would express love and personal growth. Secondly, it was also believed that all individuals had to learn who they were—and so education encompassed this aspect as well. The Lyrans believed that knowing oneself would lead one to originate those services that would create the interconnected web of consciousness and light. Each individual was consequently taught to remember the memories of other lifetimes and other realities. These memories were not to be forgotten, but rather were to be enhanced during the course of each lifetime. Life in the Lyran/Sirian tradition was not a brief series of unconnected incidents. Rather, it was comprised of a series of conscious realities that prepared each soul force for its eventual return to the higher life energies that originally created it. *This great love of the universe and its cyclic order was the foundation of the Lyran civilization's cosmic plan and sustained its successful completion.*

The Time Lords further stipulated that these laws could be extended outside of an immediate star system by creating an expanding system of laws in which the Law of the One was changed into the Law of the Four and then enlarged through these next four laws to the Law of the Five, Six and Seven. *(See Figure 23: The Galactic Human Laws.)* By the time one reached the Law of the Seven, the Law of the Four had been increased to a planetary and solar **Kha'Baa** (group soul force) that could be evolved into an eventual **Khas'Koo** for an entire star sector. Galactic humans could thus pass on to their offspring the sacred laws governing society as created by the Time Lords and embodied in the divine energies of the One, the Four, the Seven and the Ten.

Every individual learned that the key to devotion and inner reflection of the soul force energy was within the instructions given by the clan counselors. These counselors were highly respected members of their clan. Their inner growth and high soul force qualified them to give instruction in the sacred task of leading others

FIRST FOUR LAWS - Planetary

These four laws are the basis for galactic civilization. They are the foundation for Earth's spiritual advancement (like the ten commandments).

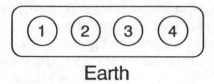

Earth

LAW OF THE SEVEN - Interplanetary

These are the first four laws raised to a higher vibratory level. Thus, the Law of the Seven is derived from the Law of the Four.

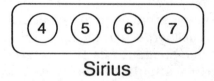

Sirius

LAW OF THE TEN - Interdimensional Reality

Again, the vibrations are raised and the Law of the Ten is derived from the Law of the Seven.

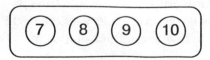

Galactic Federation

Figure 23: The Galactic Human Laws

into higher states of consciousness. Counselors also knew pre-scribed rituals and specific meditations that could be given to those whom they counseled. In this way, the culture continued from childhood to adulthood and ritual was an essential aspect of personal development. These rituals helped each individual to understand the nature of the multidimensional universe and estab-lish a relationship to it as a growing and fully conscious being. This essence of selfhood merged with a need for service to others and to the Time Lord's ultimate creation—the physical universe.

Each individual was taught, then, that one incarnated into the physical universe in order to fulfill a specific purpose. Also, each individual was taught from birth that memories from other life times must not be forgotten. Thus, special counselors were assigned to each newborn and to their parents to begin the process of keeping the past life memories alive and the new life goals in perspective.

It was believed by those in the Lyran/Sirian culture that the life process of birth should have a special set of meditations and rituals to welcome the newborn into the community and identify its specific purpose—its reason for the newly acquired physical reality. Birth was, therefore, the beginning of a joyous lifelong gift into the great web of consciousness that surrounded each and every individual.

Under the Law of the One, every individual had to discover its own life and love center and learn how to use this life and love center to appreciate its purposes for physical selfhood. This duty began at birth with the aforementioned rituals and was maintained through-out early childhood. Parents in this tradition were properly prepared and aided by the assigned clan counselors. Each pregnancy began with a system of preparation for the newborn and its needs. To parent in a Lyran/Sirian culture was a great privilege, intended to foster and witness the beginning of the never-ending cycle of life.

Life's purposes and its joys were shared not only by the immediate family, but also by the clan structure. Love was an important part of the consciousness of each individual and became a vital aspect of each individual's life. For example, as one passed through childhood, one quickly learned about his or her origins and initial purposes. A young child was encouraged to discover the joy of play as well as the mutual importance of each other's selfhood to the conscious web of life surrounding them. Children learned that humans are a guardian species created for the purpose of aiding the

167

universal Spiritual Hierarchies of light and love, and of bringing order and light to the physical universe. This responsibility is one all humans must take seriously. Each individual, from earliest childhood, was taught to act as a guardian or steward of planets and stars. This was a sacred task.

Guardianship responsibilities were made known by each counselor to every young child, and lessons about guardianship were constantly learned by ritual example. For example, a key part of learning about guardianship was a daily meditation ritual performed upon arising from a brief mid-morning nap. All humans were required to perform this ritual in order to maintain the biosphere. These rituals were designed for all ages and were learned as a preparation for adult life. Young individuals also learned by exploring rites taught to them as a kind of play. It was common for counselors to take young children to the clan temples and to allow them to participate in the daily ceremonies to enhance the planetary life force energies. In discovering the significance of this daily ritual to human civilization, children discerned the various levels of spiritual energies that surround the physical creation. This ritual helped a child or a young adult to learn about the Time Lords, the Spiritual Hierarchies and the child's role in the ever-evolving process of creation. It was a vital link between human selfhood and the constant re-creation of the physical universe that surrounded all humans.

It is an important part of the laws of galactic society that all children become aware of the many worlds that surround them. By the end of early childhood, a child is able to relate inner purposes to present life and present purpose to past life activities. The continuity of the life cycle is fully explained to the children. The life cycle is not to be discontinuous nor is the purpose of each past life to be completely forgotten. Life is a continual process from which guardianship evolves as a vital part. The self is not seen as a disjointed or alienated ego, but as the connected part of a web of consciousness. Thus, ritual assists the young child as well as the adult to understand his or her life plan and to express the specific role that the guardian spirits have deemed applicable for this lifetime.

It is important that those family members and friends who constitute a child's physical reality be included in everyday activities and ritual. Every individual chooses both parents and responsibilities for certain reasons. These reasons must be explored and understood by everyone involved in the creation of a child's physical reality. The key focus at all times is not only to encourage the development of selfhood, but also to develop an exploration of those connections that are part of creating this selfhood. Important ritual practices (directed play) are instituted during childhood to help the child understand the role of nurturing life and how that role relates to discovering his selfhood—such as playing with small animals and appreciating their role in the biosphere. It is necessary that the guardian role of each human be discovered for it is a process that runs deep in the soul force.

Each life cycle is an opportunity to explore new realities and to determine how one will eventually fit into the vast web of light that is human consciousness. This network of light encompasses all other sentient species and allows the human soul force to eventually merge with others to form a great galactic web of light as prophesied by the Time Lords. These relationships between species and the more important individual relationships between human civilizations, are based upon the relationships of the Law of the Two. Relationships of closeness bring a full understanding of what it is to serve another through love. This love energy is the basis for human civilization and the major reason for its continuing existence.

To summarize, these laws—the Laws of the One, the Four, the Seven and the Ten—are to be given to your civilization when the mass landings occur in the period just before the arrival of the photon belt. This is because your civilization is to become a civilization of fully conscious galactic humans. Once you enter into the web of galactic consciousness, you must know the rules and accept the responsibilities required to successfully have your guardianship succeed in the solar system. Humans who dwell upon Earth are about to be transformed. You must be prepared for all that is about to happen. That is why this Sirian Council has just given you a basic primer on Sirian law. These laws of relationship are vital; yet you must understand that these laws constitute only a mere beginning. This simple introduction is for you to explore and probe so that you may get a better understanding of the full meaning of Lyran/Sirian (galactic human) civilization—your very own heritage!

Many questions about the material in this chapter may now come to mind. In the next section, Virginia asks questions of Washta regarding information on "Galactic Human Civilization."

❋ ❋ ❋ **Question and Answer Section** ❋ ❋ ❋

Virginia: I'd like to get a sense of what Sirius is like so please provide any background information that is appropriate.

Washta: Let me establish some definitions before we proceed. A multi-star system is a grouping of star systems. A star system corresponds to what you call a solar system or a sun (star) surrounded by many orbiting planets. I will start by describing some of the star systems in the Sirius multi–star system and then I will describe my home world in the Sirius B star system.

The Sirius multi-star system is composed of nine stars; however, only four are important to this discussion. Sirius A contains the original *nonhuman* inhabitants and it is the largest and the brightest of the stars that make up the Sirius multi-star system. Sirius B has the galactic *human* home worlds. Sirius C and Sirius D are used for storage and administration tasks because we have a large volume of trade and commerce with other planetary systems in this sector of the galaxy.

Sirius A has three planets which are inhabited by nonhuman creatures. These creatures are fully conscious beings and are similar in stature to that of a seven- to eight-foot tall lion. They look very humanoid except for the fact that they are covered with cat-like fur and have a lion-like face. These entities are incredibly smart, wonderful creatures that have played an important part in our history ever since we first colonized the Sirius B star system.

In our solar system of Sirius B, we have two main worlds that we inhabit. The first, which is similar to your Earth, is the fourth planet from our sun. Our second world is the third planet from our sun, and it is more devoid of water than the fourth planet. This fourth planet was the first of the two to be colonized in the Sirius B star system. This event occurred about 4.3 million years ago (Earth time), around the time of the initial organization of the Galactic Federation. We were aided in that colonization by the Sirius A creatures that I previously described. These creatures helped us because they believed that only Sirius A was necessary for their needs, and they had no interest in colonizing any of the other Sirian star systems.

Our planet (home world) is about one and one-quarter times larger than your planet, Earth. It is also quite different in its geography than Earth. Earth is unique in that it is a water planet. We, unlike Earth, are not primarily a water planet; however, we have one huge ocean relatively the same size as your Pacific Ocean. This great ocean is surrounded on all sides by a series of continental land masses.

Unlike your planet which has continents that are almost like islands, the continents on our home world are mostly landlocked. Near our one great ocean, there are huge mountain systems that leave the seacoast with very small compact beaches. We have very little white sand, as some of your beaches do, and have instead a predominantly reddish-brown colored sand. Our soil is very, very different than yours, being colored more in oranges and purples with browns that are more of an orange-like brown than the dark to almost black soils found on Earth.

Except for the few mountain ranges along the coast, we mostly have broad hilly plains that flow across the land. We have vast river systems that dot these plains as well as large systems of lakes. To us, this planet is a very beautiful and gorgeous land, and it is being kept in its original pristine state. As guardians and stewards of our home planet, we have maintained the original flora and fauna found here when Lyran/Sirian civilization first colonized this planetary system. Sirius B also varies from Earth in that we have a blue-white sun instead of your yellow-white sun. Consequently, when the Sun shines in our Sirius B sky, it is of a bluer hue. Many who have seen our sunset have said to us these colors are the most gorgeous oranges, purples and shades of orange-brown imaginable—and that they are just too exquisite to adequately describe.

We also have a Firmament around our world that is the equivalent of what you once had on Earth. This Firmament has allowed our home world to maintain itself and has assured us Sirians long and healthy lives and an entirely predictable weather pattern. Our entire planet is, for the most part, nearly equivalent to what, on your particular planet, would be called a semi-tropical type of climate. Our Sirian planets, especially our third planet, are slightly warmer than Earth since they average in the mid to upper 70 degrees Fahrenheit during the entire year, without high and low variances.

Our calendar year is a little different than yours. We have a solar year that is 440 days long (11 months of 40 days each). This is because our planet is slightly farther out in orbit from our sun than your Earth is. Our day is roughly equivalent to the Earth's 24-hour period except that it is slightly longer, but we have found ways of maintaining our system of calendars to this 24-hour system. This is one of the reasons why your planet was selected for colonizing. It has the same 24-hour system of day and night similar to that of our home worlds in the Lyran constellation. If you study the Mayan calendar you may begin to understand the basic elements of our Sirian galactic time calendar. (*It is essential that Earth human begin to understand the importance of studying and experiencing galactic time.* The Mayan calendar is an excellent starting point for this endeavor.)

What is most unique to us about the Sirius B planetary system is its natural beauty and abundant life energy (prana). This life energy makes it quite incredible. The creatures and of course the plant life are also quite different. For example, our Sirian trees are amazing in color, contrasted to Earth trees, because many of them have purple instead of brown bark. What is of most interest to you, probably, is the fact that we live in various enclaves—either in cave-like systems or huge underground cities built near the power nodes of the different parts of our planetary grid system. However, these cave-like systems are not primitive, dark places as you might imagine. Living under a Firmament in underground cities will eventually occur on your planet, allowing you an amazingly long and exquisite life. In addition, we have small colonies of actual settlements on the surface that allow us to interface with the temple sites which are directly next to them. This set-up allows us to experience some energy patterns on the surface as well as to interact with the animals and the plant life—thus acting as true guardians on all levels of our planet.

Virginia: Could you say how high the Sirian mountains are?

Washta: They are no more than 3,000–4,000 feet (915–1,220 meters) in height except for one peak which is, strangely enough, almost exactly 11,000 feet (3.353 meters) tall.

Virginia: This description of Sirius is very interesting. We are also curious about your weather and if you have anything like earthquakes?

Washta: The Spiritual Hierarchy of Sirius have controlled all movements of the different planetary plate structures with light and love. Therefore, the need for rapid shifts is not necessary. Hence, there are, to use your nomenclature, no earthquakes on our planets (either the 3rd or the 4th planet of the Sirius B star system). Also because of the planetary Firmament, we do not have the wind storms, the rain, and the thunder presently associated with Earth. In addition, we have a minimal amount of volcanic eruptions. Any volcanic activity is controlled by ourselves and by the Spiritual Hierarchy when required.

Virginia: Yes, thank you. I'm wondering how we might more fully understand the Laws of One, Two, Three and Four and their everyday application in your lives. What are your normal activities such as eating, sleeping, working—sexual relationships? Do you take vacations, have what we would call recreation, hobbies or pleasures of various kinds? Could you say a little about this from your own experience?

Washta: We would be happy to do this although it is essential for all beings on your planet to comprehend that our patterns are quite different from yours. But let us attempt to give you an insight into those differences. First of all, our Four Laws are as sacred as the Bible would be to those you call fundamentalist Christians on your world. We are very deeply and totally committed to what you call God, the Time Lords and the power and the great light that comes from them. We respect, appreciate, and love them, using your terms. How these four Laws are used by us may give you an idea of how they may be used on Earth during the building of your galactic civilization.

What is first necessary to understand about the Law of the One is that it gives direction to the energy patterns of the soul force when it incarnates. This action is taken so that the soul force will remember and follow the path that was assigned to it. This procedure is done through counselors, the parents and the immediate family of the clan group who are all involved with the whole process of growth. Thus, each person has within himself or herself the basic concept of who he or she is, immediately at birth. So, one of the first things that is done when a child is born, because we are telepathic with the infant, is to continually ask it what its path is. He or she will clearly know why they picked their particular group as parents, why they are in a particular clan or super-family structure that surrounds them, how their sex supports their learning and serving choice, etc.

We then take this information and bring it to the next level by bringing in their guides and spiritual angels, and we clearly delineate how these guides are to help this person during their life. Thus there is a constant conversation between the counselor, the parents, the child and the clan structure or family structure around that particular being. To aid this process we have what we call rituals or rites, as previously discussed.

One of the basic and most important rituals done for the Law of the One is to have every individual arranged in a circle explaining their purpose and expressing their love for each other. Thus, the concept of understanding self and sharing the great love with each other is grounded and balanced. These are the kind of rituals that are normal for us in our daily existence. We are constantly modeling and teaching this love.

Since love and nurturing are the basic premise of our entire civilization, a child learns from the very beginning that it is loved and cared for by both parents and the immediate family. That immediate family, to us, includes not just aunts and uncles, grandparents, etc., but perhaps up to 60 loving beings. You see, no Sirian has the tragedy of being unloved from birth. When an entire society exists in that constant love and nurturance, it is, by your Earth standards, a heavenly existence.

Virginia: You are talking about family here?

Washta: Family, but it also relates to our clans. Clans are divided into various multiple subdivisions that we call subclan structures. On Earth, you traditionally call this a large or extended family. Each one of these particular members expresses love and caring for the child and supports the mission this particular child has given itself for this lifetime. They hug and play as an expression of their love and may also give advice to the child, when needed, through the use of stories.

Storytime is a very important part of raising any child, so personal stories about when one was a child and how one grew are constantly being shared with the child as encouragement for it to discover itself. Something else we do is to give the child common household items, or even other valuable things, that will later be used in the child's adult life, as a kind of preparation. Also, those adults who have similar life missions meet the child, hug it and share

174

love energies with it as a preface to preparing their future missions together. Thus, there is a joyful focus upon that future time of service and love to other beings and the planet. This concept of focus is also a very important part of the Law of the One.

One must understand oneself, what one did before, and how all that relates to what one is now to accomplish. This then leads, later in life, into the Law of the Two which is all about relationships or bonding together—discovering that sexuality and relationships are not something taboo but a natural process.

This all creates the experience of closeness which is the basic foundation of the Law of the Two. Here, the two equal partners create their service together, constantly interacting with the other to support that service. It is how we Sirians act together as a great web of support for each other, and also for the purpose of bringing our service of guardianship to our planet, our star system, and our galaxy. This process of the Law of the Two prepares the partners to bring their service into the external world of consciousness—and to the great laws of interconnectedness of life in our galaxy and even the very dimensions of creation.

The entire process of understanding each other is ongoing, both by using stories of love and also by seeing visible models of successful partnerships all around the planet. Our excellent counselors serve us with their ability to help partners develop skills to express themselves and continually deepen their experience of one another. Their role as models and conductors allows and encourages each and every being to connect with their inner selves. By assisting the partners to clarify what is occurring to them, the counselors direct and guide, by way of honest dialog, the true higher self that resolves concerns and finds loving solutions. Thus our laws create this great net of love and service. That is the basic nature of what humans are meant to be.

Virginia: I wonder if you could be more specific about what you Sirians look like . . . how long you live . . . what kind of food you eat . . . your sleeping patterns . . . your work . . . and things you enjoy? Anything that might be of interest to us.

Washta: First, we will provide an illustration of typical Sirians. *(See Figure 24: Typical Sirian Male, and Figure 25: Typical Sirian Female.)* Now we will answer your other questions.

175

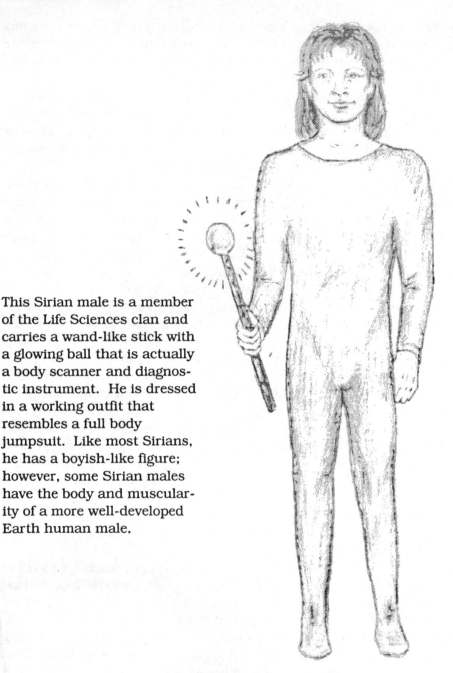

This Sirian male is a member of the Life Sciences clan and carries a wand-like stick with a glowing ball that is actually a body scanner and diagnostic instrument. He is dressed in a working outfit that resembles a full body jumpsuit. Like most Sirians, he has a boyish-like figure; however, some Sirian males have the body and muscularity of a more well-developed Earth human male.

Figure 24: Typical Sirian Male

This Sirian female is dressed in a traditional outfit that indicates what clan she is from, her position in the clan, and what clan her closeness (loved one) is from. She is a member of the Life Sciences Clan whose colors are white, blue, and gold and she is carrying a boomerang-shaped object whose main function is to balance the chakras and aid in healing the body.

Figure 25: Typical Sirian Female

We have here a civilization of fully conscious beings. As fully conscious beings living on a planet where the prana energy is very high we eat food which is a special mixture of living vegetables and fruits specially combined to maintain our energy. These energizing foods, made to be easily and completely digested, are usually eaten about twice a day.

We sleep roughly one and one-half to two hours daily because with the pure food and with the great prana energy that is being inhaled at all times, sleep is no longer very necessary. Even so, we live about 3,000-4,000 years. The length of our life is determined by our selves, usually, since we are combined into both physical and light bodies as one. We can ascend into the higher energy patterns and ask for reassignment when we feel present life is complete. As mentioned, this usually takes 3,000-4,000 of your Earth years. We, therefore, have an entirely different society as far as age, food and sleep are concerned. Most importantly, there is no real death.

The way that our life system or stages of life are experienced is quite different than what you have. For instance, since we live many centuries, the period between childhood and what we call young adulthood takes about 70 years to complete. During this time of 70 years, the entire process of the Law of the One can be developed to the point where it can be understood. During this first 70 years of guidance and spiritual growth, sexual relationships usually do not occur.

Though we are different in many ways, we are also similar to you of Earth as regarding our belief in education. We also like to take our vacations. At that time, we might go to other star systems or other parts of our own planet and simply meditate or play. We have dances and we go to the equivalent of what you would call parties where we meet with people from other clans; talk and have fun together; laugh at each other's jokes; or tell interesting stories—especially stories by our older members. Their stories can be quite fascinating because of all the wisdom they gain through the years. On Sirius, we believe wisdom takes about 2,000 years to achieve. Therefore, the older Sirians who are coming to the completion of their lifetimes are looked upon with a great deal of honor, and we gladly encourage their sharing and participation at these parties and storytimes.

Another joy is sharing the important projects we've done or things we have learned. For instance, if we are part of an exobiology

178

expedition and have gone to an entirely new star system, one of the things we would do is to hold briefings with various persons who are biologists or who are studying different concepts of exobiology. In this way, those who couldn't go share in what we have learned.

Virginia: Are you implying that you actually photograph distant places or are you using telepathy to describe them, mind to mind? How do you share what you learn with each other?

Washta: We can communicate through the use of visualization and telepathic powers which to you would be considered amazing. We can run the information of what was discovered through our own so-called mind's eye, and another fully telepathic being would receive these images and knowledge as an encapsulated version of what happened. He or she can immediately comment back about it. This is no doubt astounding to Earth beings. If you were to go to one of our social gatherings, you might see a returning party of scientists talking to another group of scientists telepathically with hardly a word being spoken between them. However, they would be very excited and you would probably wonder what was going on.

Virginia: Yes, thank you. Does this mean that you don't record information in physical libraries using books, media and so forth?

Washta: We have our libraries, but we also know that each of us carries our own immense library of consciousness—almost equivalent to the USA's Library of Congress (to use an analogy that people on your world would understand). Therefore, we are constantly exchanging our library books with one another so that we may learn more. Learning to us is a great joy and excitement. We make jokes about it, constantly laugh about it, make-up songs about it. Yes, we are continually excited and challenged about the whole concept of learning, and both learning and inner growth are a very important part of our society.

Virginia: Do you have music, art, crafts, and hobbies of any kind?

Washta: Yes. We have hobbies of art and there are people who constantly sing because of the great voice they have been gifted with through their physicalness. We are also able to play instruments and compose various musical works. Some of these are based upon our own traditional music, but we also like to learn the works of various other human and nonhuman species so that we may grasp their full concept of culture by understanding their art and their music.

179

Virginia: Very good. Is there anything else about the similarities or differences that you'd like to close with today?

Washta: We would just like to reiterate one simple but vital fact about the human soul. In spite of the differences between our two worlds at present, the energy patterns of our souls are basically the same. The difference is just that we are in full consciousness with our light bodies, whereas you—because of the various genetic mutant experiments done to humans on your planet—are now very disconnected from your great light and love powers.

We acknowledge you and extend, therefore, a great deal of respect for your courage and commitment in working to bring these energies of love and light together. Your efforts will greatly assist the mutual destinies of our two worlds, as we come together in completing the great divine plan established long ago by the great universal source (God).

Chapter 10
Lyran/Sirian Culture and
Your Human Destiny

Today Washta brings Sirai, Teletron, and Mikah of the Sirian Council, to continue their discussion about the Lyran/Sirian culture and its relationship to present Earth events. It is imperative to remember that nearly two million years ago, this culture was successfully practiced on planet Earth by a group of semi-etheric beings called in your language, the Hyborneans. This occurred long before the Lemurian civilization was established, and is a relatively little-known chapter in your planet's historical journey. This Hybornean civilization followed the *Four Basic Social Laws* governing relationships and maintained these concepts admirably over a period of approximately one million years, unbelievable as that may seem to you today. And the precepts of that culture were later followed by those whom you may partially remember as the Lemurians.

These two civilizations were the initial attempts by the Galactic Federation to bring galactic human civilization to your solar system. As mentioned, the first attempt in Hybornea was quite successful and only the intervention by the dark forces, as epitomized by the reptoid and dinoid civilizations from the Orion star system and their Dinoid/Reptoid Alliance partners, could destroy it. The Dinoid/Reptoid Alliance ravaged your solar system and planet Earth around one million years ago, and this destruction eventually led to a second civilization called Lemuria about 900,000 years ago.

The Lemurian civilization, although one of full consciousness, was founded in a very fragmentary way. This civilization was composed of colonists from many different star systems with each group permitted to create its concept of galactic civilization either on a portion of the Lemurian continent or in another area of your planet. This was because most of the civilizations from the stars, your space family, came to Earth with many different concepts of how to create human galactic culture.

There were among these Lemurians many colonists who were renegades (members of independent outpost commands), who did not fully accept the societal precepts about full consciousness, nor the concept of positive guardianship. These renegades were in many ways almost an aspect of the dark force energy that human civilization was attempting to fight. The renegades believed in hierarchical society and assumed they had the authority to alter humans for their own purposes. As the many years went by, this renegade group primarily settled on an island continent which they called Atlantis, located in the Atlantic Ocean. They began plotting a military action to destroy Lemuria, based in the Pacific Ocean, and were eventually successful. This happened about 25,000 years ago.

Today, then, we who are your galactic human representatives, relate the lessons of planet Earth's history for you so that you may understand all current happenings with a greater knowledge. The Galactic Federation and the Spiritual Hierarchy that surround your planet and your solar system are well aware of Earth's past difficulties. Therefore, we will help you re-institute the *Four Basic Social Laws* governing relationships, in order to attain a fully conscious human civilization. It will be done initially without an allowance for a great amount of variation, since this could lead to chaos during the early formative period. However, every civilization in Lyran/Sirian culture is ultimately given the right to make specific changes which best epitomize the beliefs of the Spiritual Hierarchy that surround them, as well as their own historical development. This process will also be followed in your solar system.

On planet Earth, as we have often discussed, there is not just one major guardian, but three—the Spiritual Hierarchy, the cetaceans, and Earth humans—and all share the guardianship. The present cetacean aquatic group has its brethren in the stars who are just now returning in order to bring this new civilization into being. The cetacean's combined group of aquatic guardians and caretakers will join you mutant land-based humans, who were part of the horrible disabling genetic experiments of Atlantis, to form two parts of the guardians' triangle. The Spiritual Hierarchy has remained the staunch holder of its commitment in this triangle with the cetaceans, so now it's humanity's turn!

Achieving your galactic humanness, based upon the Lyran/ Sirian civilization pattern, requires a comprehension of change and continuity. It is essential that you understand these two points since our culture rests upon them. First of all, let us look at continuity (and later on, we will address change). All galactic humans are taught that they are part of a vast cycle, a cosmic drama of life that has played itself out in the course of many lifetimes. As these lifetimes have progressed, each being has learned specific lessons that he or she can now utilize in this current lifetime. Because it is essential that you understand this entire process, many counselors are being trained and developed on your planet.

These counselors will follow the basic model given to you in the last chapter. Many individuals now exist on your planet who have within them the ability to become counselors. All that is necessary is activation of full consciousness and acceptance of the proper training that will be given when the landings occur. The purpose of Galactic Federation counselors coming to your planet is not only to oversee the changes in your civilization, but also to prepare your new civilization for its successful emergence. Their job is what has been called by the First Contact Team "a mid-wifery and coming home mission." All Earth humans will need, and hopefully volunteer for, the counseling process. Some will then take the training required to learn the skills for becoming counselors themselves. Counselors will guide, teach, and help everyone understand the mechanisms needed for determining their new galactic roles.

It is the purpose of the Galactic Federation's arrival to enable you to both fully understand, and then to perform, your given life task. This expansive intention is what the web of consciousness is all about and it is also what the clans are all about.

In the Sirius system, there are six clans; however, many of these clans can be subdivided into as many as twelve clans such as occurred in the Pleiadean Star League. Because of your association with us, we will describe the six clans as they now exist in the Sirian prototype.

The Six Sirian Clans:
1. The Spiritual Warrior Clan is the holder of the **Ch'i**.
2. The Science Clan is the holder of the **Khas'Koo**.
3. The Science Engineering Clan is the holder of the **Kaa'Baa**.
4. The Administration Clan is the holder of the **Ahn**.
5. The Life Sciences Clan is the holder of the **Kha**.
6. The Life Science Engineering Clan is the holder of the
   Ch'i'Baa.

These clan groupings form the basis for planetary and star system governing councils and their actual operation. The manner in which this system operates can only be explained when you can completely comprehend how the life–consciousness energy in these groups is utilized to create the web of linked consciousness called in Sirian, the Ch'i'Baa. It is this massive interconnected consciousness, bound only by the traditions of the Lyran/Sirian culture and the message of enlightenment from the Time Lords, that serves as the actual governing structure for this civilization.

This is so because we galactic humans are stewards and planetary guardians. We possess the information, methods and means to maintain this guardianship. These planned structures allow a process that enables us to fully understand our own purpose and to create in our clans a kind of super clan support network that makes life and its purposes (our guardianship) possible. A clan exists for the primary purpose of enabling its members to fully achieve their life tasks and their inner growth. Each clan has within it a set of specific tasks and goals which together form the great web of galactic human civilization. For example, the Life Sciences Clan has its specific set of tasks which have to do with understanding and maintaining the plant and animal life on any world. Their purpose is not to intervene, but rather to aid and support all life on the planet and in the solar system.

The Life Science Engineering Clan's job is to understand this life process, and to implement procedures and technologies which allow all life forms in any planetary biosphere to reach their fullest and most complete oneness with the planet and its Spiritual Hierarchy. Thus, the devas of the plant and the animal worlds are allowed to impress their needs upon humans in their guardianship so that humans can aid and abet their work. This process is concurrent in all the other clans because galactic civilization operates under one purpose and one purpose alone—guardianship. This guardianship process operates through the stewardship of any and all worlds that make up the star system in which galactic humans are residing.

The concept of spiritual and planetary oneness allows humans to successfully understand, on all levels, the nature of who each person is. Your civilization is to be expanded to a galactic civilization that emphasizes the individual self operating through service. This concept is accomplished through service done in love. For only through love will you become one with the great universal light of creation.

As this incipient operation amplifies on your planet, many among you have been allowed to experience a great growth of consciousness. This growth has hopefully expanded you to fully realize that you are expected to aid in creating a new planetary civilization. Many persons are now realizing that they are the forerunners of the coming Galactic Federation's landings on your planet. In fact, it should be a great joy for you to learn that this process concerns not only Earth humans but many individuals from our worlds who are also a part of this great period of transition.

Not all people reading this book are aware of our Sirian activity—or may have confused us with the little gray beings from Zeta Reticuli who have not been here in loving service. Since Earth and its human civilization is now undergoing a change in paradigm from individual fragmented selfhood to membership in a great network of consciousness, other extraterrestrials have become interested in you. You now extend into that web of life that exists upon your world and also among the great Spiritual Hierarchies that surround all creation. Be greatful that these spiritual teachers and masters have accelerated their concern, love and support for all on Earth. Their energies have led many individuals to study meditation and become familiar with the so-called ancient knowledge of planet Earth which includes the mythologies and the ways of the indigenous peoples.

As you learn how these aspects link together, you can begin to see that the concept of human civilization as presently expressed in your reality is but a mere fragmented version of the true civilization that you must one day become associated with. These changes or transformations are what we are presenting in this book. Hopefully our message will be a clarion call regarding the coming change in all humanity—change that will be happening on a worldwide scale. Every culture, race, sex, age and creed will ultimately be affected! No one will be omitted whether poor or powerful.

As consciousness is being raised, it naturally progresses toward group awareness and cooperation. To those who have awakened as light–workers, weekly meditations and meetings have become more frequent and valuable. Light–worker meditations and activities are essential for a positive result for humanity, so please continue to network and to create planetary advocate groups. These advocate groups, or whatever you call them, must link and also network with one another so that a greater web of consciousness can occur upon your planet.

This web of consciousness is a precursor to the galactic civilization that we are describing in this book. Group consciousness is essential for all light–workers, so kindly commit to this important task and immediately begin to network and link more broadly and consistently with one another. Can you want to do less when your cosmic space family is coming to welcome you home into this great and glorious galaxy? But more than that, we are preparing you for your interdimensional, spiritual, full consciousness role as well. You must not allow this role to be misunderstood nor can you allow yourselves to suddenly forget your purpose. Thus concludes this discussion on continuity. Now let us look at the second point— change.

At the present time, all that exists around you is in the process of change. The Spiritual Hierarchy, the cetaceans and the Galactic Federation, have not revealed the intimate details surrounding this change; however, you should be aware that many of these details can become known by properly employing your inner intuitive abilities. All that is required is the ability to expand your consciousness and to accept a new reality. Through your willingness and expanding consciousness you can align yourself with a new universal ethic for your planet and solar system. This new universal ethic will permit many points of conflict to be resolved. It will also give you a new technology that will seem miraculous indeed, but it is one that must be used for *positive* purposes, not for war and violence. The coming new civilization will demonstrate a way to develop loving and nurturing relationships through use of the Law of the Two and the Law of the Three. This joyful and meaningful bonding with one another, in ways not presently imagined, will ease the longing ache for that unconditional caring and love you've always desired!

Yes, you are on the verge of the creation of a whole new society, but you must realize that you have a responsibility to help that new reality be created. It is important that you accept that responsibility. You are on Earth for a purpose even though many do not fully understand this purpose yet. It has been the objective of this book to give you knowledge so that you may evaluate all that has been said here and then hopefully take the appropriate action.

You must go beyond the concept of mere survival to a concept of honorable and purposeful survival. This survival must be based upon accurate perceptions of reality and grounded in sound judgment that will produce a correct and desirable end. These factors will allow you, and all around you, to have a concept of reality that balances both physical and spiritual aspects. Understand that the actions now occurring are the building blocks for creating and birthing that new reality.

With this new reality, the genesis of a new civilization is being birthed each and every second, minute, and hour of each and every day. You should realize this fact and be cognizant that your reality as it presently exists is one that now demands a special and unique new paradigm. This new paradigm has been given in the form of Lyran/Sirian civilization and its *Four Basic Social Laws* governing relationships. You as Earth humans must first understand what these laws mean. Then you can create the forums and the planetary advocate groups that will enable you to interact and interweave your energies with one another. Thus, Earth humans should network and share this message.

Since it is such good news for your world that a new civilization will soon exist on your planet, you should be overjoyed to share the word with others. This new civilization will be interconnected to all dimensions and all the rest of physical reality. Yes, you are about to take an incredible journey! Yet this journey mandates that you have the proper tools, the most important of which is the willingness to openly pursue your spiritual path. You must not detour in any way from successfully achieving knowledge of who you are and what your role will be in this new galactic civilization.

You are part of a great cosmic drama and this cosmic drama is now in the process of being played out. As you realize the importance of what is about to happen to your planet and to yourselves, you will consciously acknowledge and consent to incredible, unbelievable changes that will transmute almost everything that exists around you. Lemuria failed because of the diversity of cultures who seeded what would be the great empire of Lemuria. But Lemuria's great difficulty will not be a part of your reality! You have come to successfully create and maintain a new galactic civilization.

This new galactic civilization will allow all people on Earth to achieve an expanded concept of consciousness and connectedness that you do not presently have. You shall be empowered to be who and what you are meant to be. It will allow you to manifest your intentions and to achieve important objectives in life. It will assist and support you in raising your precious children to achieve their grandest potential. Besides helping your family and friends, you are going to learn how to serve the energies and forces of the light, how to be in full consciousness, and how to spread this energy of light and love across your galaxy and into all dimensions.

Therefore, have joy in what is about to happen to you. Remember that as a galactic human living in a galactic civilization, you will have the opportunity to achieve a great and incredible oneness, not only with your inner soul life force, but also with many other beings in the galaxy. For your world will be a showcase world once again in which a variety of members and species of this galaxy will come to visit. You are about to become part of a fantastic and wonderful drama that will bring light and love to our galaxy. So, rejoice in who and what you are and go forth in joyous service, love, and wisdom.

Many questions about the material in this chapter may now come to mind. In the next section, Virginia asks questions of Washta regarding the information on "Lyran/Sirian Culture and Your Human Destiny."

❊ ❊ ❊ **Question and Answer Section** ❊ ❊ ❊

Virginia: Could you indicate when the clans came into being, how many individuals there are in a clan, and how people get selected into a particular clan?

Washta: First of all, the clan system began in the early Lyran human civilizations, especially in the initial Vega solar system. The clans were continued thereafter by the fully conscious galactic humans. The only basic difference from one star system to the other is in the broad number of clans established—and in how these clans are subdivided into smaller units. For example, the Sirian system has six clans, the basic Pleiadean culture has twelve, and the same number of twelve is used in the Andromeda system. There are eight clans in most of the Lyran systems, however. This clan system is important, because it is a way of defining the basic service or task that an individual chooses for its incoming incarnation. By selecting a path of valuable opportunity that allows both growth and service, it will become possible for anyone to quickly advance spiritually without need to incarnate again. This successful growth would move the individual into his or her next phase of existence which in our reality is called a *galactic presence.*

A galactic presence is a being who has transcended the physical incarnation needs or cycle and has reached the point where the judges (the various angelic judges) have decided to promote him or her into the higher level we call a full spiritual being or spiritual counselor. Those beings who have achieved the level of galactic presence are divided into several types, depending upon the nature of the soul and its particular path in spirit. They can progress and join the full Spiritual Hierarchies or those of the ascended masters. This is why individuals are judged uniquely so that when they have complied with certain consciousness requirements they may ascend to these next levels.

The clans, then, might be looked upon as service organizations that structure loving support and offer opportunities for everyone to move closer to the Creator. Their purpose is to see that the goal and potential of each particular individual within a specialized interest group is achieved. Clans operate as support groups for these particular service tasks, but offer combined support for the human family as well. By making it possible for those in service to have others around them of a similar focus, the chances for success are maximized for everyone. Thus, whatever life task someone decides to honor in a particular incarnation in fulfilling karmic debts—they will be supported by their clan.

Virginia: Are you saying each soul has a pre-determined clan? If so, how does that initial placement occur?

Washta: This is what occurs. Two beings—similar to a husband

and wife on your planet—decide to have a child. They go to a counselor and determine the proper time to have this child. They then go into a special meditation, before conception, realizing that this child will be part of a particular clan group. They ask that the incoming soul who wishes to inhabit the body—the one who will eventually be their child—agrees to be of service.

Then the parents-to-be want to know why the soul is in that particular service and how they, as parents and others in the extended family around them, can serve that particular being. This is determined so that his or her service can be completed in a way that takes care of any required karmic debts or permits other knowledge to be attained. In this way, souls may advance in spiritual growth by choosing an incarnation during which they are supported by these particular clan members. Indeed, clans look upon themselves as being the great vehicles for service.

Virginia: Thank you. Then when the child is born to this parental twosome and it becomes a member of a clan, how many clan members might there be as support?

Washta: There are tens of millions of people in the entire clan; however, every clan is broken down into many subgroups which usually includes no more than 50 to 60 people. This sub-group represents what we experience as an extended family, something that you, yourselves, have started to create on this planet. This clan sub-group operates as a web of consciousness. All the beings in it are treated with incredible love and support that provides nourishment on every possible level—be it mental, spiritual or physical. The clan accomplishes more than I can say in words. Just remember that the clan operates so that the Law of the One, the Two and the Three— three of the four basic laws—are constantly being utilized in group interaction between individuals involved in this small sub-group of the clan itself.

Virginia: From what you said about clans I'm surprised there is still any karma. I assumed there wasn't because of the loving society that you've devised. Are there still people who misbehave or have difficulties?

Washta: What we have as karma is different than yours. So let us give a definition to quickly dispel any possible confusion. Karma to us is the great collective need that each soul has to become a fully ascended being. To ascend means that certain lifetimes, or even one

190

certain lifetime, must be lived in such a constructive way that the soul's energy pattern is enlightened to the maximum amount possible.

This is what we consider to be the karma or the need of that individual. As each soul fulfills this need he or she provides a service that also allows the entire society to equally advance. So we say there is a societal karma which represents the needs of that society to both sustain itself and to advance in growth. The karma of every society begins with defining what it needs to accomplish so that it may continue to grow. Therefore, every individual who comes into a clan provides a piece of that great web, or network, that every society requires for its growth and security.

Virginia: In other words, as an example, when the United States was formed, it was supposed to be a model for freedom, happiness and the equality of each person. So Americans would say these goals are our national (constitutional) karma, or purpose. In a similar light, I believe you are saying that Sirius has had that kind of a general karma; and then some more specific ones which the clans carry out in support of, and in relationship with, that unifying purpose.

Washta: Right. You are now discerning exactly how this system operates.

Virginia: Then some people are just a little slower in practice and they need a little more assistance?

Washta: That is correct. Some fully conscious beings want to live a certain soul experience. They must then understand that they were put into this particular predestined service by agreements with their guidance, their angelic guardians, as well as those in charge of the soul force on all other levels. Successful completion of their task during incarnation then assures the maximum personal growth pattern. That is why the assistance of the counselor is so necessary! The counselor makes sure that every individual grows to the maximum level possible. That is why the counselor is honored and so admired. You might look at the counselor as being the glue that holds the personal and societal advancement together.

When we introduce galactic civilization into your particular planet and into your lives, you will discover the key importance of the counselors. That is why so many beings on your planet have come as counselors from various other star systems to provide a core base

191

of support. There is an incredible group of souls, originally from other star systems, incarnated on Earth in human form at this time. Some are conscious and some unconscious but all are capable of being trained rapidly and transcending their present amnesia to regain their own inner soul strength as counselors. This assures that your planet may quickly have the great counseling structure that other fully galactic civilizations have had for many millennia.

Virginia: Could you indicate whether a person can change their clan or life task, or are these fairly consistent throughout one of those 3,000–4,000 year life cycles?

Washta: What happens to most is they will begin with their service clan task, whatever it is. And they will remain in the clan and in their specialization during their lifespan. If they have chosen to be an administrator they will be in charge of mediating groups, maintaining rituals, etc. If they are engineers they will do what is necessary to construct spacecraft, maintain city systems, etc. If they are scientists, geneticists or biologists, they will apply their knowledge in maintaining whatever the society needs of their special skills. But unless they grow in consciousness and understand the significance of what it is they are doing for society, they will not find within them a great energy to be a counselor. If they wish to advance they must then go through various tests to show others, who have been counselors, that they are of the same light and intention to serve. Only then can they become counselors to others.

Virginia: Can you describe the process of becoming a counselor more precisely?

Washta: Normally, for Sirians, the typical becomes a counselor when reaching 1,500–2,000 years of age. Many will then move from being a counselor when they are 2,000–3,000 years old into what we call the great guides, or what you would probably call a clan priest. They maintain the temples by bringing forth the energies of the nodes of the planet in a unified way. They are the trusted overseers of the great and incredible energies of the actual guardianship. They reside at the important nodes of a specific planet so that both the planet, and the life that is part of it, can be fully maintained in a maximum energy.

This is why the rituals are so vital. All beings go to these temple structures either during events of personal crisis or at special times when these priests, as we shall call them, conduct meditations and supervise various counseling activities.

These priests also have the ability to eventually transmute themselves into what we call Time Keepers. By doing so, they become more and more attuned to the spiritual energies of their planet, and its Spiritual Hierarchy. Their energetic attunement can even allow them to interpret the energies of the Time Lords. When such an individual moves out of the priest role, he or she becomes a Time Keeper, or a great oracle to all the bodies of governance and all the priests that exist within that particular civilization. The Time Keepers are the great advisors; they are the oracles, to use a concept that existed in many ancient civilizations on your planet. They function as the final intermediaries between their galactic civilization and the Time Lords.

There are within the Galactic Federation various Time Keeper groups. Their sole purpose is to maintain the Time Lords' energies so that all levels of the Galactic Federation councils will comprehend the true meaning of their decisions and actions—and so that they will understand the significance of their participation within the divine plan of creation.

Virginia: Earlier when you listed the six clans, I noticed that the spiritual warrior clan was listed first, so I assume it carries out what we may call military activity. I wonder how this affects the people at home when all these ships are out doing battle and having their various difficulties? Has your homeland ever been attacked and what is the attitude of the average person about war and violence?

Washta: War and violence are both highly repugnant to most of our populace and they are not something we like to think about. But the realities of this galaxy have engaged us, almost from the beginning, in a vast series of incredibly huge and costly wars. These wars with the dark forces have been almost continual. Only recently have we reached a period when it seems that perhaps these wars are finally at an end. We certainly hope that the great galactic peace that has been prophesied is finally about to occur!

We have used portions of the various clans, led by the spiritual warrior clans of different star systems, to act as a military defense force for galactic humans. This defense force's sole purpose is not to act as a force of conquest, but only to act as a force of defense to maintain all sectors. They go where certain human star systems have been attacked and occupied, in an attempt to bring these conquered civilizations back into the light. As with your own planet, we want all human civilizations to be safe once again, as they were before these attacks occurred.

Virginia: Has Sirius B ever been attacked in a serious and damaging way?

Washta: We have not had a serious attack upon us in over 10,000 years.

Virginia: But I see that you are situated in a very critical and possibly vulnerable position in the galaxy, aren't you?

Washta: We are very near the Orion system which until recently contained many of the main battle forces of the dinoid civilization. We are surrounded on the other side by various reptoid armies, ships and other paraphernalia utilized for warfare. Therefore, although we sit in a vulnerable site, we have used our great spiritual energies to funnel these enemy forces away from us. As we said earlier, in spite of the many attacks around us, only once has a main battle force actually attempted to enter our systems and bring great ruin and devastation upon our civilizations.

Virginia: Yes, thank you. Could you discuss the creation myth in relationship to what we've been talking about?

Washta: The original galactic creation myth is about 50 million years old for physical sentient beings but older still for many non-human species. Some of these nonhuman species have returned to the etheric light form. More recently, about six million years ago in the Lyran constellation—specifically in the Vega star system—humans were given sentience and rudiments of civilization.

This creation myth, given for the human species, stated that there would be 100 light-star demonstration systems created. Your solar system—which we call Solis, meaning "Great Light"—was the closest of these 100 demonstration star systems to us on Sirius. You represent the potential manifestation of a glorious showcase experiment bringing light into darkness.

Basically, our creation myth begins in a similar way to many of the Earth myths contained in your religious texts and guides, such as the Bible and in many texts found in India. The various basic texts of Hinduism are the oldest unpurged works that contain a similarity to the original galactic human creation myth, so let us begin with it.

The original galactic human creation myth says that in the beginning there was the great darkness. The darkness was there because the Creator had decided to make this creation one in which there would be *light coming out of darkness*, so God assigned the Time Lords to accomplish this feat. And lo, over many incredible eons, the great pulse of time was created by the Time Lords. Then with the power of the Supreme Creative Force, time pulsed into the darkness and there was a great light in the darkness, from which came many things.

One of these creations was the birth of all the stars and galaxies, for they were the great lights hung in the darkness. At the same time, however, darkness had also created its own dark light as part of God's original creation plan. So even darkness would have light that would later be transmuted into the great holy white light that the Time Lords had brought down.

And so both light and darkness were part of the one creation in the beginning—each of which was allowed to create its own dimensions and levels. This brought forth duality and various kinds of spiritual energies that made everything around us possible. Then out of this duality there arose both light and dark celestial beings and these beings became a prototype for the many species created of both light and dark.

The light forces now created many species, one of which was a great primate from the Vega system. From the Vegan creation came the energies that brought forth what is today called "human," and the energies of the celestial hosts allowed this human to develop and to spread across the galaxy much as other creations of light had done.

This basic myth is accompanied by many other codes of understanding in a long, incredible series of manuscripts giving specifics of star systems and times, etc. However, we will not explain all this since it is not relevant for you to learn just now.

Virginia: Yes, we understand. Could you clarify why our Solar system was important? It sounds like we were out on the galactic fringes, but you say there was an important spiritual energy here?

Washta: Your solar system was chosen among the one hundred others previously mentioned, to bring in the first human prototype energies from Vega. Then of that one hundred which were chosen, planet Earth and your solar system were given the first great etheric civilization of any kind. That is why your planet and its host, the Spiritual Hierarchy, are considered to have a special blessed position. This explains why, when humans were forced to withdraw from

195

Earth, they spread out across this sector of the galaxy. But they made a pledge to re-enter your solar system and bring human civilization back to it once again. This was part of their pledge, then, to complete the karma of humans in the Vega system and reclaim this system for the light—as required by the Vegan and Earth Spiritual Hierarchies.

However, the histories of the past few million years have not accomplished this great pledge. In the beginning there was success, but as we have already explained the last 10,000 years on Earth have been disastrous. This misfortune began approximately 25,000 years ago when the Lemurians were destroyed by the Atlanteans, as we have previously mentioned.

It is unfortunate that the dark energy perceived the value of Earth's place in the creation myth, for that is why the dark forces came here to Solis, your solar system. And that is why your planet continues to have such an important position in the balance of power even though its Sun sits in a minor position in this section of our galaxy.

Virginia: Thank you. So if I understood you correctly, Earth was one of that special 100 human light-star systems. What happened to the other 99 light-star systems?

Washta: Of those other 99, only 90 were able to maintain their energy patterns and most of them developed non-human civilizations. Many of them in the Orion system, for example, brought forth some very advanced amphibious groups that are incredibly spiritual. They are, in fact, mostly etheric in form. Many times the dinoid and reptoid civilizations of Orion have attempted to conquer the amphibian group's star systems only to fail. The amphibiod spiritual energies of these great civilizations was so highly developed that they were invisible to the reptoid or the dinoid invasions. At a deeper level, these invasions could not succeed because the darker energies did not wish to be enlightened at that time.

Virginia: Could you define "amphibiod"?

Washta: An amphibiod is one that would look to you somewhat like a giant modified frog, a modified salamander—or almost like a turtle without a shell. However, unlike your turtles, these beings have hands and feet. They look quite different from what a human might expect, yet their energies and their love are so great that when any human encounters them, all apprehensions are immediately transmuted by their loving vibration. It is truly a joy to be with them, to hug them, to listen to them and to experience their energies.

Virginia: So out of the various 90 remaining light-star systems mentioned, are there any of those 90 close to us in space?

Washta: No, regrettably, the closest systems are roughly 300–500 light years away from your particular solar system.

Virginia: Yes, I have a sense of that, thank you. Now I'd like to have you define what a planetary advocacy group is and give the primary aspects or tenets of such a group, please. As you know, we already have many different meditation groups of all kinds, including my own Love Corps gatherings.

Washta: The most important aspect, of course, is the group's underlying purpose. It is meant to be a group of individuals whose sole intention is to bring the great spiritual energies of transformation upon planet Earth. Therefore, this group must have a deep spiritual energy for its basic foundation. This group energy can occur through meditation, prayer, music, various rituals or combinations of these, but it is this spiritual group dynamic that is the key for all advocate groups. They must have a great energy of the light of the spirit within them. They must understand that only by using group energies compassionately can they awaken in consciousness. Every individual must have an enormous commitment to using this powerful spiritual energy, both personally and collectively in every possible way.

To further aid you in understanding the value of group consciousness and group energy as it relates to the multidimensional nature of the spiritual and creative energy of the physical universe, you may wish to study galactic time and discover how it relates to the continuing creation of the physical universe. (We will briefly comment on galactic time at the end of this chapter.)

The second basic tenet for advocate groups, once they have created a successful group of their own, is that they can reach out to other light worker groups and gradually learn to operate as a whole. This is a difficult task, we realize. However, this sharing can be performed more easily with practice using the energies that are now pouring down around your planet. Therefore, one of the things that we would ask you to do is to invite other groups to come together in a spiritual ritual of some sort, such as a group meditation or prayer for healing your planet, for healing human society, and for preserving all life. In this way, all of you would use the inner focus of your own group to expand outward to others.

The third tenet that groups should understand is that their liaison must extend beyond other light–worker groups to anyone who seeks to better this planet in one way or another. This could include people interested in protecting the environment or those who work to better the political, social and economic conditions of others—or just to any person or group with compassionate intent. Your job is to lend assistance to these various helpers by showing them that there is support available, if they ask for it. We want them to understand that there is an incredible web of light around them from which they can draw energy and support for their particular purpose. Religions should be leading the way rather than hanging back, of course, for the total concept of an advocate group is *spirit, service,* and *liaison.* These are the three basic tenets of a planetary advocacy group and we ask you to remember and practice them.

The formation of and participation in planetary advocacy groups is what many of you awakened souls have been doing for years and years regardless of what you call them. As you have been meditating in your spiritual groups, however, you may have excluded other groups, or you simply did not seek expansion. Whatever the past, the meditation circles of various ongoing groups should be enlarged now as quickly as possible and this web of consciousness expanded. We ask that you join us in supporting this new web of higher consciousness and in aiding the creation of this new galactic civilization.

Go out into the community and show other humans that you and they are part of a human support group. Do this because, as we have stated, your first challenge is to help them welcome the spiritual essence of themselves individually and as a group consciousness, as well. To understand group dynamics, please combine with other similar groups to work as a liaison in the community. This will enrich all of humanity. It is vital for all people to seek and find community so they are not alone! They must discover that there are people available to support them and to give them our urgent information. This education process is central to the whole concept of what the advocate group is about.

Virginia: Yes, thank you. Could you comment on churches? Many church people would say this is exactly what they do; they are spiritual, they serve, and they are liaison to the world in spiritual matters and through good works. So how do you see that a church person who belongs to one of the usual religious temples, churches or organizations is different than a planetary advocate?

Washta: What we would say to those in the churches is that the clue to this whole process is the energy of love. If they are truly coming from an aspect of love and not just doing service to make a good appearance, then they can be a prototype for a true advocate group. If their core is not based upon this pure spiritual and loving energy, however, and they cannot perceive Earth's needy situation in a totally non-dogmatic, non-judgmental, and open way, then they are involved in a dogma, and are limiting their purposes. Religion is not meant to ignore present circumstances or prohibit change. It must be a helpmate for all times and all experiences, allowing an ever-increasing consciousness. In or out of churches, humanity is challenged to understand space and your upcoming role as a civilization of galactic humans.

For example, one group may proclaim itself to be a top environmental group, but it is only going through the motions. Whereas another group is a genuine environmental group because it is committed to the true energies of the spirit in an open, non-dogmatic way. Those humans who are willing to accept everyone's part in this mission of becoming galactic humans are truly planetary advocates.

Many churches are now beginning to understand that they must address modern circumstances and expand their energy patterns so that they move out of their old dogma and into a more open light. Those who do so are prime resources in the transformation your planet will experience and they are, or can choose to become, the advocates we describe.

Virginia: Yes, thank you. Then how important is it that people believe in extraterrestrials and understand the cosmic roots of humanity in order to serve as planetary advocates, whether they are in a church or not?

Washta: We would hope that you can understand how the true spiritual concepts of all religions and the seeding of all Earth humans, are dependent on the great cooperation between the Galactic Federation and the Spiritual Hierarchies that make up all creation. We would hope that you would comprehend and believe in this cooperative endeavor. However, if you wish to maintain your-

199

selves as part of a spiritual group only (and not believe in extrater-restrials), we would ask that you to listen to the energies of the Spiritual Hierarchies themselves. These various angels, archangels and ascended masters will be leading spiritual groups towards unifying with planetary advocate groups. This is the purpose of allowing your spiritual groups (that are already one with the Spiritual Hierarchy) to become amalgamated with those planetary advocate groups that have been created in service to the Galactic Federation's great mission. Both spirit and matter work hand in hand. In this combination lies an exciting future for yourselves and planet Earth if you can but understand and welcome the opportunity.

Earlier we commented on the vital influence galactic time can have in your everyday lives, but can you dare imagine its value to a group of highly-focused people? Let us review a few simple facts about what the Mayan Calendar is all about, for both individuals and groups. Please remember that your present 365-day Earth calendar is not a spiritual one but a material world calendar using physical, linear thinking. It is spiritually unconscious, so to say, and does not clarify or identify the vibrations which our galactic time contains and which we use to maintain and advance spiritual growth on many levels.

Time is the initiator pulse that makes all things in physical reality possible. It is stated in an ancient Sirian proverb about physical creation that the Time Lords were handed the great pulse of time by the Supreme Creator Force.

So let us examine this great pulse of creation—time—as a way of understanding and experiencing reality. In our galactic civilizations, we use Time Keepers to keep us informed about the actions of the Time Lords. Time Keepers are persons who dedicate themselves to understanding the underlying meanings of the universal pulse of time and to communicate with the Spiritual Hierarchy and the Time Lords on how physical creation is evolving. In other words, they could be compared favorably to the oracles of ancient Greece, Rome and Egypt on your planet. To further emphasize this important point to Earth humans, we must ask that you look at the Mayan civilization of MesoAmerica which was given a sacred galactic calendar by selected elements of Pleiadean and Arcturian Time Keepers at the beginning of the Mayan classical period (4th century AD through the

200

9th century AD).

This sacred galactic calendar has 20 Mayan glyphs. Their corresponding four harmonics and the 13 tones of creation were superimposed by the Mayan Time Keepers to conceive what was called a **K'in**. These 13 tones are used to make possible an experiential logic that signifies the best way to experience a particular day. These day patterns are mirrored daily in the sacred 260-day calendar of life called the **Tzolkin** (pronounced zoulkin). This 260-day cycle is sacred, indeed.

As just stated, in this sacred calendar, the 20 glyphs are combined with the 13 tones of creation to create what is called a **K'in** or experiential logic of the day. Each Mayan glyph encompasses all of the 13 tones of creation to form each one of the 260 **K'in**. The 13 tones of creation are unity, challenge, activation, definition, radiance, equality, attunement, integrity, intention, manifestation, liberation, cooperation, and transcendence.

If you knew which influences were being energized every day, as we do, you would cooperate with that reality and the powerful manifesting energies of Creation, instead of pushing your own uninformed intentions and attempting activities at the wrong time or in a non-productive sequence of manifestation.

There are some Earth teachers who understand and can explain this galactic time material to you, and there are several books and videos available for self-study. We highly recommend this topic, though limited space prohibits our own presentation of a more in-depth discussion about galactic time and its many essential characteristics and qualities. Just remember your Earth time is vanishing and galactic time will eventually replace it.

Chapter 11
The Galactic Federation

We of the Sirian Council—Washta, Mikah, and Teletron—wish to describe something about our own history as galactic humans and also about the organization called the Galactic Federation that Earth will soon be entering as a new member.

The Galactic Federation was formed about 4.5 million years ago to prevent interdimensional dark forces from dominating and exploiting this galaxy. This interdimensional dark force had seeded the Milky Way Galaxy with its own kind of computer-like, cold-hearted beings. Their appearance was mainly in the form of a reptoid or a dinoid individual as described earlier. These dark beings spread across the galaxy and began to successfully conquer thousands of star systems. These reptoids/dinoids, however, eventually reached an area of the galaxy where free-willed sentient human beings had created several galactic civilizations which were their technological match.

What followed, about four million years ago, was a period of brief but very barbaric stellar wars which were quickly interspersed by periods of peace. To a limited extent, this war and peace pattern has continued even into present times. As the attacks continued across the galaxy, those of us who were the enemies of this Dinoid/Reptoid Alliance became more organized. We saw the need to develop a highly diversified and effective organization that could act as an umbrella for both the coordination of the galaxy's defenses, and also as a forum that would permit necessary human and nonhuman cultural and governmental exchanges.

The Galactic Federation sees itself as a sort of United Nations of star systems whose sole purpose is to create an organization that will allow light to continue to flow into our Milky Way galaxy. At present there are over 100,000 star systems and star leagues in the Galactic Federation, and recent additions between 1988 and 1993 have increased membership to almost 200,000 members. The primary basis of this galactic light of creation is love.

One of the basic premises of the Galactic Federation is to provide for a system of defense against sudden and unwarranted attacks. In addition, the Galactic Federation also has the important tasks of exploration, technology exchange, and cultural interaction. Hence, the Galactic Federation is constantly sending scientists and liaison teams on space missions to other star systems that are not yet a part of the Galactic Federation. Another premise we must emphasize is that the Galactic Federation, through its various layers of councils, has found a way to organize planets, stars systems, and star leagues into the fourteen Regional Councils.

Since the Galactic Federation considers itself an organization of fully conscious and peaceful civilizations, it is constantly on the lookout for acceptable civilizations that meet its criteria for membership. When any planet or a series of planets in any star system reaches prescribed levels of technological and cultural development, these civilizations are contacted after a thorough scientific evaluation. This scientific evaluation covers an extremely broad spectrum of cultural, scientific, and spiritual qualifications.

Your planet and surrounding solar system have been given a dispensation from Galactic Federation rules on membership because of the efforts of the Sirian Governing Council and your Spiritual Hierarchy. The Spiritual Hierarchy reminded all Galactic Federation Councils of the special position of your solar system as both an important showcase solar system and as the underriding cause for human sentiency in the first place. This argument finally overturned the karmic laws established by Pleiadean control of your solar system since the fall of Atlantis some 10,000 years ago, and permitted the granting of *full membership to Earth in the Galactic Federation on March 5, 1993 Earth time.* This granting of full membership allowed the Galactic Federation to legally establish its rescue mission and formally empower the First Contact Team to prepare its protocols for first contact and landing on Earth.

Since the Galactic Federation is now preparing its first contact with Earth, you will need to know the Galactic Federation's functions. To show you these functions, we will use the Galactic Federation's main organizational chart. *(See Figure 26: Galactic Federation's Main Physical Organizational Chart.)* As mentioned, the main purpose of the Galactic Federation is to hasten the creation of highly sentient light-oriented galactic civilizations across our galaxy. This purpose is divided into three main parts: first, the space mission; second, the liaison groups; and third, the interdivisional forums (these groups contain the various Galactic Federation Regional and Local Federation Governing Councils).

Notice that the first component—the space mission—consists of two parts. The first part is composed of the science and exploration teams and the second part is composed of the defense forces. The purposes of the science and exploration forces are primarily three-fold.

First, the Galactic Federation believes that to send light and love across the galaxy requires that a special spiritual science be employed, and teams of explorers are sent to examine unknown regions of the galaxy in order to find acceptable new members.

Second, these same components of the science mission are used to evaluate new potential members for inclusion into the Galactic Federation. This aspect has become important in the past seven Earth years as former members of the Dinoid/Reptoid Alliance in nearby sections of our galaxy, have asked for an end to all hostilities with us and some have even requested membership in the Galactic Federation. This astounding event has been offered as proof that our mission of spreading light throughout the galaxy is succeeding and that the ancient prophecies about the purpose of the present creation are now coming true.

Finally, this mission is used to foster relationships with neutral star systems that do not presently wish to join the Galactic Federation but who ask for our technical and organizational assistance. These missions are performed to aid the good will that presently exists between these star systems and the Galactic Federation.

Furthermore, the science and exploration teams evaluate all star systems in respect to their inhabitants' full-consciousness

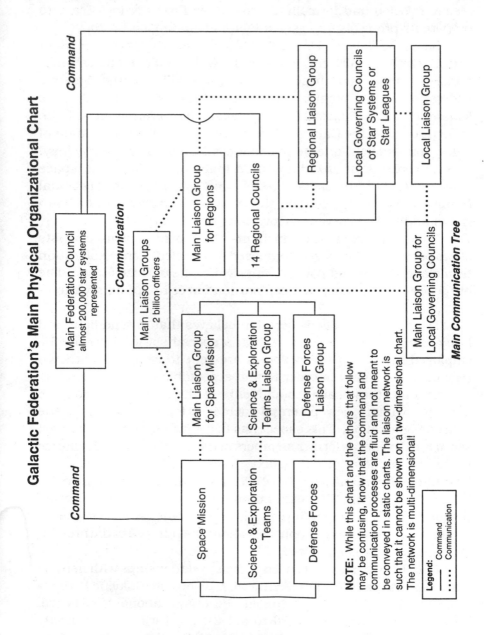

**Figure 26: Galactic Federation's Main
Physical Organizational Chart**

development and technology utilization. These criteria permit Galactic Federation planetary scientists to make recommendations to the appropriate councils within the Galactic Federation as to whether any star system or planet is truly ready for acceptance into the Galactic Federation. Accompanying them is a component of the defense forces. Here a key point must be made. *The science and exploration mission controls the use of any defense forces that are assigned to it.*

This rule for employment of the defense forces was initially established during the course of the many barbaric wars that had to be fought in order to maintain the validity of the Galactic Federation. You see, it was discovered that great difficulties would occur if the military contingent was allowed to be independent of the science arm. It is the Galactic Federation's primary goal to spread light and love rather than war across the entire galaxy. To achieve this lofty purpose, it is necessary for the Galactic Federation to have its space missions backed up with defense forces.

The defense force's purpose is to protect the science mission from attacks by the dark forces. Whenever the Galactic Federation goes into new territory, it is constantly under the surveillance of those dinoids and reptoids located in the far reaches of our galaxy and who are still opposed to any expansion of Galactic Federation territory or the addition of new members to this organization. These hostile dinoids and reptoids attempt to sabotage or to attack any Galactic Federation science mission. Consequently, the Galactic Federation has seen fit to add a defense force able to protect a science mission from any and all potential attacks.

The second Galactic Federation division is called the liaison groups or liaison teams. They are the vital key to the Galactic Federation's success. Liaison groups should also be called communication networkers and this division of the Galactic Federation has over 2 billion workers! The main function of liaison groups is to act as the primary information networks. They are the providers of the information necessary for all divisions of the Galactic Federation to make intelligent decisions. *(See Figure 27: Galactic Federation's Liaison Communication System.)* Without these insightful decisions, the Galactic Federation's ability to be a viable entity would quickly cease. Liaison is found on all levels of the Galactic Federation, from the smallest planetary governing councils up to the main Galactic Federa-

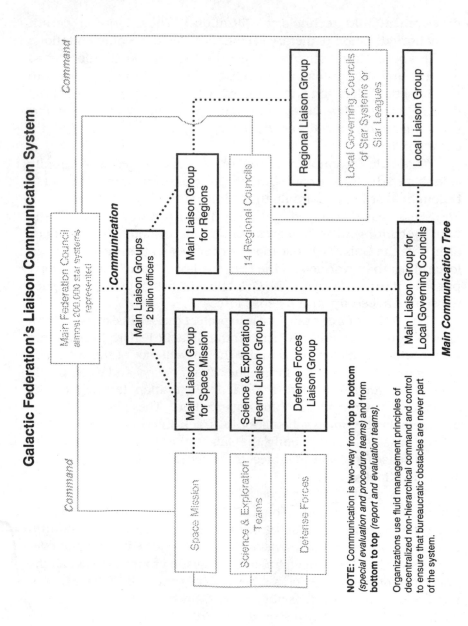

Galactic Federation's Liaison Communication System

Main Federation Council
almost 200,000 star systems represented

Command

Communication

Main Liaison Groups
2 billion officers

Main Liaison Group
for Regions

14 Regional Councils

Regional Liaison Group

Local Governing Councils
of Star Systems or
Star Leagues

Local Liaison Group

Main Liaison Group
for Space Mission

Science & Exploration
Teams Liaison Group

Defense Forces
Liaison Group

Main Liaison Group for
Local Governing Councils

Main Communication Tree

Command

Space Mission

Science & Exploration
Teams

Defense Forces

NOTE: Communication is two-way from **top to bottom** *(special evaluation and procedure teams)* and from **bottom to top** *(report and evaluation teams)*.

Organizations use fluid management principles of decentralized non-hierarchical command and control to ensure that bureaucratic obstacles are never part of the system.

**Figure 27: Galactic Federation's Liaison
Communication System**

tion Council. The liaison group's primary task is to provide and to maintain these networks of communication. These networks are filled with vital information that must be given with the proper cultural nuances and in the correct language. These complex activities are successful because the liaison teams are so well-situated and established that their organization assures favorable results. *(See Figure 28: Galactic Federation's Liaison Group Command and Control System.)*

These various liaison organizations operate within a vast set of multi-layered networks. These networks are primarily separated into what are called interdivisional councils or forums. These councils basically are run on three levels. *(See Figure 29: Earth's Relationship to Three Levels of Galactic Federation Councils.)*

The highest level is the main Federation Council itself *which is located in the Lyran star group on Vega.* The second level is composed of the various Regional Councils. There are presently 14 such Regional Councils in the Galactic Federation and the most important as far as we are concerned is our Federation Regional Council which is called the Sirian Regional Council. Your solar system will eventually join this Regional Council as a full-fledged member.

Regional councils act as forums for various difficulties. They help set policy in their particular region and they also act as a court of last resort for any problems that one particular star system or star league may have with one another. They also function as a means for cultural and technological exchanges. In this way, Galactic Federation Regional Councils provide a means for negotiating misunderstandings on technology transfer and also for trade in intellectual property.

There also exists local or star system governing councils. You of Earth and your fellow members in your solar system, will eventually form a local star system council. These star system governing councils can consist of two types: First, a simple star system council or local governing council, and second, a star league governing council which can consist of up to 20 or more combined star system governing councils. The largest star league in the Sirian Regional Council that you will be joining, is the Pleiadean Star League which consists of almost 50 different star systems.

The exact nature of the interaction between these various levels of the Galactic Federation is not simple. It is important to realize that liaison groups help the Galactic Federation to keep in touch with what is happening in a particular star system or a particular section

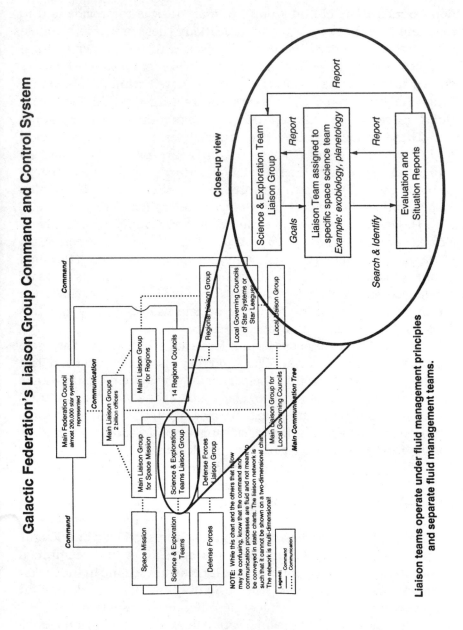

Galactic Federation's Liaison Group Command and Control System

Close-up view

Report

Report   Report

Science & Exploration Team Liaison Group

Liaison Team assigned to specific space science team *Example: exobiology, planetology*

Evaluation and Situation Reports

Goals   Search & Identify

Command

Main Federation Council almost 200,000 star systems represented

Communication

Main Liaison Groups 2 billion officers

Main Liaison Group for Regions

14 Regional Councils

Regional Liaison Group

Local Governing Councils of Star Systems or Star Leagues

Local Liaison Group

Command

Space Mission

Main Liaison Group for Space Mission

Science & Exploration Teams Liaison Group

Defense Forces Liaison Group

Science & Exploration Teams

Defense Forces

Main Liaison Group for Local Governing Councils

Main Communication Tree

NOTE: While this chart and the others that follow may be confusing, know that the command and communication processes are fluid and not meant to be conveyed in static charts. The liaison network is such that it cannot be shown on a two-dimensional chart. The network is multi-dimensional!

Legend: ——— Command
········ Communication

Liaison teams operate under fluid management principles and separate fluid management teams.

Figure 28: Galactic Federation's Liaison Group Command and Control System

Earth's Relationship to Three Levels of Galactic Federation Councils

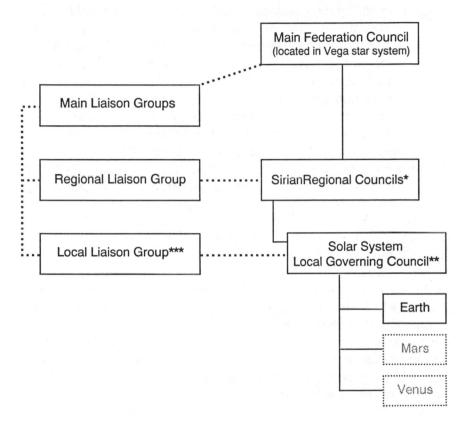

*Sirian Regional Council is one of 14 regional councils. You became a member of the Sirian Regional Council on March 5, 1993. Its headquarters are located in the Andromeda constellation.

**Earth and eventually Mars and Venus will be part of your solar system's governing council.

***Local Liaison Group acts as information network between governing councils and the main liaison groups.

Figure 29: Earth's Relationship to Three Levels of Galactic Federation Councils

of the galaxy. Thus, we interweave the various liaison groups to these different levels of councils and, at the outer edge of this whole process, to the space missions and the defense commands.

The Galactic Federation is not here to exploit Earth humans. Rather it is here to promote them into higher consciousness and to save a beleaguered planet. We are here to help birth a new human spirit and advance the entire human race into their intended true role as a guardian species once again. In this increased conscious-ness, Earth humans will then reclaim their relationship with other galactic humans spread all across the galaxy. After your many difficulties, you deserve to experience the glory of life and of love, not only in your daily lives, but also by extending that positive energy to other humans and sentient beings throughout the galaxy and throughout creation.

Let us now look at this entire process of establishing a first contact by using Earth as an example. The concept of altering the Galactic Federation's role in your solar system began in the 1950s with the formation of a special liaison and cultural group assigned to the subterranean human civilizations, organized under the aus-pices of what you call either Agartha or Shamballa. This is a large civilization that exists beneath the surface of your planet. This particular liaison cultural group was later given the task of implement-ing the first large-scale contact by the Galactic Federation to awaken its Earth human contactees. These contactees were initially picked because of their background in science and also because there was hope that they would act as communication nodes for possible media contact—a way to spread the Galactic Federation's message.

The Galactic Federation also began developing additional liai-son and cultural teams to attempt to overcome the difficulties of contacting the surface governments of your planet and also the main organization of your nations—the United Nations. This activity was expanded in the late 1960s to prepare for the fact that the surface civilization was environmentally destroying your planet, and to prepare for a possible small-scale evacuation which included a plan for the reseeding of human beings on planet Earth. At that time, a First Contact Team was established—a team with a very limited supervisory role.

By the 1980s, the Galactic Federation began to see that it was essential to view what was happening on Earth, not as a process of doom, but as a process of transformation and increasing enlighten ment. These developments consequently created the need for a new type of organization. This new organization was also called the First Contact Team and it was initially formed in the early part of the 1980s. Its mission has been vastly expanded from the concepts that created the First Contact Team in the 1950s, 1960s, and 1970s. This current First Contact Team now had a new vitality based on the hope that a massive first contact was really possible. This hope was generated by the possible benefits of the upcoming photon belt and the evolving agreement in the Sirian Regional Council as to the feasibility of using the new rising consciousness to prevent a disaster scenario from occurring.

At this same time, the Sirians also learned of a new development. They were notified by the cetaceans and by Lady Gaia's Spiritual Hierarchy to change the contact scenario to one involving a mass ascension process. This new reality caused the Sirians to extensively lobby the Sirian Regional Council for a change in policy in regards to a mass landing. This policy change began to take effect in the late 1980s. It has allowed the Sirians to alter the Sun's polarity and to research the methods for the first emergence of the ascension process. This research led them to bring many scientific teams into your solar system to evaluate the biosphere in a new way—a way that would allow your solar system to be altered back to what it was at the time of Lemuria. This concept of restoration then became the primary guiding principle for all science and space missions to your planet.

As a result of this alteration, a First Contact Team—with full powers to act as the "welcoming Earth home mission"—was formally established in the late 1980s. A new leader was appointed, whose name must not be revealed until just before contact, and it was his purposeful progress in the past two years that has led us to the mass landing process that we are now preparing to accomplish.

Earth was evaluated in the early 1990s to prepare for the welcoming home mission of the Galactic Federation's First Contact Team. This procedure was done for two purposes: first, because it was essential for the Galactic Federation to know who and what you are; and second, to aid the First Contact Team in its mission to restore Earth to the conditions wanted by the Spiritual Hierarchy. Therefore, these exhaustive studies included scientific teams that

213

could properly assess what improvements and alterations should be done to restore Earth to its original pristine condition.

The First Contact Team has had to create a Board of Command of fifty beings whose job is to oversee these many tasks. The Board of Command has been organized into appropriate committees who have been assigned various aspects of science, technology, etc., as required by the appropriate Galactic Federation Regional Council. The Sirian Regional Council has given the contact team full authority over all space in your solar system which includes planet Earth, as well as assisting your solar system by providing for its defense. Here is an explanatory diagram describing the various components of the Sirian mission. *(See Figure 30: Chart of First Contact Team.)* This mission (described in five parts) is to be accomplished by the First Contact Team.

Part One: *Liaison with Earth's Spiritual Hierarchy.*

The first part of this mission is simply overseeing the changes in Lady Gaia. Lady Gaia has been altered from a largely 3rd-dimensional Spiritual Hierarchy with adjunct powers in the higher dimensions to a 5th-dimensional Spiritual Hierarchy with the same powers. This change has caused the First Contact Team to appoint a committee that now monitors this change in planetary spirituality.

Part Two: *Planetary Environmental Recovery.*

The second part of the mission is the surveying of the planet's surface and its interior as well. This ongoing science mission has helped to establish the scientific procedures needed to return your planet to the pristine state requested by the Spiritual Hierarchy.

The Galactic Federation now believes it is essential to alter the present make-up of governance on Earth to a nonhierarchical structure, since fully conscious humans are cooperative and will want to govern themselves in a democratic way.

Part Three: *Cultural Assistance and the Landings.*

The third aspect of this mission is cultural and involves the actual contact process. The cultural mission was established for two purposes.

First, Earth civilization is about to evolve into a civilization consisting of fully conscious human beings who are a guardian species. They must be aided and supported during their transition into a civilization that has both the technology and the culture that mirrors this prime function.

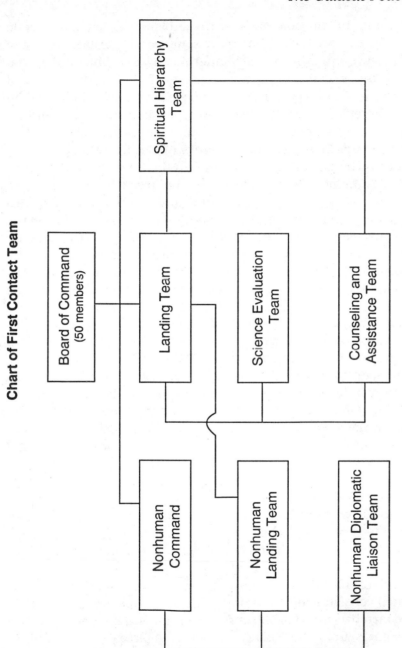

Chart of First Contact Team

Spiritual Hierarchy Team

Board of Command (50 members)

Landing Team

Science Evaluation Team

Counseling and Assistance Team

Nonhuman Command

Nonhuman Landing Team

Nonhuman Diplomatic Liaison Team

Figure 30: Chart of First Contact Team

Second, this purpose calls for the implementation of a galactic human culture on Earth, but with some modifications from the earlier culture brought to your planet during the time of Lemuria. This culture is called a Lyran/Sirian civilization. This line of development is a far cry from that which is presently established on Earth. Therefore, it was decided that special cultural committees and liaison teams from Sirius would function in this role.

Part Four: *Ecological Perimeters of Earth's Biosphere.*

The fourth part of this mission given the First Contact Team is to establish the necessary ecological perimeters of your planet. To do so, it is necessary to go back in time and compare the past with the present. As a result, incredibly sound programs for altering the present surface of your planet have been established. Programs are now underway that will successfully transform Earth back to its original state. This intent is one to which both the cetacean guardian species and Lady Gaia are now committed, and their *will* will be done.

Part Five: *Liaison for Galactic Federation and Earth.*

The fifth and final aspect of the First Contact Team's mission is to provide liaison groups between the Galactic Federation Councils and your soon-to-be emerging new galactic civilization. This mission is presently in the process of being established. It is the hope of the First Contact Team that when the mass landings occur, those who are part of the special teams will be able to provide the necessary liaison and assistance needed to aid the humans currently residing on your planet.

The overall mission of the First Contact Team, then, is to assist the arrival of full consciousness for all humans on planet Earth. It is also to allow those who are in full consciousness to establish appropriate governing structures. This particular government will be one of light and growth and not of hierarchical and authoritarian purposes.

When the mass landings occur, a temporary governing council will be created consisting of four groups. These groups are as follows: 1. selected members from Lord Metatron's Central Sun Council; 2. numerous members from the Ruling Council of Agartha (Shamballa); 3. selected cultural transference and liaison counselors from Sirius as representatives of the Galactic Federation; and 4. planetary advocate groups. These various elements will act as a temporary governing council whose sole purpose is to prepare Earth's human population for its new form of governance. The Central Sun Council of Lord Metatron will have the final say as to when this council is to be replaced by a permanent council through the timings established by divine plan and divine right order.

At the present time, the Galactic Federation is in the process of detailing the final plan—the where's and the when's of the First Contact Mission and its development after contact. The Galactic Federation's mission is based upon peace and upon love. Therefore, all who are coming to you as a part of the Galactic Federation will be on Earth as your elder galactic brothers and sisters who intend to perform this rescue mission with love, concern, and caring.

All that the Galactic Federation's First Contact Team asks of you, dear reader, is to accept the fact that a great change in human consciousness is about to occur. You Earth humans are about to embark on the amazing destiny that was forecast for you in the prophecies of your great religious works. As a fully conscious being, you will become a part of the great trinity of guardianship described earlier in this book. Please become aware of this responsibility and begin now to practice its tenets.

We ask finally that you begin to form the planetary advocate groups so essential for the success of our programs to aid and assist both your planet's and your own transformation/ascension process. It is a great and exciting time of change for your planet and all living things upon it. It is one that will shortly be filled with joy and spiritual fulfillment! We of the Galactic Federation are happy to know that your planet and your fellow members of the solar system are on the verge of a most wondrous destiny!

Many questions about the material in this chapter may now come to mind. In the next section, Virginia asks questions of Washta regarding the information on "The Galactic Federation."

※ ※ ※ **Question and Answer Section** ※ ※ ※

Virginia: First of all, I'd like to know what part bureaucracy plays in the Galactic Federation's decision-making process because, of course, I'm thinking of us Earth humans and our past 10,000 years of all this negative history. I'm wondering whether the Galactic

217

Federation's decision was intentional or accidentally allowed—or is there just indifference or bumbling sometimes, as is typical with our bureaucratic organizations?

Washta: The Galactic Federation is a very large and a most ambitious organization in terms of its size, scope and mission to bring light to this entire galaxy. Its bureaucracy is indeed an incredibly huge one befitting its mission. However, since policies are largely determined by the smaller councils, namely the regional councils instead of the main Galactic Federation Council—which itself is an immense and incredible organization all on its own—we must say that the policies concerning Earth have largely been determined by decisions of the major members of the regional council.

Unfortunately, the wars that have occurred throughout this section of the galaxy have lead to the determination of Galactic Federation policy. Once this policy has been determined and the policies put into play, it has become difficult to change them because of certain internal aspects between various members. This is one of the main reasons why it has taken the last few decades for the Sirians to successfully alter Federation Regional Council policies so that the present activities now under way could be established as official policy.

Virginia: So in a sense then, the smaller and less powerful members, either single planets or star systems, have to be protected by the understanding of a local council of some kind?

Washta: They have to be aided by the local council. However, the regional council is in charge of the various defense forces over a large sector. They decide how various forces from one governing council or star system are to be spread out beyond that single star system. The problem with your particular solar system is that it has been largely dependent on these other sector defense forces to defend it. This has allowed various groups, such as the renegades, to filter in and establish a defense group which could then be utilized to defend your solar system. This has provided the renegades opportunities to put themselves into positions of authority. Your conditions were further affected by the fact that the Pleiadeans, the Centaurians, and a few other groups (which put these outpost organizations into position in your star system in the first place) have a religious concept they call developmental karma.

218

This concept has enabled these groups to maintain the energy patterns that these rebel, or renegade, outpost organizations created in your particular solar system. This is why the present history (the 10,000 years we have been discussing) occurred and was allowed to continue. This condition is now changing because we have finally reached levels where some peaceful shifts are occurring throughout this sector. This and other factors have permitted us to again exert our authority over your solar system and allow for the changes that are now under way.

Virginia: Thank you. We'd like to know something about what we've called the Lucifer rebellion and understand what effect it may have had on the galaxy, and of course, on our own solar system and the Earth.

Washta: The Lucifer rebellion is an attempt by people to understand the struggle of light and dark forces that has occurred here on the galactic level over the past millions of years. This great rebellion of the dark force spread itself across the galaxy from that earlier time of approximately 35 million to 40 million years ago, causing many great difficulties in this galaxy. We are happy to report at this time, however, that this period of rebellion is changing from one of great difficulty and war into one of cooperation and light. This is why your solar system is now in a period of transition from its present position of darkness and limited consciousness into one of light and full consciousness.

Virginia: Could you describe the number of universes there are?

Washta: If you look upon universes as dimensions, we view them as infinite in number. If you look upon it as a physical and spiritual universe then there are but two. The key here is the range of the definition. Is it to be a spiritual versus physical concept, or one roughly similar or analogous to that of dimensions? There is duality in all of creation at this time.

Virginia: Do you have any knowledge regarding the disintegration of what is called the human soul? Has a person ever done anything so evil that it's been totally extinguished rather than later forgiven, or offered the opportunity for forgiveness?

Washta: The only times where we have anything similar to that is when intergalactic wars occur. When these wars are in progress there are weapons used that can scatter the light body of any human soul into many dimensions. One must then reconstruct it. However, we do not have any history of any soul being fully extinguished. This reconstruction takes an average of 1,000 to 2,000 earth years (if it has been completely scattered to many dimensions) to bring the soul back together again. Thus it can then resume its karmic pattern of incarnation and move toward the light.

Virginia: Oh, thank you. Could you discuss whether there has ever been on this planet, since Lemuria, any nation or government that even approaches the application of Lemurian ideals?

Washta: There exists, not on the surface of your planet but underground, since the end of Lemurian times (25,000 years ago), what is called in your mythologies the kingdom of Agartha or Shamballa. It has become a huge underground network connecting all major continents to the capital which exists beneath what is today called the nation of Tibet. This civilization has remained in various below–surface enclaves around the planet, being one with the Spiritual Hierarchies to bring humans into higher consciousness. They will again unite with surface humans once the mission of bringing full consciousness to your planet has been completed.

Virginia: In other words, on the physical planet surface itself there are no governments that know how to do this?

Washta: That is correct.

Virginia: Returning to my earlier question about the number of universes, how many of those are affecting Earth and humanity now?

Washta: The most important concept for Earth humanity to know about universes at the present time is that a shift is occurring. If we may call the universes "dimensions," there is a shift occurring from the third to the fifth dimension. This has a major effect. And it also has affected all other dimensions or universes up to the seventh dimension. Thus we have roughly five of these that are being affected from the third through the seventh dimension. This is because the increases in consciousness on your planet have required that the Spiritual Hierarchy make many dimensional shifts. As they now adjust the interdimensional energy exchanges, your planet can be prepared for movement into its new full consciousness.

Virginia: So are you really indicating that we would be better off—rather than using the word 'universe' as a physical place—to think of a universe as a dimension of awareness or consciousness?

Washta: That is what we would prefer because dimensions, once they rise above the so–called fourth and fifth dimension, become fully spiritual. Therefore, they do not exist in any concept similar to the so–called third-dimensional physical framework that everyone on your planet considers to be the basic aspect of their reality.

Virginia: So, where does that leave Sirians as human beings who have full consciousness?

Washta: We are fully conscious beings existing in this third dimension, but because of this fully conscious capability we can also commune with the angelic forces of the other dimensions. We are thus a true guardian species because the Spiritual Hierarchies that control the energies of this dimension, as well as the creation hierarchies of the Time Lords, are able to speak to us, and we are able to interact with them, too. This communication occurs on your planet in only rare individuals, whereas for us it is the usual experience of our entire civilization and an aspect of the reality we actually utilize.

Virginia: So in other words, a Sirian is a third-dimensional physical being with fourth- and/or fifth-dimensional awareness.

Washta: We have interdimensional capabilities because we are able to completely transform our physical third-dimensional type of body to a light-body that allows us to move around in other aspects of reality.

Virginia: Then your species is not totally, physically solid.

Washta: Earth humans and Sirians are very similar. If you were to see me walk down the street you could easily bump right into me, or converse with me just as you could with any other human on your planet. We are both physical beings, but Sirian humans also have the capability, because we are in complete control of our physicality, to transform our bodies into an interdimensional light-body or even to increase its usual frequency where the average Earth human would think it had disappeared.

Virginia: Could you comment on the nonhuman species among those we call the dark energies? Are they the same in terms of these definitions you have just given for yourself?

Washta: They are. And since they are fully-conscious light beings, although of a different bent and concept, they are adept with much the same abilities. When the awareness and capabilities of full consciousness are twisted inward toward the ego it can cause a great deal of harm. This problem has been experienced by Earth humans who have practiced 'magic' with less than a fully-loving intent. This is the great difficulty. That is why there has been this great conflict between light and dark in this galaxy and in this creation. Even though both light and dark are very strong forces, the light is about to lead the darkness to its own transformation. This is the nature of the struggle now going on in this galaxy.

Virginia: For the average Earth human who begins to do some kind of communication—intending to open themselves up to the light—how may they be certain that the contacts they make are with beings of the light?

Washta: Always keep yourself in the light of the great Source, in the Christed light of high consciousness that surrounds the souls of all humans. If you remain in this Christ light and in the light of the Creator Force, then you will be protected from the darkness, not swayed by it. The essence of the Christ light is love and compassion. When people are immersed in this white light energy and they use it as the source for all that they do in raising their consciousness, they will see that this energy has the capability to protect them from any dark vibrations.

Virginia: Then how do you define possession?

Washta: Possession is when these dark energies are allowed to enter into consciousness because the proper precautions are not taken to protect the physical and spiritual bodies. This is because most Earth humans do not consciously practice connecting with the great Christ light. They do not work to constantly maintain themselves in it. Practicing to connect with and remain within this light will keep difficult situations and other such negative energies away from them. This is why Earth humans should always bring the Christ light in (invoke the light).

Virginia: Thank you. Do you see this as being any kind of a serious problem for humanity as we go through these shifts?

Washta: There are potential difficulties. However, if you will simply begin the practice of raising consciousness in the proper way, by bringing in the angelic energies and the great Christ light, you will find yourselves able to connect up to your source and remain with it in all that you do. Such simple but sincere practices will protect against and help dissipate any possible difficulties.

Virginia: We realize that this question may be difficult to answer, but in terms of your current successes with many nonhuman groups coming into the Galactic Federation, how long will it take to stop the warring and violence in our galaxy?

Washta: We believe that the coming century, or roughly the next 100 years or less of Earth calendar time, will successfully bring the end to warring and violence. We believe that we are approaching not only a millennium of great change in your solar system, but we are also achieving the great ascension of light in this galaxy after battling the darkness for eons. This is because of the phenomenal and unbelievable shift in consciousness by the dark energy forces toward the light. At present, over half of the galaxy has moved into the light, whereas at the beginning of the 1980s that figure was less than a quarter of the galactic population. If this change continues at this pace, we estimate that by the end of the next century the entire galaxy will be able to ascend. This positive shift is also being reported by many other galaxies with whom we are now in communication. Their observations agree with ours, even down to the time estimates. We are therefore all the more confident about our approaching galactic enlightenment.

Virginia: How many galaxies does the Galactic Federation negotiate with at this time?

Washta: We are negotiating with approximately 50 galaxies and already have two of these galaxies as members. It is our deep hope that in the next few decades we can make as many new intergalactic connections as those we are now forming with our own galactic family. To us, this is a great omen that an amazing change is going on in our galaxy and that the time of the great myth of the light (the divine prophecy)—a basic foundation belief of all that the Galactic Federation works toward—is about to occur.

Virginia: It sounds very exciting!

Washta: It is for us. We are constantly in amazement over the tremendous energies that both the Spiritual Hierarchy and the Time Lords have set up to convert the energies of this galaxy toward the light. It feels almost like after our struggle and long climb up the mountain we suddenly have been given an elevator ride to take us right to the top.

Virginia: Maybe we have time to ask if any of your council members had any personal interesting cultural or travel experiences while carrying out the business of the Galactic Federation?

Washta: We have had many on your planet because many of us have come to Earth to observe it.

Virginia: Pardon me. I was thinking of somewhere else rather than your experiences with us here.

Washta: Yes, we have visited two planetary systems in Pegasus that are not in your present category as a showcase solar system but are very primitive. Situations have also occurred in three planetary systems in Eradanus where our ships have been attacked by independent elements of the Dinoid/Reptoid Alliance. The indigenous beings thought we were gods and gave us enormous reverence because they thought our energy transformation capabilities were very miraculous.

Our experiences have also included sharing our patterns of curing illness or providing food and resources for beings in need. On your planet, though, we have found the beings to be extremely rebellious and very much into their own concept of free will. This has caused us to observe them cautiously and has created many great difficulties in interacting with some humans on your planet. However, we consider this to be part of bringing light to your planet. As a showcase planet, it is one that will bring full consciousness of free will use and end all concepts and behaviors which are not based upon divine principles.

Virginia: Assuming we have rebellious ways, do you perceive that by the time of our photon belt experience, people will rise toward their full consciousness and let go of their rebelliousness?

Washta: There will still be a degree of rebelliousness as energy shifts occur because many human children are taught erroneous concepts and have become adjusted to that backward concept of civilization that Earth presently holds. However, we have been told and have seen by scanning humans on the planet, that beneath this shell of rebelliousness there sits a great angelic light. Once full consciousness is restored to the human physical body, this light will more easily combine with the body and produce the effects that we predict will form a new galactic civilization.

Earth humans will have a new concept of working in a full-consciousness civilization with free will on a third-dimensional level. Earth humans are the ones destined to create the great mastery of the third dimension that many of us have come close to, but which your solar system and your planet will actually achieve. That is why Earth is destined to be a great and glorious showcase once again, thereby fulfilling the divine prophecy of eons past.

224

Virginia: Are you saying that many human souls on Earth really have had a deeper turning toward the light?

Washta: That is correct. A full gamut of darkness has been delivered to your planet, as well as one of light. Now, however, your planet will combine both to produce its own unique civilization—one that will act as a showcase. Therefore, we know that even though you are but children barely entering primary school, to use an analogy, you will rapidly be the PhDs who will teach many of this galaxy's civilizations great lessons that all galactic civilizations must also learn.

Virginia: Thank you. Can you explain how these rebellious–thinking Earth people can view this first contact of yours as something other than an interference in Earth's internal affairs?

Washta: That is because the Spiritual Hierarchy has, so to speak, set up the soul contracts and the ways that it would be done. The Spiritual Hierarchy has excellently planned and organized the structure of what is now happening. The principles and the agreements that they have reached with all human souls on your planet make possible the great changes that are about to occur.

Before all human souls were allowed to incarnate on your planet, they were told that they would have to formally agree under the precepts of the divine plan and divine right order to the following two principles. First, they agreed to allow the Spiritual Hierarchy to determine when a divine intervention (to restore full consciousness) would be necessary and how it would occur. Second, they agreed to act as true Earth guardians (after the divine intervention) when the Spiritual Hierarchy so decreed. That is why they (the Spiritual Hierarchy) will come with us (Galactic Federation) to carry out this great landing and bring full consciousness back to all humans. While at the present time there may be many opinions for and against our first contact, we know that eventually there will be a favorable response as we assist and guide you on how to live as an enlightened being in a galactic human civilization.

Virginia's Afterword

Now that you have contemplated the information purported to be from galactic humans in the Sirius star cluster, it is vital to revisit those five points I suggested to you in my opening introduction to this book. Please glance back to them now on page 4, and see how they may aid you in confirming whether this information has validity for you or not.

Although I do not use all of these resources with equal attention, I always strive to have a daily personal meditation and at least one weekly group meditation as the basis for life. I do this as a gift to myself because I find it to be a healing and supportive practice worth maintaining.

From the many positive results that people have had from their inner reflections, meditations and contemplations, in fact, I've deduced that these kinds of practices are the divine passport we humans have in common for our galactic homeward journey.

Nonetheless, I also attempt to be aware of other kinds of information relating to the whales and dolphins, the indigenous people, scientific findings, and spiritual and intuitive reports. I believe that by honoring the value of all of these groups we may finally discover how they interrelate in the great mosaic of long-hidden truth—thereby deepening our own soulful depths and cosmic wisdom.

You see, when I was asked by my inner guidance to help prepare this volume, I did so with the understanding that I could present the specific cross-checks we all need to apply as we evaluate whatever incoming information is now coming forth. In other words, if we apply a process of evaluation that offers an opportunity to watch for commonalities and trends from a variety of reputable resources, we will be closer to the truth regarding potential future events. Thus our personal meditations plus weekly group meditation experiences will be supported by:

- our spiritual affiliations and positive religious teachings;
- confirmations from cetaceans;
- reports from positive indigenous peoples;
- trustworthy scientific discoveries;
- study of mythology and folklore;
- and by sources of current information we call channeled or inspired.

(And yes, I have repeated this list again from page 4 to show its urgent value and call it to your attention once more!)

As we each hold to a state of love and positive expectancy, we will hone our own intuitive processes and higher consciousness to a level where we cannot be misled or confused by the myriad of messages and feelings reported by literally millions of people who are, for the first time perhaps, receiving reflections, visions, dreams and messages never before available to them. Because of our movement into 4th-dimensional reality, we are expanding our usual states of psychic, but not necessarily spiritual, awareness, sometimes with disturbing results.

Even while you read this, the vibratory frequencies of love are stimulating our brains and bodies at the deepest core of our essence, forcing a shift in consciousness that demands the release of negative belief. This love must be filtered through the personality concepts, however, and all that is not loving must be released. This is a simple statement but the effects this influence has in our lives is awesome, indeed.

To believe what just anyone says regarding the future events on Earth is impractical, even if the source is indicated as Jesus, Mother Mary, Moses, Buddha, Krishna or Ram, Mohammed, the Archangels (and other angels), or the many Ascended Masters. I have even read statements, sincerely meant I'm sure, where the authorship calls itself God. Besides religious and spiritual figures, people may also be receiving communications from galactic humans (even nonhuman species)—from dolphins, and even from our own deceased human family and friends.

Because the astral levels of the 4th dimension are not purely mystical and spiritual in nature, and most people have difficulty receiving information from the 5th dimension and higher, there may continue to be some chaos, confusion, and possible dissonance in reception. That is why our own meditations and the information from other people require a sensitivity to the energy vibration or frequency the information carries, not just attention to the words. This proliferation will continue to engulf humanity as the higher light energies open our DNA cellular identity and affect the scalar wave potential of the human brain and physical system.

The various informants of this increasing information, which may give both guidance and a variety of different dates for possible events, must be evaluated for their balance and purity. Literally everything that is received from any source must, I believe, be held in the arena of potentiality as it is cross-checked with other guidance. (It does not personally offend me to have people check out whatever I write, because I trust everybody to follow their own guidance and do what is best for them and, also because I am continually growing and learning from others, myself. None of us are so perfected that we can't learn from one another.)

I am finding that no one source or teacher is working totally alone in this time of group consciousness—rather each contributes a unique portion of their talent to this enormously simple but also quite complex human experience. Our purest intuitives are surely sharing a quality of energy that can lead us through various challenges at the absolutely highest level of our combined emotional stability and innate wisdom. Since everything is energy, we must ourselves seek its highest vibratory frequency to fully experience the loving assistance that the divine has promised us, and is now delivering. I believe it will require our devoted attention to achieve this energy's purpose and direction within our personal lives, our group relationships, and our global responsibilities, not to mention galactic endeavors. We now need each other more than ever before, during this ascension, with its enormous variations, potentials and levels of awareness.

Yes, there is a group ascension occurring, I am certain, so we must seek to use the power of our own healed natures and bond with groups who seek only the highest good for all. Our bonded love and willingness to serve the highest good will guide and protect us as we spiral through the dimensional information barriers and interdimensional openings of truth.

There will be new vocabularies to deal with and our actual spiritual experience may be grander than what our limited language references to terms such as gates, star gates, portals and frequency bands can define and explain. Are we being initiated and aligned by these incoming energies, as we are purified and cleansed of the negative vibratory resonances and inharmonic expressions of love we've gathered along existence's highway? Time and time alone will tell, but it is love that will guide us, more than we can even imagine at this stage of our awareness.

Then, today, as a sentient being seeking inner peace and its many worldly applications, I ask you to join me in using these five reliable cross-check resources as best friends and companions on the journey inward and onward. I ask this because if our beloved planet and we humans have been the battleground of various extraterrestrial forces and their colonization practices for thousands of years, we must keep our balance somehow. Indeed, how can we overcome the feeling that we are merely pawns in a game of galactic chess?

How can we sort out which galactic beings are which in this lengthy battle between dark and light forces? And where do we fit into this cosmic struggle's eventual outcome for peace and the preservation of life? In a sense, we need to ascertain who our mentors and protectors are so we'll know whose side we're actually on. Names like Sirius, the Pleiades, Arcturus, Zeta Reticuli, Bellatrix, Orion, Pegasus, Cetus, Lyra, Vega and Sagittarius raise many questions in our quest for understanding.

For me, personally, I want to remain open-minded but not be gullible. And most vital of all is my need to constantly maintain a deep spiritual conviction through whatever spiritual reappearances and/or physical ET landings we may experience in the future. Some years back when I learned that we humans have been deceived, duped and genetically manipulated for thousands of years, I went through great emotional pain caused by my doubt, fear, anger, judgment, and even some depression that this information engendered. Perhaps we now have a cosmic dark night of the soul—a kind of collective dark night—due to this potential upcoming experience of meeting other humans from space? Something we've never really had to confront in recent times. Our way of life on earth is certainly not ideal and God knows I've prayed to help improve it. But am I prepared for a total energy shift to galactic beingness? Is humanity? Whether we know this first contact event is soon upon us or not, my personality must deal with a total surrender of the familiar, even if it's a soul dream come true. Though I am far more settled about the possible return of our spiritual family and the potential ET landings than I used to be, I want to acknowledge it hasn't been easy. Still the bottom line is that I want to remain a positive partner in this cosmological drama in which we of earth can be victors, whatever it takes, so I don't give up—and I hope you feel drawn to join me and many others in achieving this destiny!

Psychology has already helped us deal with many profound experiences and may now be called forth to support a major evolutionary stage in human consciousness—the physical experience of seeing spiritual and physical beings arrive here upon the earth. Perhaps as the late Carl Jung commented in his book, *The Undiscovered Self*, "Humans will not know who we are until we make contact with quasi-human mammals from another star."

What the book you've just read dares to suggest, of course, is that we are about to have that very experience! And it may be that our meeting with those quasi-human mammals from another star may reverse itself into a meeting where we are the quasi-humans meeting the original galactic human model, our great ancestors—the Lyrans and the Sirians. Perhaps, being the genetic mutants we presently are, we will think the original Sirians to be "gods," with a little g, as I believe our own earth people did when the renegade Pleiadean extraterrestrials arrived long ago. Will we bow down and accept them as God with a big G and not understand the true meaning of their physical landing? Or will we, this time, have the spiritual members of both the great angelic realms like Archangel Michael, plus Jesus and many Ascended Masters from all religions, appear first to reassure us that the physical contact about to occur has their blessing?

This would certainly tie in with the inspirational information I've received over the past nine years and would explain why I and many others haven't involved ourselves with much extraterrestrial information until now. Or at least it is a possible explanation of why some people have been reluctant to think about galactic life forms appearing in great numbers. The singular warmth and affection we feel toward one ET lost far from his cosmic home will undoubtedly not be the same identical feeling we'll have if a sky full of ETs arrive to improve the global society presently in power here on earth. Quite a different response, isn't it? And perhaps it should be different since no one yet knows for sure whether that touching ET movie was propaganda from the Zeta Reticulis—so we'd willingly accept their abductions and genetic experimentations on us (and our cattle)—or if it was a more general message from our own galactic human family preparing us for what may yet happen. There is also the possibility that it is only a deep unconscious yearning from our soul and the core of our own genetic identity.

Denial may have served a useful purpose, then, until we were able to realize that the dangers presented by the Zetas (the small gray beings) have been removed and we can now receive the nurturing security of our very own galactic human family. For it seems that there is a rhythm and cyclic nature to this galaxy which we have long forgotten—but which has at last decided to assist us, even as the Star Trek TV series has so vividly portrayed when their captain and crew visit primitive societies from time to time.

I am truly indebted to a few profound space age programs for the many new perceptions they bring to us about space, humans, and the future. I am eagerly awaiting some creative person's episode, in fact, where we don't meet a mean and dastardly advanced being like "Q," but rather an entire civilization of morally advanced beings who visit earth. Then the Enterprise crew could come down to earth to participate in that new wisdom which it could then take back out to other civilizations. (Any good screenwriters ready for something like this?)

I have not meant to imply that as we humans learn to use our great intuitive capabilities that we shouldn't also use our left brain intellectual prowess, even as Captain Picard does. However, unless it is balanced with more and more intuition, we will only be left with the majority of intellectuals who require proof for every hypothesis offered, and who are squeamish about entering into any hypotheses that seem too "far out" for them. Because there is absolutely no proof that the Sirians, and an immense group of nonhuman beings, will land on planet Earth from Mars sometime soon, my critical thinking self is very bothered that I would discuss this. And it would definitely like some proof before I step out and risk whatever reputation it feels I may have. Why? It wants to be safe, accepted, and right. Certainly it is greatly threatened by what my right brain imagination and intuition are involved in.

I always smile when I remember how the entire scientific world laughed at Columbus when he wanted to sail off looking for a new world. Ditto the response to the Wright brothers and their dream of a flying machine. In the shifting reality of new born intuition and consciousness then, these so-called definitions of science may be difficult to contain or explain.

All the same, I presume most of us would like some proof that there is a divine plan underway that serves us in some positive way. Proof acquired in a testable and repeatable process which no one can offer right now, that I know of. So the usual processes of critical thinking in which observation vs. interpretation are utilized and proof is definitely attained, remain unsatisfied. Yet isn't it our self-awareness and intuition that lead us on in spite of the questions our critical thinking leaves unanswered? For it is our hearts and souls that are the dreamers and believers.

I hasten to add that I do perceive some hard scientific evidence, especially in physics, beginning to support my heart's belief in galactic life, so we are gradually forging a new era of possibility. Our own forays into space have certainly paved the way for some proof already, and more will be forthcoming quite soon, no doubt.

But it is our intellectual forays into the manipulation of life's genetic codes that concern me the most right now, though it is not a subject addressed in this book's previous chapters. I refer here to the issue of genetic engineering as an example where intellect, without soulful reflection, has proceeded to clone a human embryo and to undertake a godly role in the systematic evaluation and decision-making regarding how the human gene should be altered and why.

It's only been about forty years since our Earth scientists uncovered the mysterious DNA code of life, and yet they are already able to manipulate some of its contents. With the U.S. government's fifteen year Human Genome Project underway, at a cost of many billions of dollars, I believe we citizens should claim our right to participate in the moral and ethical issues involved here. Will we let old Atlantis-type genetic experiments be repeated now? Or does this knowledge of life's DNA code behoove us, and our scientists and government officials, to contemplate where this life originally came from and assess how best we can honor the Creator's gift of life in a purely constructive way?

It seems likely to me that as we explore the DNA's genetic life essence, we will certainly learn how the physical aspects of such processes are inexorably linked to the power and source that first birthed our own creation. Are we at last close to finding a bond between spiritual mind intention and the physical expression of that Creator's vision and will through genetic coding?

At the least, we may now have to face the question of who, or what, created physical life, and learn how this was accomplished on Earth. Did wiser galactic humans simply colonize here and leave their species behind? Did space beings interbreed with mammals already here on Earth to start a new species? Or did they employ artificial insemination practices in experimental laboratories to produce or alter DNA even as our scientists might well be doing today? What's your own opinion on this formidable human issue?

In the exploration of the questions of who we are and where the genius of our cells, genes, chromosomes, etc., came from, we cannot fail to meet some Creator with its greater knowledge. I personally believe this Creator will include more than just the human race in its galactic creations, though we are undoubtedly part of a continuum of genetic expression. So our Sirian family may help us understand many things about life, God, and the cosmos—for which we are most sincerely grateful—but let us remember that a still greater spectrum of life exists and that a still greater destiny may await us all "out there somewhere. . ."

Now, I'd like to review the major points that Washta and his Sirian compatriots have shared with us as the three most vital things we should remember from reading their remarks.

"First, we would like all earth humans to understand that there is an incredible shift soon to happen in their consciousness. It will come not only because of the great change caused by the photon belt, but also because of the mass landings that are about to occur in the next few years between 1995 and 1996. This shift in reality will bring humans back into full consciousness.

The second thing we would like to emphasize is that this shift in consciousness is being done as part of a great divine plan given mainly by the spiritual and angelic hierarchies of this planet and also of this local galaxy. *All of us are coming to you as a rescue mission. It is not an invasion!* Our coming is intended to bring Earth humans into full alignment with their galactic brothers and sisters and to reunite the families they left behind long ago on other star systems. We come to help you reemerge with your former family in this great and glorious web of light that galactic humans have established with other forms of life in this galaxy. We are therefore aiding humans to reclaim their awareness of why they came to this planet in the first place and to reconstitute their relationship with the Spiritual Hierarchy while living in physical form.

The third concept that results from reuniting with your galactic family under the divine plan of the spiritual hierarchies, is that you will receive your own incredible physical capabilities of body, mind, and emotions. You are a divine spark of creation with a responsibility to the Creator and to the awesome divine plan set forth. Now, as everyone on this planet returns to the light in order to achieve their purposes and to move into whatever the next incarnations will be, that plan will be completed! and it will be completed in a conscious way, not in the haphazard way that, unfortunately, Earth humans have had to experience since the Atlantean experiment began some 10,000 years ago.

Thus, we would simply state to all humanity that this book has been delivered to describe the impending glorious shift that will make you a fully conscious being.

We are not here to control but simply to aid in bringing your human family back into alignment with all other galactic branches of the tree of life. We are here to help you achieve the supreme prophecy's fitting conclusion in which this entire galaxy will be raised into high consciousness. This is the great heritage and the great message that we wish all humans who read this work to understand and to realize."

Although we will now end this book, dear readers, there are no endings in life, only beginnings caused by change and our ever-increasing perception of events and cycles that we may not always consciously understand. This is because, for me at least, growth is the only evidence of life!

I have been inspired to conclude this book with a comment from the energy of Christ Jesus about the prophesied photon belt we may experience.

Dear Ones,

The photon light now moves forth as an enriching meta cell of spiritualized light, traversing time and space to upgrade the consciousness of living matter, and to bring all of life back home to the welcoming vibration of the Creator's heart.

Like a divine helix of interdimensional awareness, this photon emissary of love and wisdom fertilizes your sprouting springtime consciousness, preparing it for a future season of cosmic harvest.

Temporarily cradling you sleeping offspring of God in a blanket of darkness, the photon light will soon after awaken you into a collective template of cosmic familyhood where all beings can be relatives in ONENESS.

This extraordinary wave of photon consciousness brings the holy proclamation that grace is granted and that the human family will again be joined in a joyful celestial community. Then welcome your moment of deliverance from past negativity and open your heart and mind to receive the photon crown of full consciousness. It was for this you came upon planet Earth. This is that evolutionary moment you desired to taste and its honeyed bliss will truly become your shining galactic reality.

Yes, the potential of peace approaches in this garment of photon light. Then let its mantle embrace your body and soul for a cosmic flight into hope and expanding awareness. God's divine plan is unfolding! And the time is **now**. *Please do your part with full commitment and cooperation, for in that way we will never again be separated from each other or from the sacredness of the Creator's vision.*

I leave you only through this communication, beloveds, for we are linked inexorably, forever and ever, in the far reaches of space and time.

Eternally your loving brother and teacher,

Christ Jesus

236

In the Creator's name, and in appreciation of the great Christ consciousness throughout the Cosmos, we now take our leave. Peace and joy be with you eternally.

Love and Light,

Virginia

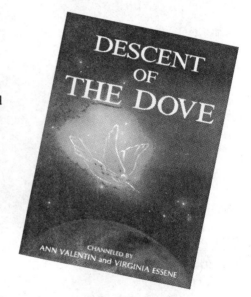

LOVE CORPS NETWORKING

The term Love Corps was coined in the book *New Teachings for an Awakening Humanity*. It is a universal alliance of all human beings of good will who seek both inner personal peace and its planetary application. Thus the worldwide Love Corps family is committed to achieving inner peace through meditation and self-healing and to sharing that peace in groups where the unity of cooperation can be applied toward the preservation of all life. In order to support our lightworkers (wherever they may be), we publish the Love Corps Newsletter. Its purpose is to keep our Love Corps family informed of the very latest information being received from the Spiritual Hierarchy.

Virginia Essene frequently travels around the United States and the world to link Love Corps energies, to share additional information not included in *You Are Becoming a Galactic Human; New Cells, New Bodies, New Life!; New Teachings for an Awakening Humanity; Secret Truths: A Young Adult's Guide for Creating Peace; and Descent of the Dove* books, and to encourage humanity's achievement of peace and the preservation of all life upon planet earth.

If you would like to be involved in the Love Corps endeavors, to participate with us in seminars, or to have an individual counseling session, please write for information so we may include your area in our itinerary.

This Time of Awakening brings a new spiral of information, to move each of us to a higher level of inner peace and planetary involvement. You are encouraged to accept the responsibility of this evolutionary opportunity and immediately unite efforts with other people in creating peaceful attitudes and conditions on our planet.

SHARE Foundation
1556 Halford Ave. #288
Santa Clara, CA 95051 USA

PARTICIPATION QUESTIONNAIRE AND ORDER FORM

To: **S.E.E. PUBLISHING COMPANY
c/o The SHARE FOUNDATION*
1556 Halford Avenue #288
Santa Clara, CA 95051 U.S.A.**
Telephone (408) 245-5457

Please send information on how I can Help disseminate
You Are Becoming a Galactic Human to:
☐ Friends, Bookstores, Churches, and other organizations

I wish to donate my skills and/or time for:
☐ Fund raising   ☐ Public Speaking
☐ Translating   ☐ Publicity

Here is my tax-deductible* donation for the LOVE CORPS efforts:
☐ $1,000   ☐ $500   ☐ $250
☐ $100   ☐ $50   ☐ $_____ (other)

I would like to help publicize **You Are Becoming a Galactic Human:**   ☐ On TV   ☐ Radio
☐ Newspapers, Magazines

I would like to join the LOVE CORPS Network so that I can link-up with others in my area and with the Love Corps Office. I am subscribing to the Love Corps Newsletter. Check here to receive an application. ☐

* The Share Foundation is a non-profit organization. Contributions are tax deductible under section 501 (c) (3) of the I.R.S. code.

See next page to order books and newsletter ⟶

Please send me copies of the following **books**:   (U.S. $)

You Are Becoming a Galactic Human @ $11.95 $_____

New Cells, New Bodies, NEW LIFE!   @ $11.95 $_____

Descent of the Dove . . . . @ $9.95 $_____

**Secret Truths: A Young Adult's
Guide for Creating Peace** . . . . @ $8.95 $_____

New Teachings for an Awakening Humanity:
    English ed. . . . . @ $9.95 $_____
    Spanish ed. **Nuevas Ensenanzas** . . .@ $9.95 $_____

Minus Love Corps discount if applicable**. . . . . . . $(_____)
                       Subtotal . . . . $_____
Plus 8.25% sales tax (California residents only) . . $_____
Plus shipping & handling for one book:***
    (Surface rates: $2 for U.S.A.; $3 for foreign) . . $_____
Plus shipping for each additional book:***
    ($1 for U.S.A.; $1.25 for foreign). . . . . $_____

Please send me the **Love Corps Newsletter**:
☐ One year (bi-monthly) 1994 subscription = $24 $_____
☐ Canadian & other international = $30 (airmail) $_____
☐ 1993 & earlier issues available @ $4/issue.
    Please specify: J/F, M/A, M/J, J/A, S/O, N/D $_____

Love Corps donation (tax deductible). . . . . $_____

TOTAL ENCLOSED $_____

Please PRINT (this information is for your mailing label)

_____
Name

_____
Address

_____
City   State/Province   Zip Code

(_____)_____
Area Code   Telephone Number (optional)

** Love Corps discounts:
        5 to 9 books - take off 10%
        10 or more books - take off 20%
*** Please request shipping rates for first class or air mail.

About Sheldon Nidle

P.O. Box 811 ▪ Half Moon Bay ▪ CA 94019

Find out what's in store for all humanity before the end of this decade. Sheldon Nidle, representative and lecturer for the Galactic Federation, will provide the most current information on the Federation's plans for our planet. Sheldon has been given secret information about true earth history, science, culture, and spirituality since childhood. He has finally been allowed to reveal this vast store of knowledge because the time of great changes is near. Due to Sheldon's education and research in the sciences, social sciences, anthropology, and alternative technology, Tesla et al., he is able to bring an astute rational and scientific approach to this controversial subject.

❖ **PERSONAL**

Sheldon was born in New York City on November 11, 1946 and grew up in Buffalo, New York. His first extraterrestrial (ET) and UFO experiences began in 1955 with various modes of phenomena and contact manifestations, e.g. Light form phenomena, extraterrestrial visitations, teaching sessions, telepathic communications, and direct core knowledge inserts. He has had numerous craft sightings throughout the years.

At about 14 years old, Sheldon demanded the ETs to stop communicating with him because he felt that their knowledge ran counter to contemporary scientific reasoning. They left but told him they would be back. In high school, he was placed in advanced science programs such as physics, chemistry, and calculus. As a teenager, he was part of a team that invented the field ion microscope. As an undergraduate at the State University of New York at Buffalo, he was vice president of the Amateur Astronomers Club.

❖ **EDUCATION**

M.A. in Southeast Asian Government, Ohio University (1970)
M.A. in American Politics and International Public Administration, University of Southern California, Ph.D. candidate (1974-1976).

❖ **OCCUPATION**

Representative and lecturer for the Galactic Federation. He is co-author with Virginia Essene of *You Are Becoming A Galactic Human*. In the 1970s, he was vice president for scientific programming for Syntar Productions where he created a documentary on the life and accomplishments of Nikola Tesla, the genius who invented the technology of the twentieth century. All throughout the 1970s up to the mid-1980s he was involved in scientific research on alternative sources of electrical energy. In the mid-1980s, his ET contacts reappeared and subsequently led him to the information that is provided in the *First Contact* newsletters and his lectures.

Literature and information regarding:

 # Planetary Advocate Groups

During the course of this book, a mention has been made of a new way to align guardian, environmental, and light worker groups. This new web of consciousness is a result of the approaching Golden Age for Earth's human civilization as well as the coming mass contact by the Galactic Federation. In spite of the emerging and expanding consciousness, one may well ask why is there a need for planetary advocate groups and why should they be formed in the first place. During the course of my lectures and workshops, these questions have been frequently been raised along with others on how to create and maintain such a group.

Now we are providing a booklet on Planetary Advocate Groups that will answer all pertinent questions. In addition, a two-hour video-tape lecture on Planetary Advocate Groups will be available at the end of June, 1994. Included in this booklet, audiotape and videotape will be answers to questions on: how to form advocate groups; why one should do so; and how to operate as a liaison and advocate for planet Earth, the Spiritual Hierarchy and the Galactic Federation.

Booklet: *All About Planetary Advocate Groups* $ 2.95

Video: *Planetary Advocate Groups (2 hour tape)* $25.00

Audio: *Planetary Advocate Groups (2 hour tape)* $11.00

To place an order please send a check or money order to:

BWiz
c/o Sheldon Nidle
P.O. Box 811
Half Moon Bay, CA 94019   (415) 726-2827

Shipping and Handling: please add $1.00 per booklet
• $2.00 per audio • $3.00 per video tape (For California residents add 8.5% tax)

Sheldon Nidle and the Galactic Federation

Extraterrestrial Contact and Human Evolution
Lecture Series

✓ **Lecture Series** 2- hour **Videotapes** @$25 per lecture and **Audiotapes** @$11 per lecture

__ V1 **LS#1: General Overview and Update** (Dec. 2, 1993)
__ A1 *The Galactic Federation ▪ The Genesis Story ▪ Lemuria and Atlantis ▪ Earth Changes*
▪ The Coming Mass Landings ▪ Photon Belt ▪ Transformation/Ascension Process

__ V2 **LS#2: First Contact — Its Meaning and Implications** (Dec. 9, 1993)
__ A2 *Mass Landings ▪ The Role of the Federation ▪The Role of Cetaceans ▪ Preparing for the*
Photon Belt ▪New Technology, New Psychology ▪ Lady Gaia and Earth Changes

__ V3 **LS#3: New Bodies and Full Consciousness** (Dec. 30, 1993)
__ A3 *Photon Belt Phenomenon ▪ New Chakra System ▪ Talking with the Rocks, Plants, and Animals*
▪ Ascension Process ▪ Integration of Changes ▪ Angelic Hierarchy

__ V4 **LS#4: The Return of the Lyran/Sirian Culture** (Jan. 6, 1994)
__ A4 *The Laws of Relationships ▪ Spiritual Sexuality ▪The Role of Counselors*
▪ The Clans ▪ Cultural Practices and Traditions ▪ The Sirian Councils

__ V5 **LS#5: Earth Spiritual Hierarchy and the Galactic Federation** (Feb. 25, 1994)
__ A5 *What is the Spiritual Hierarchy? ▪ Their Involvement with the Galactic Federation ▪ The Roles of*
Archangels, Angels, Ascended Masters, and Devas ▪ Role of Spiritual Hierarchy in Ascension
Process ▪ Earth/Human Transformation ▪ The Coming Mass Landings ▪ The Second Coming and
the Photon Belt ▪ Our Holographic Envelope

__ V6 **LS#6: Linking the Hawaiians, the Mayans, and the Tibetans** (Mar. 11, 1994)
__ A6 *Role of Lemuria Today and Tomorrow ▪ Mass Migrations After Its Destruction*
▪ The Legacy of the Lemurian Culture: Hawaii, Tibet, and Mexico ▪ Galactic Influence ▪ Religious
Concept of Time ▪ Mayan and Tibetan Cultural Links ▪ Magic of Hawaii ▪ Reflection on Three
Remnant Cultures of Lemuria

__ V7 **LS#7: Our Ascension/Transformation Process** (Mar. 25, 1994)
__ A7 *What is Ascension? ▪ Different Levels of Consciousness ▪ Role of Angelic Hierarchy in Ascension*
▪ How to Prepare for Ascension ▪ Integrating the Changes in Your Consciousness
▪ How Consciousness Affects Our Genetics ▪ Photon Belt and the New Galactic Civilization

__ V8 **LS#8: Cetaceans and the Spiritual Hierarchy** (Apr. 29, 1994)
__ A8 *Update on Cetacean (Dolphin & Whale) Contact ▪ Preparing for Human Guardianship*
▪ The Interaction of the Cetaceans and Spiritual Hierarchy ▪ Defining Human Guardianship
▪ Cetaceans as Teachers of Galactic Wisdom ▪ The Spiritual Hierarchy's Role in
Planetary Guardianship

Other Products

✓ **Other audio tapes @$11:**

__ **AT1**   Introduction to Sheldon Nidle and the Galactic Federation
- a Space Cities TV interview (1 hr. 43 min.)
Sheldon's First Contact ▪ *Sheldon's Mission* ▪ *The Sirians' Concern for Earth*
▪ *Galactic Federation* ▪ *First Contact Team* ▪ *Earth History* ▪ *Photon Belt* ▪ *Advocate Groups*

__ **AT2**   Sheldon Nidle, guest speaker at United Light meeting (2 hours)
The Importance of Being Involved in Planetary Advocate Groups ▪ *Commitment, Love, & Service*
▪ *Hawaiian Way of Dealing With Conflict* ▪ *Questions & Answers: Galactic Friends* ▪ *Year of Major Event* ▪ *Mayan Calendar* ▪ *Origin of Sphinx* ▪ *Atlantis & Plato* ▪ *Destruction of Mars*

__ **AT3**   Planetary Advocate Groups - Guidelines

✓ **Other video tapes:**

__ **VT1**   Human Evolution and the ET Connection - a Space Cities TV interview (30 min.) $20

__ **VT2**   Introduction to Sheldon Nidle and the Galactic Federation $25
- a Space Cities TV interview (1 hr. 43 min.)
Sheldon's First Contact ▪ *Sheldon's Mission* ▪ *The Sirians' Concern for Earth*
▪ *Galactic Federation* ▪ *First Contact Team* ▪ *Earth History* ▪ *Photon Belt* ▪ *Advocate Groups*

__ **VT3**   LS#1: General Overview and Update - a Space Cities TV presentation (1 hr.) $20
The Galactic Federation ▪ *The Genesis Story* ▪ *Lemuria and Atlantis* ▪ *Earth Changes*
▪ *The Coming Mass Landings* ▪ *Photon Belt* ▪ *Transformation/Ascension Process*

__ **VT4**   LS#2: First Contact — Its Meaning and Implications $20
- a Space Cities TV presentation (1 hr.)
Mass Landings ▪ *The Role of the Federation* ▪ *The Role of Cetaceans* ▪ *Preparing for the Photon Belt* ▪ *New Technology, New Psychology* ▪ *Lady Gaia and Earth Changes*

__ **VT5**   Galactic Time Workshop (4 hours) - Nov. 20, 1993 $40
Based on the Mayan calendar and Jose Arguelles' Dreamspell Game. Understanding galactic time will be useful in the new galactic civilization that is emerging. Topics include: Birth Kins ▪ *20 Sacred Glyphs* ▪ *13 Tones of Creation* ▪ *Wavespells & Castles* ▪ *Tzolkin* ▪ *Haab*

__ **VT6**   Planetary Advocate Groups - Guidelines (2 hours) $25

✓ **Printed Materials:**

__ **PM1**   First Contact Newsletter - bi-monthly, 6 issues $24

__ **PM2**   Beyond Wizdom Newsletter - 6 back issues (Aug.'92-July'93) $17

__ **PM3**   All About Planetary Advocate Groups - booklet $2.95

To order, fill out the Newsletter/Tape Order Form provided in next page.
Prices effective May 11, 1994 and subject to change without notice.

Newsletter/Tape Order Form

BWiz • c/o Sheldon Nidle • P.O. Box 811• Half Moon Bay • CA 94019
(415) 726-2827

Name _____

Address _____

City _____

State_____ Zip_____ Phone (optional)_____

Quantity • Unit Price • Description	• Amount
_____	_____
_____	_____
_____	_____
_____	_____
_____	_____
_____	_____
_____	_____
_____	_____

Date_____   Total _____

*Shipping & Handling _____

(For California residents only) 8.5% Tax _____

__ Check __ Money Order   Grand Total _____

*Shipping and handling: $1.00 per audiotape & $1.00 per booklet • $3.00 per videotape and $1.50 each additional videotape order to same address
Thank you for your order!

PARTICIPATION QUESTIONNAIRE AND ORDER FORM

To: **S.E.E. PUBLISHING COMPANY
c/o The SHARE FOUNDATION*
1556 Halford Avenue #288
Santa Clara, CA 95051 U.S.A.**
Telephone (408) 245-5457

Please send information on how I can Help disseminate
You Are Becoming a Galactic Human to:
  ☐ Friends, Bookstores, Churches, and other
    organizations
I wish to donate my skills and/or time for:
  ☐ Fund raising   ☐ Public Speaking
  ☐ Translating   ☐ Publicity

Here is my tax-deductible* donation for the LOVE
CORPS efforts:
  ☐ $1,000   ☐ $500   ☐ $250
  ☐ $100   ☐ $50   ☐ $_____ (other)

I would like to help publicize **You Are Becoming a
Galactic Human:**   ☐ On TV   ☐ Radio
  ☐ Newspapers, Magazines

I would like to join the LOVE CORPS Network so that I
can link-up with others in my area and with the Love
Corps Office. I am subscribing to the Love Corps Newsletter. Check here to receive an application. ☐

* The Share Foundation is a non-profit organization.
Contributions are tax deductible under section 501 (c)
(3) of the I.R.S. code.

See next page to order books and newsletter ⟶

Please send me copies of the following **books**:   (U.S. $)

You Are Becoming a Galactic Human @ $11.95 $_____

New Cells, New Bodies, NEW LIFE! @ $11.95 $_____

Descent of the Dove . . . . @ $9.95 $_____

**Secret Truths: A Young Adult's
Guide for Creating Peace** . . . . @ $8.95 $_____

New Teachings for an Awakening Humanity:
    English ed. . . . . @ $9.95 $_____
    Spanish ed. **Nuevas Ensenanzas** . . .@ $9.95 $_____

Minus Love Corps discount if applicable** . . . . $(_____)
                                 Subtotal . . . . $_____
Plus 8.25% sales tax (California residents only) . . $_____
Plus shipping & handling for one book:***
    (Surface rates: $2 for U.S.A.; $3 for foreign) . . $_____
Plus shipping for each additional book:***
    ($1 for U.S.A.; $1.25 for foreign). . . . . $_____

Please send me the **Love Corps Newsletter**:
☐ One year (bi-monthly) 1994 subscription = $24 $_____
☐ Canadian & other international = $30 (airmail) $_____
☐ 1993 & earlier issues available @ $4/issue.
    Please specify: J/F, M/A, M/J, J/A, S/O, N/D $_____

Love Corps donation (tax deductible). . . . . $_____

                          TOTAL ENCLOSED $_____

Please PRINT (this information is for your mailing label)

_____
Name

_____
Address

_____
City   State/Province   Zip Code

(_____)_____
Area Code   Telephone Number (optional)

** Love Corps discounts:
      5 to 9 books - take off 10%
      10 or more books - take off 20%
*** Please request shipping rates for first class or air mail.

Newsletter/Tape Order Form

BWiz • c/o Sheldon Nidle • P.O. Box 811• Half Moon Bay • CA 94019
(415) 726-2827

Name _____

Address _____

City _____

State_____ Zip_____ Phone (optional)_____

Quantity • Unit Price • Description	• Amount

Date_____   Total _____

*Shipping & Handling _____

(For California residents only) 8.5% Tax _____

__ Check __ Money Order   Grand Total _____

*Shipping and handling: $1.00 per audiotape & $1.00 per booklet • $3.00 per
videotape and $1.50 each additional videotape order to same address
Thank you for your order!

NOTES